ADULT BILITERACY

Sociocultural and Programmatic Responses

ADULT BILITERACY

Sociocultural and Programmatic Responses

Edited by
Klaudia M. Rivera • Ana Huerta-Macías

Lawrence Erlbaum Associates
Taylor & Francis Group

New York   London

Lawrence Erlbaum Associates
Taylor & Francis Group
270 Madison Avenue
New York, NY 10016

Lawrence Erlbaum Associates
Taylor & Francis Group
2 Park Square
Milton Park, Abingdon
Oxon OX14 4RN

© 2008 by Taylor & Francis Group, LLC
Lawrence Erlbaum Associates is an imprint of Taylor & Francis Group, an Informa business

Printed in the United States of America on acid-free paper
10 9 8 7 6 5 4 3 2 1

International Standard Book Number-13: 978-0-8058-5362-9 (Softcover) 978-0-8058-5361-2 (Hardcover)

Library of Congress Cataloging-in-Publication Data

Rivera, Klaudia M.
    Adult biliteracy : sociocultural and programmatic responses / Klaudia M. Rivera and Ana Huerta-Macías.
        p. cm.
    Includes bibliographical references and index.
    ISBN-13: 978-0-8058-5362-9 (pbk. : alk. paper)
    ISBN-10: 0-8058-5362-6 (pbk. : alk. paper)
    ISBN-13: 978-0-8058-5361-2 (hardcover : alk. paper)
    ISBN-10: 0-8058-5361-8 (hardcover : alk. paper)
    1. Education, Bilingual--United States. 2. Linguistic minorities--Education--United States. 3. Literacy--Social aspects--United States. 4. Bilingualism--United States. I. Huerta-Macías, Ana. II. Title.

LC3731.R58 2007
370.117--dc22   2007013983

To our parents

Contents

Preface

This volume brings to the forefront linguistic, demographic, sociocultural, workforce, familial, academic, and other issues surrounding the development of bilingualism and biliteracy in the educational spaces occupied by adults in the United States. As such, it helps to fill a gap in the research literature on language development among adults, which has traditionally placed more emphasis on the development of English as a second or other language. Most importantly, it brings to light issues that are integral to the success of immigrant populations in the United States—issues that politicians, policy makers, educators, and employers must place at the top of their agendas as immigration reform is formulated and implemented. To not do so is to ensure failure not only for those adults who come to the United States seeking a better life and who make the success of our own day-to-day lives possible through their labor, but also for the future of this country.

Background

The most recent National Assessment of Adult Literacy (NAAL) has brought increased attention and urgency to the issue of adult literacy. The survey indicated that the number of adults who have those basic skills necessary to perform simple, everyday quantitative tasks rose from 75 to 79% since the last National Adult Literacy Survey (NALS), in 1992. Prose literacy scores increased among African Americans by 6 points and among Asian/Pacific Islanders by 16 points. Document literacy scores also increased for African Americans by 8 points—as did overall quantitative literacy skills from the 1992 survey. What is troubling is that the average prose scores for Hispanic[1] Americans fell by 18 points, and the document literacy scores for this same group fell by 14 points, since the last NALS (National Center for Education Statistics, 2005).

This is of great concern, as Latinos form the largest so-called "minority" ethnic group in the United States, and yet they are the ones who seem to perform at the lowest levels, not only in terms of adult literacy but also in terms of educational achievement overall. Furthermore, the grim statistics do not end with the national assessments. Hispanics have the highest high school dropout rates. National dropout rates in 2001 were 65.7% for Hispanics compared to 7.3% for Whites. Statistics further indicate that in this same year, 68.7% of high school completers were White, 13.7% were Black, and 11.9% were Hispanic (National Center for Education Statistics, 2005). Not surprisingly, Latinos also fall behind on a number of issues, including income, employment, and college degrees. In

2001, for instance, 24.9% of Hispanics lived in poverty, compared to 23.1% of Blacks and 7.9% of Whites (Poverty Gap, 2004).

Literacy is at the core of educational and economic advancement as well as health and general well-being. Clearly, we must do a better job of providing access to literacy development for all groups, but particularly for Latinos—including Mexicans, Puerto Ricans, Salvadorians, and all Spanish-speaking populations—being that the gaps are greatest in this group, which is, at the same time, as noted above, the largest ethnic group in the United States. Thus, the emphasis in this volume is on Latinos, while recognizing that the issues discussed apply to other ethnic, linguistic minority and immigrant groups as well.

The notion of *immigrant* also merits some discussion, for one cannot generically classify all Latinos or other groups who speak little or no English as simply immigrants. Demographers distinguish between individuals who are foreign born versus those who were born inside the United States, or are native born. For example, in many families the parents are foreign-born immigrants while the children are native born. This distinction is made, where appropriate, in the research literature and is also reported in this volume wherever relevant to the discussion.

Regardless of the immigrant classification, our Latino adult population must have increased access to education that assists them not only through adult basic education, but also through transition to college and an associate's or bachelor's degree, and ultimately to sustainable employment. This is not only an issue of basic human rights that provide access to literacy and education, but also an economic issue. Consider that in 2005, the Department of Labor reported 150 million people in our workforce. In 2005, the National Center for Education Statistics reported that 3 million students graduated from high school. Thus, at best, only 2% of our workforce comes from public schools each year. Therefore, the source of workers must be the adult population today (Adult Competitiveness Challenge, 2006). Consider also reports indicating that within the next decade the United States will be 12 million short of the types of workers that will be needed—those with a GED or a high school diploma plus some college (Carnevale, 2002, cited in Adult Competitiveness Challenge, 2006). Couple this with the current demographics showing that Hispanics comprise 12.5% of the population in the United States (U.S. Census Bureau, 2001), and it becomes crystal clear that we must focus more attention on this group in order to maintain a successful economy in this country. It is imperative that we research and implement the most effective ways to help this population raise its educational, literacy, and biliteracy levels, and thus its economic status through increased education and attainment of jobs that pay sustainable wages.

Immigrants have always recognized that English language development is key to advancement in this country, and the long waiting lists for English as a Second Language (ESL) classes that are typical in our large urban areas are a testimony to their hunger for English. Trejos (2006) reports, for instance, that in

Maryland the waiting list for adult education services includes over 5,000 people, with most of them seeking ESL classes. It is incumbent upon us, as educators, policy makers, and administrators, to provide them with English while also validating and building on the Spanish language abilities that they bring with them. Additionally, we must advocate for a stronger and better funded adult education and literacy system in the United States that will better support our efforts toward literacy and biliteracy development. Sticht (2004) reports that

> There is a grossly underfunded and underdeveloped adult education and literacy system in the United States with over 3,000 programs and close to 3 million enrollees per year. But the federal level of funding is less than US$225 per enrollee. Even with state contributions added in, the average funding per enrollee across the United States is only about US$650. (p. 1)

The lack of resources and educational attainment for Latino adults points to the need to use nontraditional methods of instruction that will accelerate their learning—methods that build on those strengths that our learners bring with them in the area of language development or learning of new knowledge. This includes linguistic, factual, and experiential knowledge. In the linguistic realm, learners bring with them knowledge of Spanish that can be utilized as a springboard for both literacy/biliteracy development and new knowledge. Even though the exact nature and role of transfer are not yet known (Cook, 1996), linguistic and educational research has indicated that literacy and learning in a second language are facilitated when there is a source of transferable skills from the native language (Cummins, 1980; Lanauze & Snow, 1989, cited in Baker, 2001). We also know that cognitive development takes place when we learn in a language that we understand. Additionally, the activation of schema and background knowledge as critical to new learning—whether a language or other new knowledge—has been highlighted by the National Research Council (2000). Therefore, the implication is that the use of two languages in the adult education and literacy classroom is sound pedagogy, and thus the need to look at not only literacy but also biliteracy in the education of adults—for one cannot ignore the linguistic and other knowledge of our learners as they engage in new learning. Previous knowledge must be accessed and developed if our students are going to acquire new knowledge in a sound and efficient manner. Use of the native language of the student then becomes a key piece in the process of literacy/biliteracy development and the acquisition of new knowledge.

We must additionally explore diverse learning environments and program designs when providing access to education by Latinos and all language minority groups. Community-based organizations, family literacy, and workforce education programs, for example, provide additional opportunities for matching student needs and interests with an educational program. Eisner (1994) in his discussion of concept formation and an expanded view of knowledge indicates that "a broad array of opportunities represented by a wide array of forms of representation and modes of treatment ... increases educational equity for students by increasing the probability that they will be able to play to their strengths" (p. 89). The implication for adult education and literacy is thus the need to expand and contextualize learning for our adults, so that they may find different entry points to education and economic advancement.

Overview of the Volume

This volume is founded on the notions discussed above: our basic human right to access to education and literacy, the significance of previous knowledge, and the need for diverse learning environments in adult literacy, including ESL. Thus, by virtue of these ideas, we expand the discussions in this volume to biliteracy and not solely literacy. Biliteracy is the ability to read and write and otherwise use two languages in socioculturally appropriate ways. Foundational information that enhances the understanding of these ideas, such as a discussion of theoretical notions on literacy and biliteracy development and a critical analysis of today's demographics, is also provided herein. The book is structured in four sections.

Part I, "Adult Biliteracy: Perspectives and Policies," includes two chapters and a photo essay. In Chapter 1, "Adult Bilingualism and Biliteracy in the United States: Theoretical Perspectives," Klaudia M. Rivera and Ana Huerta-Macías discuss those linguistic, cognitive, and sociocultural theoretical notions surrounding literacy and biliteracy development that are so significant in our work with adults who are acquiring a second language. Literacy and biliteracy development as a transactional process is a basic point in this chapter.

Chapter 2, "Adult Biliteracy and Language Diversity: How Well Do National Data Inform Policy?" by Mario Castro and Terrence G. Wiley, guides readers through an examination of the demographics in the United States. Their discussion helps us to uncover trends that in turn can help us develop sound policy for the education of adults. The authors highlight the significance of Spanish in the United States, being that it is second only to English in terms of the number of speakers in the language. They further indicate that more attention needs to be paid to literacy and job skills development that can be mediated in another language; traditionally, the emphasis has been on oral English language skills.

The photo essay, "Literacy and Biliteracy: Expressions in Environmental Print," by Klaudia M. Rivera and Ana Huerta-Macías, depicts a series of images illustrating the use of literacy and biliteracy in environmental print, including, for instance, advertising, public announcements, and billboards. The images highlight the use of languages for sociocultural, economic, and political purposes. They also provide a sampling of the many types of linguistic variations that are created in writing with the integration of two languages, variations that are now commonplace in our culturally and linguistically diverse society.

Part II, "Adult Biliteracy in Diverse Contexts," comprises five chapters. Chapter 3, "Adult Biliteracy in Community-Based Organizations: Venues of Participation, Agents of Transformation," by Klaudia M. Rivera, highlights the roles that community organizations play as partners in the educational services provided to adults. Community-based organizations are central to our work in adult literacy and biliteracy. Rivera offers a rich discussion of how community-based programs, among other things, provide leadership and economic development as well as multiple avenues for the use and development of the native language and English through literacy-building activities ranging from popular theater to leadership development and the establishment of cooperatives.

In Chapter 4, "Workforce Education for Latinos: A Bilingual Approach," Ana Huerta-Macías provides a discussion of how the native language skills can be tapped to accelerate learning in workforce education. She describes a dual-language approach to learning that builds on the cognitive and linguistic skills that students bring to the classroom. An important element of this approach is that students are provided with opportunities to apply what they have learned through partnerships with business, industry, or other entities, such that the learning is contextualized through real-life experiences.

Elizabeth Quintero provides snapshots of two family literacy programs in Chapter 5, "A Crossroads: Family Education Programs." She describes critical literacy activities in which culture, language, prior knowledge, and current dilemmas are addressed, and emphasizes the need for such programs to provide opportunities for personal and social transformation.

Issues of adult literacy and biliteracy have traditionally been discussed in circles outside of academics, where the native language has most often been viewed as problematic to student success. In Chapter 6, "Academic Biliteracies for Adults in the United States," Ellen Skilton-Sylvester highlights two examples of university programs that move beyond this view and discusses how U.S. educational institutions seeking to develop academic literacy can create a space for the native language. Within this context, the native language is seen as a resource and not a problem.

Civics education brings yet another opportunity for the development of adult literacy and biliteracy. In Chapter 7, "Civics Education and Adult Biliteracy," James S. Powrie problematizes citizenship education and describes how civics programs can address the dual-language needs of learners in a way that is systematic, coherent, and educationally sound. By examining two EL/Civics programs, the chapter presents a framework for categorizing various types of services and strategies that build on and help develop bilingualism and biliteracy.

Part III, "Themes, Issues, Challenges," concludes the volume. A discussion of adult literacy and biliteracy would be incomplete without some perspectives on the role that assessment plays in adult learning. In Chapter 8, "Capturing What Counts: Language and Literacy Assessments for Bilingual Adults," Heide Spruck Wrigley emphasizes that no single measure should serve as the basis for assessing and evaluating student abilities and growth. She highlights the complexities embedded in assessing what students are able to do in two languages. Wrigley also provides examples of how alternative assessments can fill gaps left by large-scale standardized tests.

Chapter 9, "Issues and Future Directions," by Ana Huerta-Macías and Klaudia M. Rivera, threads together the different themes presented in the previous chapters and recommends additional avenues for research in adult literacy and biliteracy education.

Endnote

1. The authors use the term *Latino* throughout this volume when referring inclusively to all Spanish-speaking ethnic groups in the United States. However, the term *Hispanic* is sometimes used when referring to the research literature that uses Hispanic rather than Latino.

References

Adult Competitiveness Challenge. (2006, February 16). Retrieved April 26, 2006, from http://www.naepdc.org/NAAL/NAAL%20White%20Paper%20021606.doc

Baker, C. (2001). *Foundations of bilingual education and bilingualism.* Clevedon, England: Multilingual Matters.

Cook, V. (1996). *Second language learning and language teaching* (2nd ed.). New York: St. Martin's Press.

Cummins, J. (1980). The cross-lingual dimensions of language proficiency: Implications for bilingual education and the optimal age issue. *TESOL Quarterly, 14*, 175–187.

Eisner, E. W. (1994). *Cognition and curriculum reconsidered* (2nd ed.). New York: Teachers College Press.

National Center for Education Statistics. (2005). *National Assessment of Adult Literacy (NAAL): A first look at the literacy of America's adults in the 21st century* (NCES 2006-471). Washington, DC: U.S. Department of Education.

National Research Council. (2000). *How people learn: Brain, mind, experience, and school.* Washington, D.C.: National Academy Press.

Sticht, T. (2004, February/March). Can massive injections of adult literacy education improve children's reading skills? Retrieved April 25, 2006, from http://naepdc.org/february.htm#A_Sticht_Must-Read

Trejos, N. (2006, February). *Adult-ed programs inadequate.* Retrieved May 16, 2006, from http://naepdc.org/february.htm#Adult-Ed_Programs_Inadequate

U.S. Census Bureau. (2001). *Census 2000 PHC-T-10. Hispanic or Latino Origin for the United States, Regions, Divisions, States, and for Puerto Rico: 2000* (Summary File 1 and unpublished data; Internet Release date: October 22, 2001). Retrieved February 19, 2005 from http://www.census.gov/population/cen2000/phc-t10/tab01-00.pdf

Acknowledgments

We are grateful to those who came before for what they taught us and to the many who teach us today.

About the Editors

Klaudia M. Rivera has more than twenty years of experience creating and implementing adult native language literacy and ESL programs that foster bilingualism and biliteracy for Latinos and other language minorities. These programs apply critical pedagogy, participatory and popular education in community-based contexts. Her research and publications are in the areas of native language literacy, ESL, critical literacy and biliteracy, and popular education. Her most recent research is about the role of worker centers in providing education to day laborers. Dr. Rivera is a professor of language and literacy at Long Island University in Brooklyn, New York.

Ana Huerta-Macías is a professor in the Department of Teacher Education at the University of Texas at El Paso. Her research interests are in the areas of bilingualism, literacy and biliteracy, and workforce education—particularly with English language learners who are native speakers of Spanish. Dr. Macías has numerous publications in the areas of TESOL (Teaching English to Speakers of other Languages), bilingual family literacy, and workforce education. Her most recent book is *Working with English Language Learners: Perspectives and Practice.*

Contributors

Mario Castro
College of Education
Arizona State University
Tempe, Arizona

Ana Huerta-Macías
College of Education
University of Texas at El Paso
El Paso, Texas

James S. Powrie
LiteracyWork International
Las Cruces, New Mexico

Elizabeth Quintero
Steinhardt School of Education
New York University
New York, New York

Klaudia M. Rivera
School of Education
Long Island University
Brooklyn, New York

Ellen Skilton-Sylvester
Arcadia University
Glenside, Pennsylvania

Terrence G. Wiley
College of Education
Arizona State University
Tempe, Arizona

Heide Spruck Wrigley
LiteracyWork International
Las Cruces, New Mexico

PART I

Adult Biliteracy

Perspectives and Policies

1

Adult Bilingualism and Biliteracy in the United States

Theoretical Perspectives

KLAUDIA M. RIVERA AND ANA HUERTA-MACÍAS

The Immigrant Profile

The influx of immigrants to the United States over the past few decades has had a profound impact on the country. The dramatic increase in immigration in recent years has impacted the demographic, economic, educational, and linguistic arenas in this country. The immigrant population is growing 6.5 times faster than the native-born population. The Census in 2000 found 31.1 million immigrants in the United States—more than triple the 9.6 million in 1970 and more than double the 14.1 million in 1980 (Population Resource Center, 2002a). Additionally, estimates are that undocumented immigrants numbered 9.0 million in 2003, with Mexican unauthorized immigration alone growing at about 500,000 immigrants per year (Immigration Facts, 2003). Not surprisingly, Hispanic immigrants, designated as Spanish speakers, accounted for 45% of the 25.7 million increase in the Hispanic population growth in the United States between 1970 and 2000 (Suro & Passel, 2003). While the largest number of immigrants in the United States comes from Latin America (51%), large numbers were born in Asia (25.5%) and Europe (15.3%), with the balance of 8.1% born in other countries (National Institute for Literacy, n.d.).

There is great disparity in terms of economic status between immigrants and native-born populations. Almost 17% of those who are foreign born live below the poverty line, compared to 11% of the native-born population. The poverty rate, however, is lower for European and Asian immigrants (9 and 13%, respectively) than for Latin American immigrants, which stands at 22% (Population Resource Center, 2002b).

Immigrants also have lower levels of formal education than do the native-born populations. Estimates are that 33% of immigrants lack a high school diploma. The figure, however, varies for foreign-born immigrants from different areas and waves. Only 5% of African immigrants, for instance, lack a high school diploma, while the figure is closer to 20% for immigrants from Asia, Europe, and South America. However, the picture is actually more complex when one includes native-born immigrant populations who also lack a high school diploma or General Educational Development (GED). The National Center for Education Statistics (2002), for instance, states that the dropout rate for foreign-born Hispanics, ages 16 to 24, is 44.2%; for native-born first-generation Hispanics, 14.6%; and for native-born second-generation Hispanics, 15.9%.

The generally low levels of educational attainment by immigrants impact their employment and earnings. The picture for wage disparities again becomes very complex when one considers earnings for both foreign- and native-born immigrants. The earnings figures separated by ethnic group and immigrant/generation status are difficult to find because the definition of *immigrants* becomes nebulous in terms of generations. Do we still consider, for instance, second- or third-generation Hispanics[1] or Asians to be immigrants? Nonetheless, the figures that are available for ethnic groups reflect large gaps in earnings. The Pew Hispanic Center, for example, reports that the average full-time Hispanic (foreign- and native-born) worker earned about $31,000, or about 60% of what non-Hispanic Whites earned. The overall pay gap between Whites and Hispanics is $7,000 for men and $5,000 for women (Pew Hispanic Center Fact Sheet, 2002). Additionally, nearly half of all foreign-born immigrant workers earned less than 200% of the minimum wage, compared to 32% of native workers, and they compose 20% of low-wage workers, while they comprise 11% of all U.S. residents (Capps, Fix, Passel, Ost, & Perez-Lopez, 2003).

What about literacy levels among immigrant groups? The 1992 National Adult Literacy Survey found large gaps ranging from 67 to 75 points in composite literacy scores between Hispanic populations (both native and foreign born) and White native-born adults. One report indicated that if the scores were adjusted to exclude all foreign-born adults and native-born Blacks and Hispanics, then the mean scores of the remaining native-born population would greatly rise to rank second highest among all countries. That is, the scores of the Anglo native-born population would jump to second highest among all countries. The most recent survey, the 2003 National Assessment of Adult Literacy, found the percentage of adults who spoke English before starting school decreased, while the percentage of adults who spoke Spanish or Spanish and another non-English language before starting school increased. Scores for the latter population group dropped 17 points for prose and document literacy, compared to the 1992 survey. Therefore, while the assessment did not specifically look at immigrants, the figures for those speaking Spanish or Spanish and another non-English language are suggestive of lowered literacy levels among immigrants (National Center for Education Statistics, 2005).

However, currently the United States is "characterized by an extraordinarily high degree of inequality" (Sum, Kirsch, & Taggart, 2002). Thus, language is a barrier for educational and economical advancement for immigrants, the majority of whom are Latino and speak Spanish as their native tongue. Wrigley, Richer, Martinson, Kubo, and Strawn (2003) report that spoken English appears to be important for economic stability and overall success in the United States. They report that a 1999 refugee survey, for instance, showed that only 26% of refugees who did not speak English were employed, as opposed to 77% of those who spoke English. Likewise, the same study reports that the Welfare-to-Work Program in Los Angeles reflected employment rates for Hispanic and Asian English proficient workers to be 10 to 30 percentage points higher than employment rates for Hispanics and Asians who were not proficient in English. It is no surprise, therefore, that English as a Second Language (ESL) programs are the fastest growing components of adult education programs nationally; in 1997 to 1998, 48% of enrollments were for ESL classes (National Institute for Literacy, n.d.). The need to develop English language skills among immigrants is a common element of this population, as well as proficiency in Spanish or another language. This population of adults in the United States is bilingual, although to varying degrees. Their literacy levels in the native and English languages also vary greatly, given that there are great discrepancies in their levels of formal education. Therein lies some of the complexity of meeting the language and educational needs of the immigrant populations in the United States. An additional challenge lies in the inextricable ties between language, culture, and social context. Literacy and biliteracy development implies not only the learning of a second language,[2] but also different ways of viewing and interacting with the world. Both perspectives, linguistic and sociocultural, are explored in this chapter. It is appropriate to first discuss some of the linguistic issues that adult learners face as they strive to acquire English and to develop biliteracy.

Development of Biliteracy

A general definition of biliteracy is the ability to read and write in two languages. A broader definition, however, includes more than reading and writing; it includes the ability to construct and communicate meaning in two languages across diverse social contexts and in socioculturally appropriate ways. The ability to do this in one language is, in itself, a challenge for many adults. The ability to do the same in two languages is a major challenge to many. The theoretical processes involved in the development of biliteracy, however, are not unlike the processes of literacy development in the first language. Many of the strategies used in the development of literacy in the native language are also used in the development of literacy in the second language; in fact, biliteracy development builds on the linguistic knowledge acquired in the first language.

Traditional psycholinguistic views of literacy considered it to be primarily a static process that involved the reader's knowledge of sound-symbol relationships. If a reader was able to decode a word or phrase, then she could pronounce it and thus read it. A starting point for literacy development was therefore to learn the letters of the alphabet and the study of phonics. However, there is an extensive body of literature that supports the notion that literacy is much more complex than what traditionalists might lead educators to believe. Learning phonics is only one small piece of the reading process. Knowledge about all of the components of language is critical to reading comprehension and writing. These involve knowledge about how the language works in terms of the sound system (phonology), the syntactic system (grammar), the morphology (word formation), and the semantics (word meaning), for all of these systems of language play a role in the literacy development process. This knowledge about the systems of language is acquired in a natural and subconscious manner by children as they are exposed to and begin to interact in their native language.

Knowing and drawing upon the linguistic systems, however, is only one of the various literacy behaviors of readers and writers of a language. Kucer (2001) summarizes the following strategies and behaviors exhibited by readers as they engage in the reading and writing processes:

- Generating and organizing major ideas and concepts and their corresponding supporting details and, when writing, expanding and elaborating on ideas
- Organizing or integrating meanings across the text into a logical and coherent whole
- Sampling and selecting visual (print) information, such as word beginnings and endings, that is necessary for the formulation of meaning when reading or for the expression of ideas when writing
- Selecting and using a variety of linguistic cues from a range of linguistic systems (semantic, syntactic, morphemic, etc.) to formulate meaning
- Using their knowledge of language and of the world, as relevant, to make sense from print or to create meaning through print
- Making meaningful predictions based on what has been previously read, or planning future meanings when writing, as based on the visual information sampled and selected, and on background knowledge
- Monitoring and evaluating the meaning that is generated to see if it makes sense

- Revising predictions or meanings when something does not make sense
- Using a variety of strategies to make revisions, such as rereading, consulting a dictionary, or deleting ideas when writing
- Generating inferences by building links between prior knowledge and what was read, or discovering new meanings when writing
- Reacting to what is read or written
- Varying the manner in which a text is read (e.g., skimming vs. looking for details) as based on the purpose for reading, or varying the style of writing depending on the purpose and the audience

A learner who is acquiring literacy in a second language is engaging in the same behaviors listed above that are exhibited in the native language. However, there are also differences that are brought about by the interaction of two languages, the native language and the second language, in the biliteracy development process. The following section elaborates on the notions of difference and linguistic interaction.

The Role of Transfer

This linguistic storehouse of knowledge acquired in the native language is used in a supportive role as adults acquire a second language. Studies in bilingualism have indicated that linguistic knowledge transfers from the first language to the second. Some of this knowledge is directly applicable to the second language, where the languages are similar. For instance, a Spanish-speaking student can directly apply grammatical notions from Spanish to English that function in the same way, such as subject-verb-object word order (e.g., *El perro se comió el hueso* and *The dog ate the bone*), the use of pronouns in subject position (e.g., *Ella es casada* and *She is married*), and the use of auxiliaries to form the present perfect tense in English (e.g., *Ella ha viajado a Guatemala* and *She has traveled to Guatemala*). The learner will hypothesize and reformulate rules about how the second language works where there are differences, such as in adjective placement (e.g., *el libro grueso* vs. *the thick book*). It has been suggested, moreover, that this transfer from the first to the second language occurs primarily in the early stages of second language development, with decreasing reliance on the first language in later stages of development (Ovando, Collier, & Combs, 2003).

The research literature on bilingualism also indicates that the linguistic knowledge that a student acquires in the development of a second language is cumulatively stored with knowledge about the native language. This storehouse of linguistic knowledge has been referred to as a common underlying proficiency (CUP) that bilingual and biliterate individuals possess (Cummins, 1981, cited in Baker, 2002). Students draw on their CUP in the course of learning a second language. This notion that two seemingly different languages actually have common properties at a deeper, structural level, and that students draw upon this knowledge in the development of bilingualism and biliteracy has also been referred to as the interdependence theory (Cummins, 2000, cited in Baker, 2002).

Likewise, knowledge gained about literacy in the first language transfers to the second language. The higher the levels of literacy in the native language, the higher the level of transfer will be to English literacy skills. An adult who has sixth grade literacy in Spanish, for instance, already knows much about reading and writing that can transfer to English. The reader knows, for example, that in Spanish one reads from left to right, top to bottom, that sentences begin in capital letters and end in periods, and that the first line of a paragraph is indented. More sophisticated literacy notions also transfer. For example, the same reader will also use context clues to guess the meaning of unknown words, predict events from titles and illustrations, skim for main ideas, and monitor her own meaning making as she reads. The same literacy strategies that have been learned and utilized in the first language are thus used in the second language once the learner has acquired the linguistic systems of English. The strategies from Kucer (2001) listed above are a source of transferable literacy skills for the biliteracy development process. Monitoring for meaning, for example, is one such strategy that can transfer. When a passage read in English does not make sense, the student might opt to go back and reread for increased understanding. Knowledge gained in the first language about the reading and writing processes can thus be applied to the second language, to the degree that an adult has developed literacy in the first language. This notion that the development of language and literacy in a second language is facilitated to the degree that one is literate in the native language is a function of the interdependence theory mentioned earlier.

Krashen (1996a), in his exploration of literacy and biliteracy development, elaborates on supporting evidence for this notion of transfer. He states that there are positive correlations between literacy development in the native and second languages in studies where confounding factors (such as length of residence in the United States) are controlled. These studies show that first language reading ability is a good predictor of second language reading ability. Those who read well in their native language also read well in the second language, as evidenced by reading performance in Chinese, Japanese, Vietnamese, Turkish, Spanish, and English. Krashen (1996b) adds that the underlying process of reading in different languages is similar as based on miscue analyses, the average number of eye fixations per word, and reading strategies utilized across languages. He also found that the literacy development process is similar in different languages. A print-rich environment, for example, produces better readers across different languages, and readers across languages can develop literacy without explicit instruction.

Adult students developing bilingualism and biliteracy thus come to the classroom with a body of previously acquired knowledge and strategies that are available to them in the second language as soon as they begin to develop proficiency and are able to express themselves in the second language. This transfer about literacy skills also occurs between languages that have significant differences. Ovando, Collier, and Combs (2003) write that "not only are L1 literacy skills important to L2 literacy in languages with obvious transfer possibilities, but also literacy skills from non-Roman alphabet languages (such as Arabic, Hindi, Korean, and Mandarin Chinese) assist significantly with acquisition of L2 literacy in a Roman-alphabet language such as English" (p. 130). Burt, Peyton, and Adams (2003) indicate that the levels of oral proficiency in English also impact the development of literacy in English. The implication is that it is easier to read and write about what one can already talk about.

Transfer also applies to the learning of content, or subject matter. Knowledge gained through the native language does not have to be retaught in a second language. A student who learned algebra in Spanish does not have to relearn it in English. Likewise, a student who has learned a trade (such as an electrician or a carpenter) does not need to relearn that trade in English. Both students will, however, have to learn corresponding language in English relevant to the subject area or occupation.

Literacy as a Transactional Process

Another aspect of the complexity of the reading process has to do with current notions about literacy that describe it as a transactional process that involves not only linguistic, but also cognitive and sociocultural factors. The process is transactional because the reader constructs meaning as she reads a given text by drawing on different sources of knowledge, such as knowledge about the text, the reader's own background knowledge, and knowledge about the author and her intent in writing the text. This is contrary to traditional views of literacy, which consider that the reader simply absorbs meaning, in a unitary fashion, as it appears on the printed page. Thus, given the traditional view, all readers interpret a given text the same way, while a transactional view of literacy acknowledges that a given text will be interpreted differently by different readers depending on their linguistic knowledge, their background knowledge about what they are reading, and their knowledge about the text itself. Perceptions about what the author is trying to convey also influence the interpretation of a text (Kucer, 2001; Smith, 1997). A Mexican student who encounters the word *wedding*, for instance, will have a very different understanding of a wedding celebration than an Anglo American student. The Mexican student may consider a wedding celebration to go on for 24 hours and entail a large wedding party, a religious celebration, lots of food and spirits for the guests, a dance that includes children and not just adults, a *menudo* (beef tripe with red chile) breakfast for all at about 4 A.M., and a get-together for dinner the following day. The Anglo American student may think of a different, lower-keyed, and shorter wedding celebration. The very different notions of wedding may cause confusion for a reader who is trying to make sense of a narrative that describes a wedding as well as several unrelated activities all taking place in a single day in the life of a protagonist.

Likewise, a student encountering the word *lunch* may not only think of very different foods than what a typical American lunch consists of, but also be mystified by a narrative that describes a manager going out to lunch and then attending a meeting at 1 P.M. Lunch in some Latin American countries occurs anywhere between 1 and 3 P.M. and may last two hours—thus the contradiction.

The notions of a common underlying proficiency, linguistic interdependence, and transfer are significant for adult literacy programs that strive to develop not only literacy in English, but also varying types of conceptual knowledge. One implication is that conceptual knowledge can more effectively and efficiently be taught in the native language. Family literacy programs, for instance, can implement parent enrichment instruction in Spanish, and thus build on the parenting knowledge already brought by participants; likewise, workforce literacy programs can discuss complex and more abstract notions, such as critical thinking in the face of workplace accidents (e.g., a chemical spill) in Spanish.

The notion that literacy involves a transactional process that includes the reader's cumulative background knowledge, knowledge about the text, and knowledge about the writer also has significant implications for the development of biliteracy. One implication already alluded to above is that the knowledge that students bring with them serves as a springboard for additional learning. This is true whether it is linguistic knowledge, conceptual knowledge, or experiential knowledge; it does not have to be retaught, although the expression of such knowledge in the second language does need to be taught. Another implication is that adults from diverse linguistic and cultural backgrounds will bring alternative bodies of knowledge to the learning situation, as opposed to what might be considered mainstream knowledge that native English speakers bring. Thus, they bring diverse "literacies," or ways of knowing, to the classroom. Because one's background knowledge and lived experiences play a highly significant role in the literacy development process, by extension, the curriculum and instruction for the learner must not only acknowledge and integrate these diverse literacies into the classroom, but also help fill in gaps of knowledge to assist students in the biliteracy development process, for literacy is a sociocultural construct.

Sociocultural Perspectives on Bilingualism and Biliteracy

We start to name the world as our parents and caretakers give us the words to represent it. These seemingly simple words or mere nouns, however, carry the meanings and emotions associated with particular experiences. Freire (1987) expresses this vividly when describing his growing up and learning to read in Recife, Brazil:

> The text, words, letters of that context were incarnated in the song of the
> birds—tanager, flycatcher, thrush—... in the color of foliage, the shape

of leaves, the fragrance of flowers ...—the green of the mango when the fruit is first forming, the green of a mango fully formed, the greenish-yellow of the same mango ripening, the black spots of an overripe mango ... (p. 30)

Knowledge of the world is acquired throughout our lives, and it is expressed through language. Feelings, values, and emotions are engraved in the language through which experiences are first named. As children develop language and ways to name their experiences, they are also developing a view of the world and ways to make meaning as they interact with it. When individuals acquire a second or additional language, they add more lenses through which they perceive and name their world. For bilinguals, the naming of one reality, such as the one connected to emotions, may be associated with the language they learned from their parents, while other realities, such as that of school, may be associated with a second language. The development of literacies among bilinguals is also complex. A Spanish-speaking immigrant, who learned English as an adult, may feel more comfortable writing in Spanish, but the same individual may feel more competent in English when writing about her job and other academic-related matters that she learned in English.

Successful bilinguals choose between languages, in their oral and written forms, depending on the social context in which they are functioning. For example, when encountering a friend who is monolingual, the choice of language is obvious. However, when meeting a bilingual friend with whom the speaker shares a similar cultural background, the choice of language is not obvious. A Latino speaker may choose Spanish, English, or both for the linguistic interaction. Languages are chosen depending on many variables, including the topic of conversation, the level of intimacy between the speakers, and the need to denote subtle meanings and identities. Moreover, these choices are compounded by the use of sophisticated sociolinguistic skills such as code switching (Zentella, 1997) to relay specific sentiments and meanings that are culturally bound. "I was very upset because él me faltó al respeto" was overheard in a conversation between two bilingual young adults. The reason for the switch between languages is obvious to many Puerto Rican New Yorkers. *Respeto* is a word for which, although there is a cognate in English, *respect*, the English does not meet the meaning demands that the word in Spanish fulfills for Puerto Ricans. The linguistic choices embedded in the use of a first, second, or both languages come naturally to bilinguals and depend on the languages known by the interlocutors and their cultural affiliation. Sometimes a language is chosen for other sociolinguistic reasons. For example, one might include others in a conversation by switching to English when there is a monolingual English speaker in the group, or might exclude others by switching back to Spanish to mark cultural boundaries. Bilinguals and speakers of dialects utilize these linguistic strategies.

The individuals described above share a linguistic and cultural repertoire that allows them to navigate in and out of two systems to transverse across linguistic, cultural, social, and academic contexts. The linguistic theory that underlies the biliteracy development process and dual-language use of these individuals was described above. The following section will make an attempt to describe the social and cultural foundations of bilinguals' linguistic competencies and dual-language use.

Literacy as a Sociocultural Construct

Paulo Freire (1987) in the following quotation emphasizes the complex and dynamic connection between literacy and social reality: "Reading does not merely consist of decoding the written word or language; rather it is preceded by and intertwined with knowledge of the world. Language and reality are dynamically interconnected" (p. 29).

Street has proposed two models to explain different notions of literacy, the autonomous and ideological models. The *autonomous* model of literacy focuses on discrete elements of reading and writing skills and conceptualizes them in technical terms, which are independent of social context (Street, 1993). This model narrows the definition of literacy to sets of transferable skills involved in learning to read and write in a particular language that can be taught and measured in standardized ways. In the United States formal literacy has been understood not only as literacy in English, but also, more specifically, in a particular, idealistic, and unaccented variety of English (Wiley & Lukes, 1996). The autonomous view of literacy, coupled with restricting the value of literacy skills to those learned in American Standard English, has too often meant English-only instruction for children and adults. These beliefs have also obscured the ways in which literacy is represented in other languages and their varieties because they overlook how literacy is used in diverse communities. Moreover, constricting literacy to literacy in the "dominant" language leads to the perception that other types of literacy are inadequate, impoverished, and need to be remediated by schooling (Street, 1994). Such a narrow frame of reference impedes the understanding of the many uses that individuals, bilingual or otherwise, make of being literate and active in the world, and it also represents their actions as static.

The *ideological* model of literacy proposed by Street (1993) views literacy practices as inextricably linked to culture and power structures in society and recognizes the variety of cultural practices associated with reading and writing in different contexts. In order to understand literacy in a broader perspective, one that includes a view of the world, social interaction, and culture, one must go beyond the "autonomous" definition that treats reading only as psycholinguistic processing skills. It requires a view of language that is connected to experience and situated action and interaction in the world (Gee, 2001). This view provides the space to understand the cultural practices and uses that bilinguals have of literacy in two languages and problematizes English-only instruction.

Sociocultural views of literacy such as those developed by the New Literacy Studies (Street, 1993, 2000) and the New London Group (Hamilton, 2000; New London Group, 1996) and as described in cultural-historical or Vygotskian approaches (Cole, 1996; Moll, 2000) propose inclusive ways to understand literacy. The New Literacy Studies (NLS) pay attention to the social practices and conceptions of reading and writing and the rich cultural variation in these practices. Street (1993, 2000) contends that reading and writing only make sense when studied within the social and cultural contexts in which they take place. Two immigrant workers in a factory may use two languages orally and in writing to discuss and take notes about the workings of a particular machine. They complement each other's knowledge of the working of the machine and of English to make sense of its operational manual.

The concept of multiliteracies proposed by the New London Group is concerned with cultural and linguistic diversity and the integration of the different modes of communication channels and media available in the new global order (Cope & Kalantzis, 2000; New London Group, 1996; Street, 1993). The immigrants described in the preceding section, for example, may use pictures to complement their note taking at work. The same persons may share their knowledge about the machine (in English and Spanish) with a cousin in Mexico through electronic mail. Since there are multiple ways to be literate in a language (multiliteracies), literacy in additional languages will expand the contexts, channels, media, and uses for bilingual and biliterate individuals to express what they know and are able to do.

Cultural-historical theory posits that learning is essentially social and that linguistic interaction and mediated experiences are central to the development of literacy (Vygotsky, 1986). For bilinguals the mediated experience may take place in the first, second, or both languages, and thus, the engagements with literacy can be multiple.

These views provide sociocultural and historical lenses through which one can understand the complexities embedded in the development and use of biliteracy. They are inclusive of the multiple channels and contexts in which individuals express themselves orally and in writing and take into consideration the cultural and social demands in each of these contexts. The centrality of language and mediated experience sheds light on how individuals live in literacy—how they understand, develop, and use literacies in their daily lives.

Biliteracy as a Sociocultural and Historical Activity

According to sociocultural and historical approaches, the development of literacy (in one, two, or more languages) goes beyond the psycholinguistic processes involved in learning to decode, such as knowing vocabulary and sound-letter correspondences in two languages, because it includes the interaction between languages and social worlds. For bilinguals, the interaction between the two languages and their social worlds is what makes the development of biliteracy a complex process. For in addition to the use of two languages, biliteracy demands successful participation in two cultures and their corresponding activities, values, and expectations. Brice Heath (1982) stated that what counts as literacy varies across communities. She argued that the use of oral or literate interaction depends on what is appropriate according to the setting and the participants, and that there is shifting and interplay between how individuals use oral and written language.

For biliterate individuals, the interplay between languages and literacy in these languages and contexts is ever constant, depending on the appropriateness of language use in relation to the setting, the participants, and their linguistic backgrounds. There is interplay in deciding which of the languages meets the particular communication demands of a situation and in what mode. In other words, expressing a thought in a particular language would depend on many factors. Bilinguals must consider which language best meets their meaning demands and if they feel linguistically competent to use it. Additionally, bilinguals' use of oral language and literacy (in the first, second, or both languages) depends on the contexts and functions of what they want to accomplish. For example, Sergio, an immigrant worker in a food processing plant in Canada, takes notes in English and Spanish of the procedures he follows, using *bien* or *muy bien* to note a good temperature or speed setting for a particular product in a certain tunnel (Belfiore, 2004). As stated by Belfiore, "His practice captured not only his steps in the process but, more importantly, his thinking, his considered conclusions about what was 'bien' or 'muy bien' in different circumstances" (p. 60). In other words, Sergio made choices in terms of which language best met his meaning demands and how comfortable he felt using it to document a rigorous procedure. Sergio used his biliteracy in a manner that was efficient, effective, and socially and contextually appropriate.

Children and emergent bilinguals also demonstrate attention to the relationship between language and context. Reyes (2001) described the writings of Iliana, a first-grader who was instructed in Spanish because of her recent arrival from Mexico. Iliana writes a letter to Santa Claus in English because she probably thinks he speaks English. In her letter, she writes, "She has been 'good' because she has 'obad' [obeyed] her 'Ticher' [teacher]" (p. 109). In addition to writing to Santa in a language she thinks he would understand, Iliana uses what she knows about writing in Spanish and what she knows of English to accomplish her task. Like Sergio, she focused on meaning, choosing English to make her letter comprehensible to a monolingual Santa. These examples illustrate the notion that bilinguals use biliteracy in effective, efficient, and contextually appropriate ways. Their focus on meaning guides their language choice—they choose the language(s) that best expresses what they need to communicate in a particular context.

Vygotsky (1978) posits that all human activity and learning are socially mediated and that language is the primary mediator of this activity. Parents, as children's first mediators, share with them important cultural knowledge through their social interactions. These social interactions create zones of proximal development in which children are able to access knowledge, including cultural knowledge, which allows them to reach their developmental potential. At the center of this interaction is guidance by and collaboration with more capable peers. Thus, language, culture, and knowledge are developed through mediated experiences with more capable others and are cornerstones of identity development. Encounters between experts and learners mediated by linguistic interaction and experiences are central to the development of literacy (Vygotsky, 1986), and thus, meaning is constructed through the process of articulating ideas in joint activity with others (Lee & Smagorinsky, 2000). Due to the centrality of mediated experience in Vygotsky's theory, "Language becomes the primary medium for learning, meaning construction, and cultural transmission and transformation" (Lee & Smagorinsky, 2000, p. 2). In addition to being central to learning and to the development of literacy, language also serves as a conceptual organizer or a primary medium through which thinking occurs (Lee, 2000).

According to Vygotsky's sociohistorical theory, therefore, individuals develop bilingualism as they interact with other bilinguals. Through verbal and written interactions with other capable users of two languages, bilinguals also learn cultural knowledge, including ways of thinking, meaning making, and how to organize the world. These affect how bilinguals approach, use, and interpret oral and written language. Bilinguals bring to their understanding of a reading in Spanish the conception of the world that is embedded in that language. Their knowledge of English and their bicultural knowledge inform and enhance the understanding of a particular text. One can read a text in one language, for example, and discuss it in the other, and thus, biliteracy augments the background knowledge a reader can draw from in order to comprehend texts through different sociocultural prisms. This is illustrated in an example given by Jiménez drawn from his research with fifth- and sixth-graders. Maria, in responding to the question of how what she knows in Spanish helps her learn English, states, "Si no entiendo el inglés, tengo que pensar en español y así me ayuda." Maria responded that when not able to understand a reading in English, she can think in Spanish and help herself (Jiménez, 2000, p. 993). She is able to use both languages in the process of organizing her thinking to draw meaning from text. Similarly, Huerta-Macías (this volume) provides examples of how bilingual lessons can expedite job attainment and advancement for workers with low levels of English. In an ESL lesson on safety in a construction site, for example, the teacher and the students brainstorm about what the students already know about accidents on the job. The workers can respond in Spanish or English. The instructor uses the context of the initial brainstorm to introduce job-related vocabulary in English. In addition to learning such words as *hazardous*, *spill*, and *danger zone* in the

ESL lesson, the students will encounter the same words in reading assignments in English texts that are used for the construction lessons (Huerta-Macías, this volume). The bilingual lessons allow workers to utilize their native language and background knowledge to acquire new knowledge and to learn English. The intellectual power of biliteracy is that it mediates and amplifies the cultural experiences of learners (including how they deal with text) in ways that are not possible in one language alone (Moll & Dworin, 1996). This is particularly the case for adults because they have at least one fully developed language and can draw from vast amounts of past experience and background knowledge in order to make meaning from and with text.

Biliteracy in Different Contexts

Understanding literacy in relational ways—in terms of what individuals and social groups do with literacy, how they do it, where and with whom (Hamilton, 2000)—can lead to an understanding of what biliterate individuals do with literacy in varying social, communicative, and cultural contexts. It allows to better understand, for instance, how they favor one language over the other in particular contexts or with whom. Since there is a mixture of written and spoken language in many literacy events (Brice Heath, 1982; Barton & Hamilton, 2000), the interplay between languages (the first, second, or both) in their oral and written representations is multifold. For example, a bilingual adult discussing a newspaper article that is written in English may go back and forth between English and Spanish to get her point across while supporting her ideas by referring to the English text. This complex linguistic activity would only be socially appropriate when discussing the article with a person with whom the reader shares both linguistic backgrounds. With a monolingual person, she would have to use different strategies. Moreover, there are social practices associated with the use of literacy in a particular language or when using two languages at the same time, as in code switching. Dworin (2003), Gutiérrez, Baquedano-López, and Alvarez (2001), and Jiménez (2000) offer examples of bilingual children using their bilingual, bicultural, and biliterate knowledge and skills to make sense of what they are reading and writing, thus demonstrating a sophisticated understanding of the social practices associated with literacy in one or both languages. Gutiérrez et al. (2001) describe Martha's relationship to El Maga, an ambiguous entity with whom she corresponds through e-mail. After Martha discovers that El Maga is bilingual in Spanish and English, she begins using Spanish and English in her e-mails in ways that are culturally appropriate. For example, she uses *usted* to relay respect for El Maga. Martha "displays not only her fluency in both languages but also her ability to be humorous and play with language across cultures and codes" (Gutiérrez et al., 2001, p. 135).

Smith (1997) refers to the importance of children seeing themselves as members of the "literacy club," a group of written language users. By becoming a member of the literacy club, he states that children find themselves among people who are engaged in meaningful written activities and learn to see themselves as readers and writers. Biliterate individuals must see themselves as members of a biliteracy club that includes other competent users of literacy in Spanish and English, separately or at the same time. For example, Martha, as a member of a biliteracy club, had opportunities to use and demonstrate her biliterate and bicultural knowledge through meaningful activities in her relationship with El Maga. Daniel, a second-grader who enjoyed reading in English and Spanish, when asked about his reading in two languages, reported that Spanish was his first language and added, "but I was born with a little bit of English" (Dworin, 2003, p. 37). Even though he wrote mostly in Spanish, he chose to write a letter in English to a friend because he knew his friend did not read Spanish well. Like Martha, as a result of using both languages in meaningful activities at home and at school, Daniel viewed himself as a capable user of literacy in two languages. In a biliteracy club there would be members who would be more competent in Spanish, while others would be more competent in English. There would be members for whom the hybridized language use flows naturally in both languages, while there would be others for whom literacy is more clearly defined in one language. What all members would share are the meanings, strengths, and struggles of what it means to belong to two literate worlds with their cultural and social meanings.

This has important repercussions for bilinguals, especially in terms of developing literacy in school. When only one language is used in instruction, as is often the case in U.S. schools, a bilingual may favor English over Spanish not only because of the appropriateness of the use of this language to the social context, but also because he has become more proficient with writing in English. Because language proficiency and literacy levels are also a function of use and interaction (their learning is social and mediated), a bilingual adult may become more literate in English for academic purposes, but may continue to favor Spanish in social interaction.

Biliteracy and Schooling

Literacy in one or both languages relates to the years of instruction in the particular language and personal motivation in learning and using literacy in that language (Farr, 1994). Brittany, an emergent bilingual who was assigned to English literacy instruction (Reyes, 2001), took up reading and writing in Spanish and English, motivated by her friendship with Iliana, who was a Spanish speaker. Brittany's choice of language to write in her journals and literature response logs depended on her mood, the book she was reading, and the nature of her writing. These choices suggest that she was using one or the other language in ways that were appropriate to the context and topics of her writing (Reyes, 2001). Likewise, Daniel chose to write in English to a friend who did not read Spanish well (Dworin, 2003). Instruction, motivation, mediated interaction with other bilinguals, opportunities to use literacy, and social, cultural, and meaning-making demands are important variables in the development of biliteracy. Guerra and Farr (2002) offer another example in their descriptions of Malú's writings. Malú was born in the United States, attended schools in the United States and in Mexico, and was enrolled in college in Chicago at the time of the study. She was the oldest of four children of Mexican descent and the first to attend college. In personal narratives Malú uses English and Spanish. Her shifting from one language to the other within one narrative depended on the topic and stylistic decisions. She chose English for topics that were related to school and Spanish when writing about family life. These examples, of children and an adult, show a "fluency" in how these bilinguals used biliteracy in writing that, in addition to instruction, depended on the topic, situation, style, and purpose of the piece.

Monolingual instruction and lack of opportunities to learn from and interact with other competent bilinguals and their social worlds have dire results for bilinguals. The forced use of only one language is stressful and unnatural. Imposing a monolingual environment in a bilingual context creates artificial borders for linguistic use and, as stated by Moll and González (1994), can be an annoying constraint in these contexts. Biliteracy, on the other hand, expands the possibility of accessing funds of knowledge from two or more social worlds and their immediate linguistic and ethnic communities (Moll & González, 1994).

Perceiving and acting on bilingualism and biliteracy as a problem rather than as a resource (Ruíz, 1984, 1990) or as a curse rather than a blessing (Wiley & Lukes, 1996) can have negative educational outcomes. Jiménez (2000) in a study of middle school, bilingual, low-literacy learners found that the less competent bilingual Latino readers were more apt to see bilingualism as problematic than were competent readers. These readers did not know how to capitalize on the use of their two languages when reading. On the other hand, the Latino students who were better readers created multiple connections between their two languages in reading comprehension. When the low-literacy learners were taught to use some of the reading strategies used by successful bilingual readers, they were able to demonstrate a deeper processing of text. English-only instruction for adults prevents them from accessing information that they need right away in order to have jobs, access social services, and get involved in their children's education.

The emotional and personal consequences of monolingual instruction are also negative. Wong Fillmore (2000) and Baez (2002) share moving stories of the emotional and personal loss resulting from English-only instruction. For Kai-fong and Chu-mei, two immigrant children from China studied by Wong Fillmore (2000), the loss of their ancestral language meant isolation from family members and with it their sense of belonging, knowing where they came from, and how to deal with life.

Baez (2002) describing his own schooling process, and how in order to become fluent in English he had to forget Spanish, also referred to the loss of the intimacy associated with his native language and the closeness to his family and past that it allowed. He states that, like Richard Rodriguez (1982), he too forgot his *private* identity in order to learn a new one. He warns against the continued victimization of children by requiring them to give up their home language. Once a language is lost, the ability to create bilingual worlds is thwarted, forcing bilinguals instead to choose between what is made to appear like two irreconcilable realities: the personal/familiar and the public one. Baez (2002) states, "Language made me Puerto Rican, and then American, and each had its own set of permitted (when a Puerto Rican, a member of a family, a son; when American, a successful individual) and prohibited (when Puerto Rican, a non-American; when American, a non-Puerto Rican) spaces" (p. 129). Baez refers to the permitted and prohibited spaces as the normal and the stigmatized and brings attention to the regulating role of language in making "obvious" (to parents, teachers, students) how "normal" it is to learn English, even at the expense of forgetting one's first language.

Bilingualism is looked upon as an asset in immigrant families who often have to rely on their children to negotiate new environments. The middle school students studied by Jiménez (2000) referred to the importance of maintaining their Spanish to communicate with family members, including parents, through letter writing and to fulfill their role as translators for monolingual relatives. Adults are also aware of the importance of their children maintaining Spanish. This way, their children can benefit from their parenting and from participation in family and community networks. This has been amply documented in adult education programs serving immigrants (Quintero & Huerta-Macías, 1993). Parents are mindful of the role that language plays in their children's inclusion in or exclusion from two worlds: the family and outside worlds. In the outside world, English can provide privilege or work as a gatekeeper. Therefore, adults are eager to learn English and want their children to learn English as soon as possible. This eagerness, coupled with uninformed educational advice, sometimes results in English-only instruction for the children and with it the loss of intimacy and the capacity to share knowledge, values, and traditions that are at the heart of parents' functions and roles. It can also result in ESL-only instruction for adults, which precludes them from building on what they know and transferring knowledge from their first language.

Looking at language systems as separate from their sociocultural contexts precludes teachers and researchers from noticing the wide variety of ways in which biliterate individuals use the linguistic resources available to them and limits the ways through which educators can build on and extend instruction. Furthermore, the exclusive use of English in instruction determines who produces knowledge and who has access to it, taking away students' language as a "fundamental tool for the production of knowledge, reflection and social transformation" (Rivera, 1999a, p. 490). For example, by using Spanish and English in the curriculum, students at El Barrio Popular Education Program analyzed the impact of immigration reform in their lives. They interviewed community members (in English and Spanish) about their attitudes and beliefs about immigration. They also met with lawyers, members of Congress, and other politicians and produced educational videos based on their findings. This process was possible because "the native language of the students was not abandoned as a transitional tool to develop literacy or English skills but was utilized through the process of their own education as an important resource (Ruíz, 1984, 1990) which could be developed and enriched" (Rivera, 1999b, pp. 342–343). Monolingual English instruction also thwarts the capacity that bilinguals have to draw from two or more social worlds and from the cultures that live and breathe in them.

Biliteracy and Identity

As discussed in the preceding section, literacy is developed through mediated experiences with other language users. These experiences are rooted in sociocultural practices and are cornerstones of identity development. Identity develops along with language and is acquired informally in the home and neighborhood as individuals socialize with family and community members. As stated by Street (1994), "In learning literacy practices we are not just learning a technical skill but are taking on particular identities associated with them" (p. 15). Biliterate individuals develop language and literacy as well as ways to interact with their worlds that are socially and culturally appropriate. As bilinguals use their two languages to interact with other bilinguals in a range of cultural and social contexts, their identities shift accordingly.

Requiring bilinguals to replace one language with another impacts the way that they perceive themselves, and thus their identity. Baez's (2002) experience of how when he beholds himself as a Puerto Rican he is a non-American and when an American he is a non-Puerto Rican demonstrates a lack of reconciliation in his bilingual bicultural self. Chu-mei and Kai-fong, the children studied by Wong Fillmore (2000), changed their names to Sondra and Ken to fit in at school. Skilton-Sylvester (2002) relates how Nan, a Vietnamese girl in fifth grade, seemed to tie her ability to choose the right American name to her success at school. "Nan sensed that she did not have the resources she needed to succeed in school but if she could somehow be someone else, she might be able to flourish" (p. 66). So, she first became Mandy and then Stacey.

Biliteracy allows individuals to reach a hybrid identity where they can be Puerto Rican, Mexican, Vietnamese, or Chinese and also North American. It permits them to take on two complementary rather than competing identities (Saxena, 1994). This complementary/hybrid identity provides the space to be here and there and to express oneself in one or the other language, perhaps in both, verbally and in writing, allowing literacy to shift according to what one is accomplishing. An identity is neither white, black, brown, or olive skin, nor English, Spanish, Quechua, or Mayan speaker, but rather something that biliterates are making, that is in flux.

This hybrid identity is necessary because as parents, workers, and community members, adults must play different roles and assume the identities these demand. Some of these identities are associated with the first language, others with the second, and some with a hybrid space. García, Morín, and Rivera (2001) found in their study of a Pentecostal church in Brooklyn that even though English was used informally in the church, Spanish was the language that the participants favored for the proclamation of faith, the reading of the Bible, and religious instruction. The church provided the space for a hybrid identity to exist. Even children, who were mostly monolingual as the result of being in English-only classrooms, had learned to read and write in Spanish during Bible studies, and thus incorporated a Spanish literate identity to their repertoire. This type of scenario takes place at home where a parent helps a child with homework, discussing it in Spanish while the child writes it in English. It also takes place in the workplace. Hull and Schultz (2002), Belfiore (2004), and Hunter (2004) report on how a particular identity may lead to the acceptance or rejection of certain literacy practices at work.

A bilingual's hybrid identity can also be negated during a particular literacy event. This takes place, for example, when literacy is associated exclusively with one language, such as in the case of English-only instruction, and the implied rejection of the worthiness of the bilingual's other language and culture. Being bilingual, Mexican American or New York Puerto Rican is part of one's amalgamated identity. To leave a piece of that identity behind is a threat to who one is, where one has been, and from where one has come. Benjamin Alire Saenz (2004) writes in response to the Russian poet Joseph Brodsky's suggestion that he keep Spanish, a foreign language according to Brodsky, out of his writings:

> I cling to my culture because it is my memory, and what is a poet without memory? I cling to my culture because it is my skin, because it is my heart, because it is my voice, because it breathes my mother's mother's mother into me. My culture is the genesis and the center of my writing, the most authentic space I have to write from. I am blind without the lenses of my culture. (p. 253)

Latinos in the United States are creating spaces that are more inclusive of the practices and expressions of their bilingual, bicultural, and biliterate identities. These practices and expressions will continue to change as Latino identity amalgamates to include more of the entire gamut of the cultural differences and similarities between those who are immigrants and those born and raised in the United States. Morales (2002) states, "Latino culture, which is constantly evolving both north and south of the border, involves an increasing, if nonsystemic, proliferation of identities that allow us to choose from an array of guises, accents, class mannerisms, and racial solidarities" (p. 19). For this, Latinos can draw from ethnic similarity, racial affiliations, language, accents, and fluid geographical borders as they strive to make sense of a hybridized identity and the power they have in their shared and evolving languages and the literacies within.

Programmatic Responses

In a demographically rapidly changing society such as the United States, educators face the challenge of how to best meet the needs of a diverse student population. These are some of the questions that adult educators have raised as they try to develop a culturally and linguistically appropriate pedagogy for their students. How can they use the bilingual and biliterate potential of their students as an asset in the curriculum? How can they help their students access what they know from two different languages and two cultural worlds to inform instruction? How can educators help their students to use both languages to think and learn? How can they see beyond the grammar of a particular language as students develop their biliterate potential so that they do not hinder their students' creativity? How can educators observe and learn from what adults do outside the classroom to inform and amplify the contexts for learning? How can educators help students to become mindful of the multiple ways to activate their metalinguistic and metacultural strategies to make sense of literacy in different social contexts?

The following are the shared characteristics of adult education programs that are successful implementers of a pedagogy that engenders bilingualism and biliteracy. These include providing adult students with ample opportunities to:

1. Make multiple connections between languages:
   - Activate background knowledge, knowledge acquired in the native language as well as English. During literacy instruction, adult students should learn to make text-to-world, text-to-text and text-to-self connections (Harvey & Goudvis, 2000) to activate what they know to aid their reading comprehension.
   - Apply the strategies that successful bilinguals use to make meaning across languages, such as consciously transferring and translating and activating the knowledge about cognate vocabulary in Spanish and English (Jiménez, 2001).
   - Use the native language to ask questions, explore prior knowledge and knowledge about the world, brainstorm, organize ideas, and develop outlines.
   - Engage with material and content that is interesting and relevant to adults.
   - Use language in context and learn new vocabulary in context.
   - Engage in instruction that is modified to make it accessible to the bilingual who is developing literacy in both languages.

2. Apply reading comprehension strategies that good readers use, for example:
- Use prediction, questioning, rereading, evaluating, and monitoring for comprehension. These strategies can be more fruitful to bilinguals when used in both languages. For example, when monitoring for comprehension, a bilingual may not necessarily have to do it in the language in which the text is written. The reader can do the monitoring in the bilingual's other language with the same results—or perhaps better, depending on his familiarity with the language of the text.
- Read in one language and discuss the text in both languages.
- Use graphic organizers and take notes in either language or in both.

3. Use both languages in socioculturally appropriate interactive activities:
- Engage in language activities that are appropriate to the sociocultural background of the student.
- Make sociocultural connections between the two languages. What are the differences and similarities in terms of interactional styles? What works in a language that does not work in the other?
- Use languages in purposeful activities. For example, write letters in either language to accomplish students' real tasks, engage in project-based learning, use language in and outside of the classroom.
- Engage with culturally appropriate and relevant texts.
- Use different modes of communication (oral, written, artistic, and electronic—telephone, text and e-mail messaging, etc.) in both languages.

Conclusion

This chapter has presented demographic characteristics that reflect the current dynamics of the U.S. population. The increasing numbers of immigrants who bring diverse linguistic and cultural backgrounds make it imperative that educators integrate notions of biliteracy development processes into their work with diverse student groups. The linguistic and sociocultural perspectives of biliteracy development were also discussed, along with implications for how emerging bilinguals utilize two languages across different social contexts, both in and outside of the classroom. The importance of making connections between a bilingual's two languages was emphasized as a way of assisting the biliteracy development processes. This chapter concluded with a listing of characteristics of successful adult education programs that engender bilingualism and biliteracy development. Chapters 3 to 7 provide detailed descriptions of these types of education programs. Examples include family, workforce, civics, community, and academic education programs that embody those notions described herein on biliteracy development and dual-language use.

The notions discussed in this chapter underscore the need for educators to go beyond traditional notions of literacy development in our work with immigrant adults acquiring English and to think in terms of a broader perspective of literacy development. This broader perspective includes biliteracy and issues of assessment, culture, identity, bilingualism, and language—all of which function in dynamic, interrelated ways. The multidimensional and complex aspects of the process imply the need for:

- Expanding the understandings of educators regarding literacy and biliteracy development such that their knowledge base in this area will be enhanced
- Advocating and supporting immigrant students seeking to learn English as they face the cognitive, linguistic, and affective issues that impact their learning and as they strive to navigate their way through American society
- Applying the notions of literacy and biliteracy development to classroom practice
- Applying what we know about biliteracy development to program designs
- Challenging notions that the only way to access learning and be successful in the United States is through English

The chapters that follow further discuss these ideas and present examples that describe what instruction and practice based on a multidimensional view of literacy and biliteracy look like in diverse learning contexts.

Endnotes

1. *Latinos* is used herein as an all-inclusive term to refer to Puerto Ricans, Mexicans, Salvadorans, and all Latin American subgroups. The term *Hispanic* is used interchangeably with *Latino* when discussing research that uses this term. Thus, the term used in a specific study is preserved when reporting on that study.
2. The authors are aware that some immigrants are acquiring a third or fourth language in their struggle to learn English; however, for the purpose of this discussion we will consider two languages only, given that the theoretical issues are essentially the same regardless of the number of languages involved.

References

Baez, B. (2002). Learning to forget: Reflections on identity and language. *Journal of Latinos and Education, 1*, 123–132.

Baker, C. (2002). *Foundations of bilingual education and bilingualism.* Toronto: Multilingual Matters.

Barton, D., & Hamilton, M. (2000). Literacy practices. In D. Barton, M. Hamilton, & R. Ivanic (Eds.), *Situated literacies: Reading and writing in context* (pp. 7–15). London: Routledge.

Belfiore, M. E. (2004). Literacies, compliance and certification. In M. E. Belfiore, T. A. Defoe, S. Folinsbee, J. Hunter, & N. S. Jackson (Eds.), *Reading work: Literacies in the new workplace* (pp. 19–61). Mahwah, NJ: Lawrence Erlbaum Associates.

Brice Heath, S. (1982). Protean shapes in literacy events: Ever-shifting oral and literate traditions. In D. Tannen (Ed.), *Spoken and written language: Exploring orality and literacy* (pp. 91–117). Norwood, NJ: Ablex.

Burt, M., Peyton, J. K., & Adams, R. (2003). *Reading and adult English language learners: A review of the research.* Washington, DC: Center for Applied Linguistics.

Capps, R., Fix, M., Passel, J.S., Ost, J., & Perez-Lopez, D. (2003, November). *A profile of the low-wage immigrant workforce.* Washington, DC: Urban Institute.

Cole, M. (1996). *Cultural psychology: A once and future discipline.* Cambridge, MA: Harvard University Press.

Cope, B., & Kalantzis, M. (2000). Introduction. Multiliteracies: The beginning of an idea. In B. Cope & M. Kalantzis (Eds., for the New London Group), *Multiliteracies: Literacy learning and the design of social futures* (pp. 3–8). London: Routledge.

Dworin, J. (2003). Examining children's biliteracy in the classroom. In A. I. Willis, G. E. Garcia, R. Barrera, & V. J. Harris (Eds.), *Multicultural issues in literacy research and practice* (pp. 29–48). Mahwah, NJ: Lawrence Erlbaum Associates.

Farr, M. (1994). En los dos idiomas: Literacy practices among Chicano Mexicanos. In B. J. Moss (Ed.), *Literacy across communities* (pp. 9–47). Cresskill, NJ: Hampton Press.

Freire, P. (1987). The importance of the act of reading. In P. Freire & D. Macedo (Eds.), *Literacy: Reading the word and the world* (pp. 29–36). South Hadley, MA: Bergin & Garvey.

García, O., Morín, J. L., & Rivera, K. (2001). How threatened is the Spanish of New York Puerto Ricans? Language shift with vaivén. In J. A. Fishman (Ed.), *Can threatened languages be saved?* (pp. 44–73). Clevedon, England: Multilingual Matters.

Gee, J. P. (2001). Reading as situated language: A sociocognitive perspective. *Journal of Adolescent and Adult Literacy, 44,* 714–725.

Guerra, J. C., & Farr, M. (2002). The spiritual and autobiographical discourse of two Mexicanas in Chicago. In G. Hull & K. Schultz (Eds.), *School's out! Bridging out-of-school literacies with classroom practice* (pp. 96–123). New York: Teachers College Press.

Gutiérrez, K. D., Baquedano-López, P., & Alvarez, H. H. (2001). Literacy and hybridity: Moving beyond bilingualism in urban classrooms. In M. de la Luz Reyes & J. J. Halcón (Eds.), *The best for our children: Critical perspectives on literacy for Latino students* (pp. 122–141). New York: Teachers College Press.

Hamilton, M. (2000, July). *Sustainable literacies and the ecology of lifelong learning. Working papers of the global colloquium on supporting lifelong learning.* Retrieved August 10, 2004, from http/www.open.ac.uk/lifelong-learning/index.html

Harvey, S., & Goudvis, A. (2000). *Strategies that work: Teaching comprehension to enhance understanding.* Portland, ME: Stenhouse.

Hull, G., & Schultz, K. (2002). Connecting schools with out-of-school worlds: Insights from recent research on literacy in non-school settings. In G. Hull & K. Schultz (Eds.), *School's out! Bridging out-of-school literacies with classroom practice* (pp. 32–57). New York: Teachers College Press.

Hunter, J. (2004). Implications for theory. In M. E. Belfiore, T. A. Defoe, S. Folinsbee, J. Hunter, & N. S. Jackson (Eds.), *Reading work: Literacies in the new workplace* (pp. 241–260). Mahwah, NJ: Lawrence Erlbaum Associates.

Immigration Facts. (2003, October). *Unauthorized immigration to the United States.* Retrieved July 18, 2004, from http://www.migrationpolicy.org

Jiménez, R. T. (2000). Literacy and the identity development of Latina/o students. *American Educational Research Journal, 37,* 971–1000.

Jiménez, R. T. (2001). Strategic reading for language-related disabilities: The case of a bilingual Latina student. In M. de la Luz Reyes & J. J. Halcón (Eds.), *The best for our children: Critical perspectives on literacy for Latino students* (pp. 155–167). New York: Teachers College Press.

Krashen, S. D. (1996a). *Under attack: The case against bilingual education.* Culver City, CA: Language Education Associates.

Krashen, S. D. (1996b, May, 1). Does literacy transfer? *NABE News,* 5–36.

Kucer, S. B. (2001). *Dimensions of literacy: A conceptual base for teaching reading and writing in school settings.* Mahwah, NJ: Lawrence Erlbaum Associates.

Lee, C. D. (2000). Signifying in the zone of proximal development. In C. Lee & P. Smagorinsky (Eds.), *Vygotskian perspectives on literacy research* (pp. 191–225). New York: Cambridge University Press.

Lee, C. D., & Smagorinsky, P. (2000). Introduction. In C. Lee & P. Smagorinsky (Eds.), *Vygotskian perspectives on literacy research* (pp. 1–15). New York: Cambridge University Press.

Moll, L. C. (2000). Inspired by Vygotsky: Ethnographic experiments in education. In C. Lee & P. Smagorinsky (Eds.), *Vygotskian perspectives on literacy research* (pp. 256–268). New York: Cambridge University Press.

Moll, L., & Dworin, J. (1996). Biliteracy in classrooms: Social dynamics and cultural possibilities. In D. Hicks (Ed.), *Child discourse and social learning* (pp. 221–246). New York: Cambridge University Press.

Moll, L., & González N. (1994). Lessons from research with language-minority children. *Journal of Reading Behavior, 26,* 439–456.

Morales, E. (2002). *Living in Spanglish: The search for Latino identity in America.* New York: St. Martin's Press.

National Center for Education Statistics. (2002). *Dropout rates in the United States: 2000.* Retrieved June 12, 2004, from http://nces.ed.gov/pubs2002/droppub_2001/8. asp?nav=1

National Center for Education Statistics. (2005). *National Assessment of Adult Literacy (NAAL): A first look at the literacy of America's adults in the 21st century* (NCES 2006-471). Washington, DC: U.S. Department of Education.

National Institute for Literacy. (n.d.). *English as a second language literacy.* Retrieved June 20, 2004, from http://www.nifl.gov/nifl/facts/esl.html

New London Group. (1996). A pedagogy of multiliteracies: Designing social futures. *Harvard Educational Review, 66,* 60–92.

Ovando, C. J., Collier, V. P., & Combs, M. C. (2003). *Bilingual and ESL classrooms: Teaching in multicultural contexts.* New York: McGraw-Hill.

Pew Hispanic Center Fact Sheet. (2002, January). *Hispanic economic prospects depend on education and a strong economy.* Retrieved June 30, 2004, from http://www.pewhispanic.org/site/docs/pdf/economy_pdf_version.pdf

Population Resource Center. (2002a). *Executive summary insert: 2002 demographic characteristics of immigrants.* Retrieved July 3, 2004, from http://www.prcdc.org/ summaries/immigrationinsert02/immigrationinsert02.html

Population Resource Center. (2002b). *Executive summary: Immigration to the United States: 2002 update.* Retrieved July 10, 2004, from http://www.prcdc.org/summaries/immigrationupdate02/immigrationupdate02.html

Quintero, E., & Huerta-Macías, A. (1993, Fall/Winter). Whole language: Critical curriculum for family literacy. *The School Community Journal,* 45–62.

Reyes, M. de la Luz. (2001). Unleashing possibilities: Biliteracy in the primary grades. In M. de la Luz Reyes & J. J. Halcón (Eds.), *The best for our children: Critical perspectives on literacy for Latino students* (pp. 96–121). New York: Teachers College Press.

Rivera, K. M. (1999a). Popular research and social transformation: A community-based approach to critical pedagogy. *TESOL Quarterly, 33,* 485–500.

Rivera, K. M. (1999b). From developing one's voice to making oneself heard: Affecting language policy from the bottom up. In T. Huebner and K. A. Davis (Eds.), *Sociopolitical perspectives on language policy and planning in the USA* (pp. 333–346). Amsterdam: John Benjamins.

Rodriguez, R. (1982). *Hunger of memory: The education of Richard Rodriguez.* New York: Bantam.

Ruíz, R. (1984). Orientation in language planning. *NABE Journal, 8,* 15–24.

Ruíz, R. (1990). Official languages and language planning. In K. L. Adams & D. T. Brink (Eds.), *The campaigns for English as the official language of the USA* (pp. 11–24). Berlin: Mouton de Gruter.

Saenz, B. A. (2004). I want to write an American poem II. In O. Santa Ana (Ed.), *Tongue-tied: The lives of multilingual children in public education* (pp. 253–254). Lanham, MD: Rowman & Littlefield.

Saxena, M. (1994). Literacy among the Panjabis in Southall. In M. Hamilton, D. Barton, & R. Ivanic (Eds.), *Worlds of literacy* (pp. 195–214). Clevedon, England: Multilingual Matters.

Skilton-Sylvester, E. (2002). Literate at home but not at school: A Cambodian girl's journey from playwright to struggling writer. In G. Hull & K. Schultz (Eds.), *School's out! Bridging out-of-school literacies with classroom practice* (pp. 61–90). New York: Teachers College Press.

Smith, F. (1997). *Reading without nonsense* (3rd ed.). New York: Teachers College Press.

Street, B. (1993). The new literacy studies. In B. Street (Ed.), *Cross-cultural approaches to literacy* (pp. 1–21). London: Cambridge University Press.

Street, B. (1994). Struggles over the meaning(s) of literacy. In M. Hamilton, D. Barton, & R. Ivanic (Eds.), *Worlds of literacy* (pp. 15–20). Clevedon, England: Multilingual Matters.

Street, B. (2000). The new literacy studies: from "socially situated" to the work of the social. In D. Barton, M. Hamilton, & R. Ivanic (Eds.), *Situated literacies: Reading and writing in context* (pp. 180–196). London: Routledge.

Sum, A., Kirsch, I., & Taggart, R. (2002). *The twin challenges of mediocrity and inequality: Literacy in the U.S. from an international perspective* (Policy Information Report). Princeton, NJ: Educational Testing Service.

Suro, R., & Passel, J. S. (2003, October). *The rise of the second generation: Changing patterns in Hispanic population growth.* Washington, DC: Pew Hispanic Center.

Vygotsky, L. S. (1978). *Mind in society: The development of higher psychological process* (M. Cole, V. John-Steiner, S. Scribner, & E. Souberman, Eds.). Cambridge, MA: Harvard University Press.

Vygotsky, L. S. (1986). *Thoughts and language.* Cambridge, MA: Massachusetts Institute of Technology Press.

Wiley, T. G., & Lukes, M. (1996). English-only and Standard English ideologies in the U.S. *TESOL Quarterly, 30,* 511–535.

Wong Fillmore, L. (2000). Loss of family languages: Should educators be concerned? *Theory into Practice, 39,* 203–210.

Wrigley, H. S., Richer, E., Martinson, K., Kubo, H., & Strawn, J. (2003, August). *The language of opportunity: Expanding employment prospects for adults with limited English skills.* Washington, DC: Center for Law and Social Policy.

Zentella, A. C. (1997). *Growing up bilingual.* Malden, MA: Blackwell.

2

Adult Biliteracy and Language Diversity
How Well Do National Data Inform Policy?

MARIO CASTRO AND TERRENCE G. WILEY

This chapter represents a modest attempt to begin answering the question of what we can learn from national data to better inform literacy policy. However, in order to answer that question, there is a need to understand (1) practical issues and limitations of collecting national literacy data and (2) the influence of the dominant ideology of monolingualism on the framing of national data questions. The first part of this chapter addresses the practical concerns and limitations with reference to the National Adult Literacy Survey (NALS) and the National Assessment of Adult Literacy (NAAL). The second part addresses the ideological assumptions underlining the U.S. Census and how some of the census data help refute and better inform those assumptions. The chapter concludes that a more robust focus on language diversity and literacy in other languages is needed to better inform adult literacy policy.

In the United States, there are many popular assumptions and myths that surround discussions of literacy and language diversity. The United States is often erroneously assumed to be largely an English monolingual nation where language diversity is generally seen as a problem. Populations that have facility in languages other than English are often considered aberrant. In discussions in the popular media or press, literacy is generally equated with English literacy. Thus, to better inform both popular opinion and educational policy, there is a need for data. In the absence of such data, educational policy is primarily shaped by attitudes and beliefs that are products of the dominant ideology about language and literacy in the United States, with a myopic focus on English monolingualism (Wiley, 2005). English monolingualism reflects an ideology that speaking languages other than English is aberrant and socially disuniting (Ovando & Wiley, 2003).

What National Data Do We Have to Inform Literacy Policy?

Before addressing the question of what we can learn from national data, it is useful to consider some of the practical issues surrounding the collection of literacy data. We begin with a focus on three common approaches to assessing literacy in the national population and then briefly consider the NALS and the NAAL.

Three Common Approaches to Assessing Literacy in the National Population

There are three common ways to assess literacy in the national population: self-reported assessments of literacy; surrogate measures, such as using years of schooling; and direct measures or tests of literacy. All three methods have their drawbacks, but direct measures are always preferable, although expensive.

Historically, the U.S. Census has been the principal source of self-reported and surrogate literacy data for the United States. During the 19th and early 20th centuries, individuals were asked if they could read or write a simple message in English or some other language. If they answered yes, they were considered literate. Today, most people can read and write at some level, so the emphasis has shifted to one of concern for those who indicate they cannot do so very well.

Researchers and policy makers tend to distrust self-reported information because individuals may inflate their abilities. However, there is also a tendency for those with less schooling to sometimes under-represent their actual literacy abilities in conducting daily affairs outside of school contexts (Wiley, 2005). Nevertheless, there is some evidence indicating that self-assessment can be a valuable tool when proper controls are used (LeBlanc & Painchaud, 1986; McArthur, 1993).

Surrogate measures are also problematic. The grade-level equivalences to literacy have been largely chosen for the convenience of having readily accessible surrogates for direct measures; however, there has been little agreement regarding what ceilings (6, 8, or 12 years) should be taken as equivalent to being literate in contemporary society. Critics have long noted that the number of school years completed is no guarantee that literacy skills have actually been acquired or retained (Hunter & Harman, 1979).

One of the major concerns regarding direct measures of literacy is that they involve simulations of real-world events rather than evaluations of real-life performance. Those who do well on sit-down school tests do not always perform well in real-world contexts, and those who cannot perform well in school tasks often can function in actual tasks. Thus, conclusions drawn about actual literacy abilities from the results of simulations or literacy tests must be interpreted with caution. Just because an individual cannot perform a task on a sit-down exam does not mean she or he is unable to perform the real-world task it is designed to simulate, and all tasks contrived by test makers do not represent things that people really have to do in order to function well in society (Wiley, 2005).

All three of the common approaches to assessing literacy, that is, direct measures, surrogate measures, and self-reported measures, have limitations. Nevertheless, direct measures using simulations of real-world tasks or tests, although they may lack "ecological" or real-world validity, are always preferable to self-reported and surrogate measures. But given the general dearth of national information available from direct measures of literacy, self-reported information, such as the U.S. Census collects, and surrogate data derived from information about schooling can be useful in informing policy.

The NALS: A Mixed Review

One of the more comprehensive direct assessments of English literacy undertaken in recent years was the National Adult Literacy Survey (NALS). The NALS was developed out of a Congressional initiative that mandated the U.S. Department of Education (DOE) report on adult literacy. The DOE's National Center for Education Statistics (NCES) and Division of Adult Education and Literacy undertook a national household survey to assess the literacy skills of adults in the United States, and Educational Testing Service (ETS) became the prime contractor, with Westat, Inc. as its subcontractor (Macías, 1994; Wrigley, Chisman, & Ewen, 1993). The NALS built on an approach from the prior Young Adult Literacy Survey (YALS). The model conceptualized literacy along a continuum of three domains: *prose, document,* and *quantitative* literacy. Each of these domains was assessed through simulated real-world literacy tasks and scaled on five levels of difficulty. In the document literacy domain, for example, respondents might be asked to give information about an employment application. For the prose domain, they might be asked to determine the general idea of a narrative. The documents, prose selections, and quantitative tasks were scaled based on their purported levels of difficulty (Wiley, 2005).

Although the NALS undertook only direct assessment of English literacy, it was more responsive to issues of ethnic and linguistic diversity than most previous efforts (Kirsch, Jungeblut, Jenkins, & Kolstad, 1993). In addition to the direct assessments, the NALS included demographic questions on language diversity that were later subjected to secondary data analysis. The NALS oversampled for Latinos and African Americans (Macías, 1994). It also allowed for some secondary data analysis of subgroups (see Greenberg, Macías, Rhodes, & Chan, 2001).

The initial analysis of the NALS data found very little evidence of nonliteracy but very high levels of marginal literacy performance at Levels 1 and 2 (Kirsch et al., 1993). The NALS findings attracted national attention. Headlines of many of the leading newspapers and magazines tended to sensationalize the findings. The authors of the initial report, however, had been more cautious. For example, Kirsch et al. (1993) noted,

> The approximately 90 million adults who performed in Levels 1 and 2 [on a five-level scale] did not necessarily perceive themselves as being "at risk." … It is therefore possible that their skills, while limited, allow them to meet some or most of their personal and occupational literacy needs. (p. xv)

In explaining their major findings, Kirsch et al. (1993) concluded that "twenty-one percent of the respondents who performed … [at the lowest level] were immigrants who may have been just learning to speak English" (p. xiv). The authors placed emphasis on "learning to speak English" and not on prior literacy in other languages. Critics maintained that the NALS assumed familiarity with U.S. society, and thus may have been particularly biased against newer arrivals (see Chisman, Wrigley, & Ewen, 1993).

Subsequent reports attempted to correct the original sensationalist claims. According to Mathews (2001), only 5% of those surveyed should be considered not literate, primarily because they failed to answer any questions. The test's five-level implicational scale was also supposed to increase in difficulty, such that Level 1 tasks should be easier than Level 2 tasks. Some items, however, did not appear to have scaled as predicted, thus raising concerns about the validity of the scale (see Mathews, 2001; see also Berliner & Biddle, 1996; Berliner, 1996; Wiley, 2005).

The NALS Secondary Data Analysis

Despite the concerns with the NALS findings based on its direct measures of literacy, as previously noted, positive aspects of the NALS survey were its oversampling of those who speak languages other than, or in addition to, English, and the fact that self-reported data on languages other than English, and literacy in them, were collected. Greenberg et al. (2001) undertook a major secondary data analysis of the self-reported data (see Figure. 2.1 to Figure 2.3).

Greenberg et al.'s (2001) secondary data analysis found that, among all language minorities in the United States, bilingualism was highest among those from Asia. Biliteracy rates among Hispanics were highest among those from

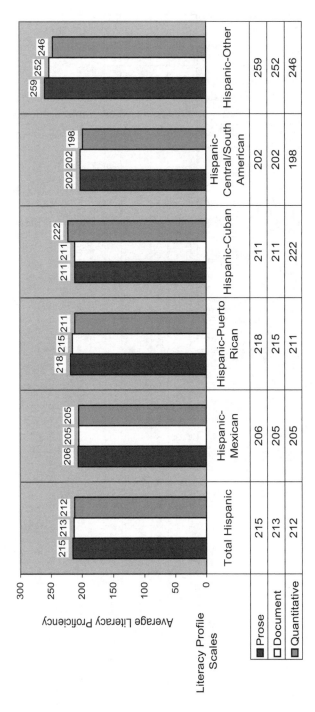

Figure 2.1   Average literacy proficiencies by Hispanic subgroup. (Adapted from Greenberg, E. et al., *English Literacy and Language Minorities in the United States*, NCES 2001-464, National Center for Education Statistics, Washington, DC, August 2001, Table 2.9, p. 45. Reprinted with permission from Wiley, 2005.)

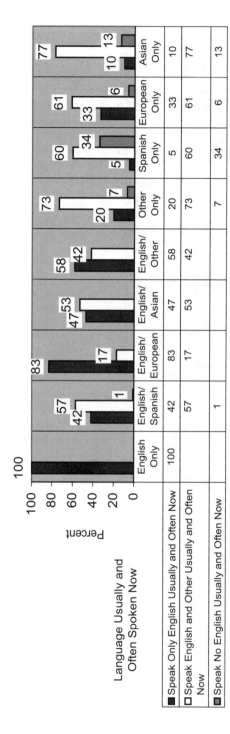

Figure 2.2   Language usually and often spoken now compared with language spoken in home while growing up. (Adapted from Greenberg, E. et al., *English Literacy and Language Minorities in the United States*, NCES 2001-464, National Center for Education Statistics, Washington, DC, August 2001, Table 2.6, p. 41. Reprinted with permission from Wiley, 2005.)

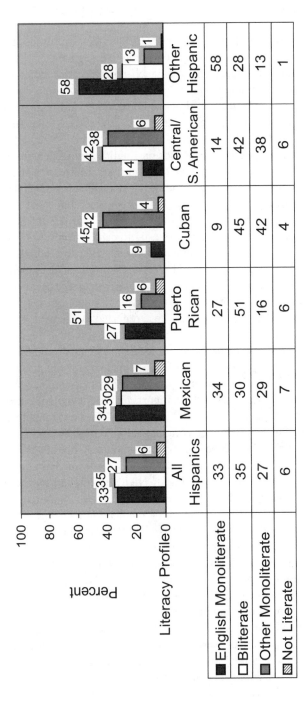

Literacy Profile	All Hispanics	Mexican	Puerto Rican	Cuban	Central/ S. American	Other Hispanic
English Monoliterate	33	34	27	9	14	58
Biliterate	35	30	51	45	42	28
Other Monoliterate	27	29	16	42	38	13
Not Literate	6	7	6	4	6	1

Figure 2.3   U.S. Hispanic literacy profile. (Adapted from Greenberg, E. et al., *English Literacy and Language Minorities in the United States*, NCES 2001-464, National Center for Education Statistics, Washington, DC, August 2001, Table 2.4, p. 32. Reprinted with permission from Wiley, 2005.)

Puerto Rico and Cuba and lowest among those of Mexican origin and other Hispanics (see Figure 2.3).

In retrospect, despite its limitations, the NALS remains one of the few direct assessments of literacy of a nationally representative segment of the population. Greenberg et al.'s secondary analysis of self-reported information provides data that would otherwise not be available. In the absence of more comprehensive information, these data are useful in providing some information on levels of literacy and biliteracy in languages other than English. A follow-up to the NALS was begun in 2003. The new assessment is called the National Assessment of Adult Literacy (NAAL). It focuses on English language assessment of U.S. adults age 16 years and older. NAAL "will provide information about background factors associated with literacy, the skill levels of the least-literate adults, and the application of literacy skills to health-related materials" (NCES, 2004).

Early analyses from the NAAL show that prose and document English literacy scores for U.S. adults did not differ significantly from the NALS (see Figure 2.4); however, prose and document scores for Hispanic adults dropped significantly from those reported by the NALS, while prose and document scores rose significantly for Black adults and prose scores increased significantly for Asian/Pacific Islander adults (NCES, 2005). Average quantitative English literacy scores increased significantly from those reported by the NALS for Black adults and White adults, as well as for the total adult sample.

Secondary analysis will be necessary to determine if the drop in English literacy scores for Hispanic adults signals advances made by the Spanish language within the Hispanic population that correspond with language use changes among the U.S. population as a whole. The NCES reports that the "language background of America's adults changed between 1992 and 2003," with a greater percentage of adults speaking Spanish before starting school and a significant decrease in the percentage speaking English before starting school (NCES, 2005).

Changes made to the NAAL provide another reason for Hispanic adults' differences in scores. Despite a rescaling of NALS results "using the criteria and methods established for the 2003 assessment," the NCES warns that caution should be taken when making interpretations based on changes in English literacy levels from 1992 to 2003. In the NALS, the easy literacy tasks at the beginning of the assessment were presented only in English; in the NAAL, "corresponding tasks were presented in either English or Spanish, although the materials to be read were presented only in English." The NAAL also included an alternative assessment where English- or Spanish-speaking adults who were unable to answer a minimum number of literacy screening tasks were asked questions orally in either English or Spanish but based upon materials presented in English only. The objectives were "to provide more accurate data about the English literacy levels of adults" and to exclude fewer adults due to the language of the interview (NCES, 2005). The inclusion of persons in the NAAL who were excluded in the NALS may explain differences in scores.

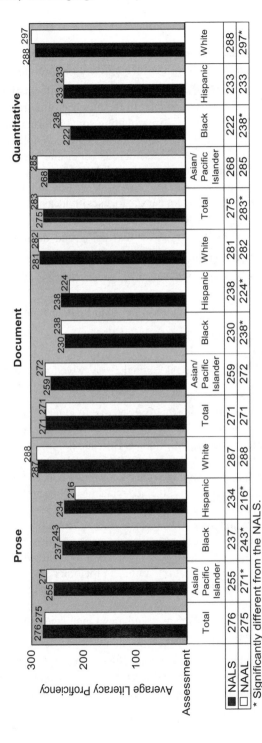

Figure 2.4 NALS and NAAL average adult English literacy scores by race/ethnicity. (From National Center for Education Statistics, *National Assessment of Adult Literacy: A First Look at the Literacy of America's Adults in the 21st Century*, NCES 2006470, Washington, DC, December 2005, retrieved May 8, 2006, from http://nces.ed.gov/NAAL/PDF/2006470.PDF.)

The U.S. Census

In this section, we consider the types of census data collected on language and language diversity as well as some of the ideological underpinnings that frame the survey. We analyze the data with specific reference to the largest language minority population, the Mexican-origin population.

Language Use Data

The U.S. Census is the primary source of national data. Historically, the census gauged whether respondents self-reported reading or writing in the English language or another language. The current census focuses on measuring self-reports of oral English language proficiency. On its Web site, the U.S. Census Bureau (2004a) summarizes the "Language Use Data" topic:

> Language Use, English Ability, and Linguistic Isolation data were col-
> lected in the 2000, 1990, and 1980 decennial censuses using a three-part
> series of questions:
> A. Does this person speak a language other than English at home?
>
> (For those who speak another language)
> B. What is this language? _____
> C. How well does this person speak English?—very well, well, not well,
>   not at all.

In earlier censuses, the questions focused on an individual's "mother tongue" (the language spoken when the person was a child) or on language used by only a select group (e.g., foreign born) (U.S. Census Bureau, 2004a). With its current focus, the Census Bureau reports that, in 2000, 47 million U.S. residents five years of age and over spoke a language other than English at home (Shin with Bruno, 2003, p. 1). This figure does not include residents of Puerto Rico, but does represent 18% of persons residing in the 50 states and the District of Columbia who are five years of age and over (U.S. Census Bureau, 2004a).

As the Census Bureau's summary indicates, comparability of recent language use variables is limited to a 20-year span (1980 to 2000). Also, the 2000 Census does not collect data on speaking ability in the other language for those who speak a language other than English at home, reading ability (in any language), and language spoken at work.

In explaining why the 2000 Census asked about language use and English-speaking ability, Shin with Bruno noted the following:

> The question on language use and English-speaking ability provides
> government agencies with information for programs that serve the
> needs of people who have difficulty speaking English. Under the Vot-

ing Rights Act, information about language ability is needed to meet statutory requirements for making voting materials available in minority languages.

The Bilingual Education Program uses data on language to allocate grants to school districts for children with limited English proficiency. These data also are needed for local agencies developing services for the elderly under the Older Americans Act. (2003, p. 10)

Thus, the reasons given for enumerating the non-English-speaking population are to help agencies and programs serve non-English-speaking populations. As with bilingual education programs, the focus is on accommodation.

The important question for this paper is: How helpful are current census data in terms of informing adult education policy? The census does collect data on self-reported oral English language proficiency. According to a Census Bureau staff member who reported at the 1989 Annual Meeting of the American Statistical Association, "Far from the 'total count' mechanism that many consider its sole function, the once-a-decade tool has been asked to address and assess numerous dimensions of the diverse fabric of the U.S. society" (Kominski, 1989, p. 1). The Census Bureau also collects education and other workforce data that are major sources for policy making in the United States.

The Census Bureau's assumptions reflect the dominant ideological assumptions about language in the United States, namely, that in the United States:

1. English is the language spoken outside the home.

2. It is desirable in the United States that non-English speakers change into or conform as English language speakers.

These assumptions structure the programs of those who work in adult literacy, workplace literacy, or English as a Second Language (ESL) instruction. The assumptions also misdirect the hope of workers who come to believe "that increased literacy or English-language fluency will positively affect their work, their goals, and their opportunities"; and incorrectly foster the belief that workforce problems like unemployment "can be solved by developing a more literate, English-speaking workforce without addressing the economic crisis and its political origins" (D'Amico & Schnee, 1997, pp. 118–119). Despite the emphasis on spoken English, we will demonstrate that the Census Bureau's own data help inform these narrow ideological assumptions.

The 2000 Census did not collect language use information from government and private service providers, schools, businesses, and so on. Nevertheless, the "Language Use and English-Speaking Ability: 2000" Census Brief makes the following assumption about language use and life's chances at the beginning of the report:

The ability to communicate with government and private service providers, schools, businesses, emergency personnel, and many other people in the United States depends greatly on the ability to speak English. (Shin with Bruno, 2003, p. 1)

The Census Brief defines a "linguistically isolated" household as one in which no person aged 14 years or over speaks English "very well" (Shin with Bruno, 2003, p. 10) and adds this caveat:

In the United States, the ability to speak English plays a large role in how well people can perform daily activities. How well a person speaks English may indicate how well he or she communicates with public officials, medical personnel, and other service providers. It could also affect other activities outside the home, such as grocery shopping or banking. People who do not have a strong command of English and who do not have someone in their household to help them on a regular basis are at even more of a disadvantage. (Shin with Bruno, 2003, pp. 9–10)

Despite the importance of English and the opportunity to learn English in the United States, there are a number of communities in the United States where one can carry on these activities and function well in languages other than English. The more relevant fact is that the census does not collect the information necessary to assess language use in languages other than English. Rather, the data collected result from overarching ideological assumptions about language. The types of data collected are framed by the dominance of the ideology of English monolingualism and a preference to focus on oral English. As we have previously observed,

National measures of literacy are influenced by the ideology of English monolingualism. ... National demographic surveys often include questions regarding oral fluency in English or other languages at the same time that they neglect to seek information about literacy in languages other than English. Similarly, adult education programs for language minority populations seem to emphasize the acquisition of oral English and fail to survey native language literacy or even English literacy. (Wiley, 1996, pp. 78–79)

Although the data on language use and enumerating information on the non-English-speaking population help agencies and programs serve the particular non-English-speaking population or provide for their rights and protect their freedom, the discourse that frames the data collection reflects major ideological assumptions about English that assume that English is the only language of importance spoken outside the home. The discourse implies a preference for changing the person into an English language speaker rather than providing services in languages other than English. Thus, this type of discourse privileges

English and speakers of English despite the fact that the U.S. Census's own data affirm that this is a multilingual society.

Similarly, given the pervasiveness of the two major ideological assumptions in discourse on language policy,

> Most discussions of language policy are framed as if monolingualism were part of our heritage from which we were now drifting. Framing the language policy issues in this way masks both the historical and contemporary reality and positions non-English language diversity as an abnormality that must be cured. Contrary to the steady flow of disinformation ... language diversity has always been a fact of life ... [and] efforts to deny that reality ... ha[ve] resulted in either restrictionist or repressive language policies. (Wiley & Wright, 2004, p. 143)

While the myths result in bleak assumptions about the ability of speakers of languages other than English to complete everyday activities without a strong command of the English language, and despite the concern that many speakers of other languages are linguistically isolated from English, census data also point to the prevalence of English language within most households where other languages are spoken. In fact, 96% of the total population five years of age and over lives in households that are not linguistically isolated from English. Second, census data show 75% of the population that speaks a language other than English at home does not reside in a linguistically isolated household. Third, census data indicate that 28% of persons who speak a language other than English at home reside in households where at least one person speaks only English. Therefore, low levels of linguistic isolation coupled with high rates of membership in households with English-only speakers point to high rates of access to persons with proficient English speaking skills. In other words, many of those assumed to be isolated by their lack of English live within households where they interact with those proficient in English (percent figures calculated from U.S. Census Bureau, 2003a).

The Significance of Spanish in the United States

According to U.S. Census data, there are 159 languages with more than 1,000 speakers in the United States, 93 languages with more than 10,000 speakers, 38 languages with more than 100,000 speakers, and 8 languages with more than 1 million speakers (calculated from U.S. Census Bureau, 2004b). These figures are for those aged five years and above, as are all language figures that follow unless specified otherwise. Among these many languages, Spanish is second only to English. The 2000 Census indicates that there are more than 28.1 million Spanish-speaking persons in the United States; this accounts for 60% of persons who speak a language other than English at home (calculated from Shin with Bruno,

Table 2.1   U.S. Population Five Years of Age and Over by Language Spoken at Home

Language Spoken at Home	Number	%
Speak English only	215,423,557	82
Speak Spanish	28,101,052	11
Speak other language	18,850,543	7
Total	**262,375,152**	**100**

2003, p. 2). Table 2.1 summarizes the proportion of the population that speaks English only, Spanish, or another language at home in the United States.

These summary data on languages spoken at home provide a big-picture view that reveals the United States to be mostly comprised of English monolinguals, but with substantial numbers of Spanish speakers and speakers of other languages. Importantly, however, the speakers of languages other than English are not necessarily immigrants. It is tempting to use "U.S. born" as a proxy for English-only speakers and "speakers of languages other than English" as a proxy for immigrants, but there are problems if we do so. To make this point, we present a close look at that portion of the U.S. population that is often the focus of ESL and adult literacy services: the Mexican-origin population.

The Mexican-Origin Population in the United States

We examine the Mexican-origin population in the United States using the 5% Public Use Microdata Sample (PUMS) from the 2000 Census (U.S. Census Bureau, 2003b). The 5% PUMS files contain individual records of responses to census questionnaires representing a 5% sample of the occupied and vacant housing units and the persons in the occupied units. Based on analysis of the 5% PUMS files, persons of Mexican origin account for more than half of the Spanish speakers in the United States, just under a third of speakers of languages other than English, and just 2% of those who speak English only. Mexican-origin persons, therefore, represent a majority of Spanish speakers in the United States, make up a substantial portion of persons who speak a language other than English, but are a very minor part of the English language monolingual population.

The Mexican-origin population in the United States is mostly concentrated in the Southwest, Illinois, and Florida, and two-thirds of the Mexican-origin population resides in either California or Texas. Table 2.2 shows that more than 90% of the Mexican-origin population reside in 14 states.

The 5% PUMS data show important differences between language spoken at home in the overall U.S. population and the U.S. Mexican-origin population. Although PUMS data show 79% of Mexican-origin persons speak Spanish at home, 82% of the overall population speak only English at home (calculated from U.S. Census Bureau, 2003a). This does not mean, however, that most of

Table 2.2 Top States by Share of U.S. Mexican-Origin
Population Five Years of Age and Over

Rank	State	Number	%	Cumulative Percent
1	California	7,598,201	41	41
2	Texas	4,609,055	25	66
3	Illinois	1,013,406	6	72
4	Arizona	955,318	5	77
5	Colorado	407,082	2	79
6	Florida	319,148	2	81
7	New Mexico	307,571	2	82
8	Washington	285,166	2	84
9	Nevada	252,061	1	85
10	Georgia	238,652	1	87
11	New York	228,487	1	88
12	North Carolina	205,881	1	89
13	Michigan	195,770	1	90
14	Oregon	185,742	1	91

Note: Cumulative percent may not match the cumulatively
added percent figure in the % column due to rounding.

the Spanish speakers are linguistically isolated because 74% of Mexican-origin
persons also speak a language other than English and speak English very well
or well (or only English), and 67% of those who speak a non-English language
at home (of which Spanish is the non-English language in 99.7% of cases) also
speak English very well or well (see Table 2.3 and Figure 2.5). Census PUMS
data thus show the Mexican-origin population to be mostly bilingual and the
overall population to be mostly monolingual.

State-by-State Comparisons and the Importance of Spanish

A state-by-state comparison of Mexican-origin persons who speak Spanish or
English only shows regional differences in the rates of speaking Spanish and
English only (see Figure 2.6). The Mexican-origin populations in western and
southwestern states, for example, as well as in states with large numbers of Spanish speakers, such as Florida, Illinois, New Jersey, and New York, overwhelmingly speak Spanish versus English only. On the other hand, the far northeastern
states of Maine, New Hampshire, and Vermont and the far north-central states of
North Dakota, Montana, South Dakota, and Wyoming show a majority of Mexican-origin persons who speak English only. The only other states with majority English-only-speaking Mexican-origin populations are Hawaii and West
Virginia.

Table 2.3   U.S. Mexican-Origin Population by Language Spoken
at Home and English Ability

Language Spoken at Home	%	Speak Non-English Language and English		
		Very Well or Well	Not Well	Not at All
Non-English language	79	53%	16%	10%
English only	21	—	—	—
Total	**100**			

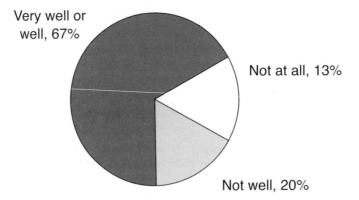

Figure 2.5   Ability to speak English for U.S. Mexican-origin persons who speak Spanish.

The nine states with majority English-only-speaking Mexican-origin populations have a relatively small number of Mexican-origin and Spanish-speaking persons residing in the state. Some states with low numbers of Mexican-origin residents, such as Delaware and Rhode Island, show high rates of Spanish as the language spoken at home. Delaware and Rhode Island both have relatively large Spanish-speaking populations that are not of Mexican origin. In the case of Delaware, Spanish speakers who are not of Mexican origin number nearly 27,000. In Rhode Island, Spanish speakers who are not of Mexican origin number nearly 77,000. The combined number of Spanish speakers who are not of Mexican origin in these two states outnumbers the combined number of Spanish speakers who are not of Mexican origin in the nine states where the majority of Mexican-origin persons speak English only (103,000 to 95,000). This hints that the rates of speaking Spanish and English only are somewhat a function of a state's Spanish-speaking population size and the state's location.

Since two-thirds of the Mexican-origin population reside in either California or Texas, as reported above, the rates for these two states are especially significant. In California, as with the United States as a whole, 79% of Mexican-origin persons five years of age and over speak Spanish at home, while only 21% speak

English only. The rates of speaking Spanish at home are even greater in Texas, where 83% of Mexican-origin persons speak Spanish and 17% speak English only.

When the U.S. Mexican-origin population is considered, PUMS data confirm that it is incomplete to use the U.S.-born category as a proxy for English-only speakers and speakers of languages other than English as a proxy for immigrants. More than 63% of Mexican-origin persons in the United States are American citizens, and an overwhelming portion (70%) of these Americans speak Spanish. Also, nearly two-thirds of U.S.-born Mexican-origin persons in the United States speak Spanish at home, and Mexican-origin persons who were born in the United States account for a majority of Mexican-origin persons in the United States (see Table 2.4).

Educational Attainment of the Mexican-Origin Population in the United States

Having verified that the greater part of the Mexican-origin population in the United States speak Spanish at home, regardless of citizenship status, we now consider census educational attainment data for Mexican-origin adults in the United States. No factor affects the prospects of workplace success more than educational attainment. For this part of the analysis, we use the 1% PUMS from the 2000 Census (U.S. Census Bureau, 2003b) due to the large size of the 5% sample. Similar to the 5% PUMS files, the 1% PUMS files contain individual records of responses to census questionnaires representing a 1% sample of the occupied and vacant housing units and the persons in the occupied units.

Table 2.5 displays educational attainment by language spoken at home and English-speaking ability for the 18 years of age and over U.S.-born Mexican-origin population. From this table, the spurious conclusion can be reached that, to elevate educational attainment, English should be the focus of workforce training since those who speak Spanish and English very well or well (henceforth S&Evwow) have educational attainment rates that nearly match those who speak English only, and since Spanish speakers who do not speak English or who speak English "not well" have educational attainment levels that are much lower than the levels of those who speak S&Evwow or English only. This conclusion is flawed for many reasons, which are brought to bear by census data. Based on Table 2.5, the more accurate conclusion can be reached that, rather than educational attainment being a function of English ability, English ability is a function of educational attainment that was obtained under English or bilingual instruction. This second conclusion is supported by the likelihood that U.S.-born persons attend or attended school under English or bilingual instruction. Table 2.5 shows that 66% of U.S.-born Mexican-origin persons aged 18 years and up who do not speak English received six years or less of schooling. To reach this high

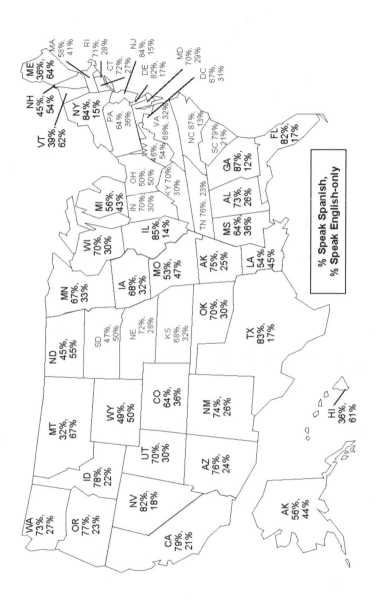

% Speak Spanish,
% Speak English-only

State or District	Number	State	Number	State	Number
Alabama	36,036	Kentucky	25,139	North Dakota	3,421
Alaska	10,890	Louisiana	30,281	Ohio	80,219
Arizona	955,318	Maine	3,199	Oklahoma	114,131
Arkansas	51,879	Maryland	38,570	Oregon	185,742
California	7,598,201	Massachusetts	23,405	Pennsylvania	50,222
Colorado	407,082	Michigan	195,770	Rhode Island	5,641
Connecticut	22,770	Minnesota	83,092	South Carolina	46,544
Delaware	10,429	Mississippi	18,247	South Dakota	4,947
D.C.	4,237	Missouri	68,116	Tennessee	65,035
Florida	319,148	Montana	10,492	Texas	4,609,055
Georgia	238,652	Nebraska	59,942	Utah	117,897
Hawaii	18,333	Nevada	252,061	Vermont	1,095
Idaho	67,300	New Hampshire	4,481	Virginia	69,267
Illinois	1,013,406	New Jersey	95,038	Washington	285,166
Indiana	134,186	New Mexico	307,571	West Virginia	4,582
Iowa	52,369	New York	228,487	Wisconsin	106,270
Kansas	126,176	North Carolina	205,881	Wyoming	15,909
				Total	**18,481,327**

Note: Spanish and English-only figures may not add to 100% due to speakers of other languages and rounding.

Figure 2.6   Mexican-origin population that speaks Spanish and English only by state.

Table 2.4 Spanish- and English-Only-Speaking Mexican-Origin Population by Citizenship

			Language	
Citizenship	**Number**	**%**	**Spanish**	**English Only**
Citizen by U.S. birth	9,821,359	53	65%	35%
Citizen by naturalization	1,904,004	10	94%	6%
Not a U.S. citizen	6,601,643	36	94%	5%

Note: Spanish and English-only percent figures may not add up to 100% due to speakers of other languages. Also, the % column does not add to 100% due to citizens who were born in an American territory or to an American parent abroad.

Table 2.5 Educational Attainment of U.S.-Born Mexican-Origin Persons Aged 18 Years+

		Speak Spanish and English		
Educational Attainment	**Speak English Only**	**Very Well or Well**	**Not Well**	**Not at All**
6th grade or less	3%	6%	35%	66%
7th grade to 12th grade, no diploma	20%	29%	30%	21%
High school graduate	31%	29%	17%	7%
Some college, less than bachelor's degree	33%	27%	14%	4%
Bachelor's degree to doctorate degree	12%	9%	3%	2%
Total	**100%**	**100%**	**100%**	**100%**

of a percent for those who speak English "not well" requires collapsing two educational attainment categories: 65% of those who speak English "not well" received less than a high school diploma. And, to nearly reach the percent among those who speak S&Evwow or English only requires collapsing three categories: 64% of those who speak S&Evwow and 54% of those who speak English only received a high school diploma or less. These data show that, rather than educational attainment being a function of English ability, English ability is more likely a function of schooling for the U.S.-born population. In other words, U.S.-born persons who have had the opportunity for schooling are likely to acquire English-speaking skills.

As seen in Figure 2.7, focusing on providing English skills to the U.S.-born Mexican-origin population as a means of providing workforce training also results in limiting the training to a very small percent of the citizenry. Of U.S.-born persons (who, as reported above, constitute a majority of Mexican-origin persons in the United States), 96% speak English only or speak S&Evwow, and only 1% speak Spanish only. Thus, workforce training that is focused on English

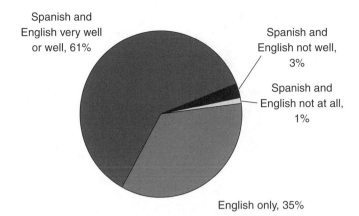

Figure 2.7   Language spoken at home for U.S.-born Mexican-origin persons 18 years+.

language development would mostly be beneficial to approximately 1% of the population. Workforce education must focus on occupational skills in order to benefit the majority of the population.

English Ability and Its Relationship to Education

A comparison of the mostly bilingual U.S.-born Mexican-origin population with non-U.S. citizens and naturalized U.S. citizens shows differences in the prevalence of Spanish and English. As reported above, most of the Mexican-origin population in the United States speaks Spanish at home, including the U.S. born (as seen in Figure 2.7). However, the prevalence of Spanish is much greater and familiarity with English much less for non-U.S. citizens, who constitute 36% of the Mexican-origin population, and, to a lesser degree, for naturalized U.S. citizens, who constitute 10% of the Mexican-origin population.

As seen in Figure 2.8, persons who speak S&Evwow or English only do not constitute a majority of noncitizens. Although those who speak S&Evwow make up the largest slice of speakers, those who speak English only constitute the smallest slice at 6% of the noncitizen population. A majority (60%) of non-U.S. citizens speak Spanish and no English or English "not well." English is less familiar to non-U.S. citizens than it is to the U.S. born, as 73% of noncitizens speak at least some English compared to 99% of the U.S. born.

Persons who speak S&Evwow constitute a majority of naturalized citizens, like they do with the U.S. born (see Figure 2.9). English is almost as familiar to naturalized U.S. citizens as it is to the U.S. born, as 93% of naturalized citizens speak Spanish and some English; however, those who do not speak English or speak English "not well" constitute a larger portion of naturalized citizens than

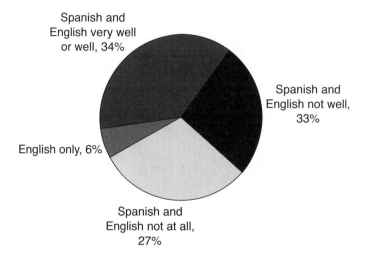

Figure 2.8   Language spoken at home for Mexican-origin non-U.S. citizens 18 years+.

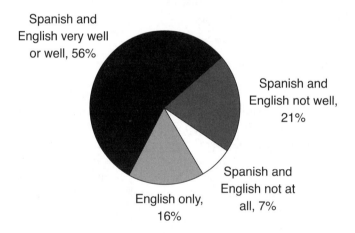

Figure 2.9   Language spoken at home for naturalized Mexican-origin persons 18 years+.

they do of the U.S. born (28% of naturalized citizens compared to 4% of the U.S. born).

Table 2.6 shows educational attainment rates for non-U.S. citizens. Non-citizens who speak some English (those who speak Spanish and English "not well" and those who speak S&Evwow) have greater educational attainment than monolingual noncitizens who speak English only or Spanish only. While 39% of noncitizens who speak Spanish and English "not well" and 21% of noncitizens who speak S&Evwow have an educational attainment level of 6th grade or less,

Table 2.6   Educational Attainment of Mexican-Origin non-U.S. Citizens Aged 18 Years+

Educational Attainment	Speak English Only	Speak Spanish and English		
		Very Well or Well	Not Well	Not at All
6th grade or less	47%	21%	39%	57%
7th grade to 12th grade, no diploma	32%	37%	37%	28%
High school graduate	14%	23%	16%	10%
Some college, less than bachelor's degree	6%	14%	6%	3%
Bachelor's degree to doctorate degree	2%	5%	3%	1%
Total	**100%**	**100%**	**100%**	**100%**

nearly half (47%) of noncitizens who speak English only and a majority (58%) of those who do not speak English have this level of education. These data show that focusing workforce training on providing English instruction to speakers whose first language is not English or who do not speak English like the local English monolinguals misses those who need workforce training—those with low levels of schooling. In the case of noncitizens, those who speak English only, like those who speak Spanish only, are also in great need of workforce training and increased schooling opportunities.

Comparing Table 2.6 with Table 2.5 shows that non-U.S. citizens who speak Spanish and do not speak English have educational attainment rates that are greater than similar speakers who are U.S. born; however, non-U.S. citizens who speak English only or who speak S&Evwow have educational attainment rates that are markedly less than similar speakers who are U.S. born. This difference strongly suggests that English ability is a function of schooling because non-U.S. citizens likely received much more of their schooling in Spanish than did the U.S. born, who likely received almost all of their schooling in English. Data thus suggest that workforce training focus should be redirected from providing English instruction to speakers whose first language is not English or who do not speak English like the local English monolinguals to providing educational opportunities to those with low levels of schooling. The data make the case for Spanish language literacy for adults and for continued workforce, GED, and college preparatory education in the first language and English.

Finally, naturalized citizens who do not speak English have educational attainment rates similar to speakers who were U.S. born (compare Table 2.7 with Table 2.5). However, naturalized citizens who speak at least some English have educational attainment rates that are less than those who are U.S. born and who received schooling in the English language. This comparison also suggests that workforce training focus should be redirected to providing educational opportunities to those with low levels of schooling.

Table 2.7   Educational Attainment of Naturalized Mexican-Origin Persons Aged 18 Years+

Educational Attainment	Speak English Only	Speak Spanish and English		
		Very Well or Well	Not Well	Not at All
6th grade or less	33%	19%	48%	70%
7th grade to 12th grade, no diploma	24%	30%	32%	18%
High school graduate	19%	24%	13%	7%
Some college, less than bachelor's degree	16%	21%	5%	4%
Bachelor's degree to doctorate degree	8%	7%	2%	1%
Total	**100%**	**100%**	**100%**	**100%**

Conclusion and Recommendations

Policies based on the two major ideological assumptions that English is the language spoken outside the home and that it is desirable that non-English speakers change into or conform as English language speakers have resulted in restrictionist and repressive language policies in the area of U.S. adult education. For example, making the assumption that persons who speak a language other than English at home are immigrants ignores that languages other than English are "native" to the United States, puts into question the legitimacy of persons who speak languages other than English as Americans, and renders invisible the reality around us. The United States, especially in the Southwest, southern Florida, and the eastern and western metropolitan seaboard, is a multilingual nation. Denying the multilingual nature of the United States, while making the assumption that non-English language diversity in the United States is an abnormality that must be remedied, fails to allow for the development of reality-based workforce and educational policies as alternatives to the restrictionist and repressive ones that currently exist.

An overemphasis on oral English language skills at the expense of literacy and job skills that can be mediated in languages other than English overtly delimits the workplace and educational policy options that would better accommodate our linguistically diverse society. Because of the assumption that only those with proficient English language speaking ability can advance in the labor market, there is a lack of research on those who daily function without it because of the vitality of languages other than English and the interaction with bilinguals who can mediate for speakers of Spanish and other languages. As the conclusion of the executive summary of Greenberg et al.'s (2001) secondary analysis of the 1992 National Adult Literacy Survey notes:

Only non-native English speakers with low levels of formal education were truly disadvantaged in the labor market by their lack of native English language skills. Most members of this disadvantaged group were not being reached by existing English as a second language and basic skills classes.

Other non-native English speakers and immigrants, *even those with low levels of English literacy* as measured by the 1992 National Adult Literacy Survey, were generally able to learn enough English to exhibit employment patterns and earnings comparable to native English speakers. (Emphasis added, Greenberg et al., 2001, p. x)

Thus, lack of access to education is more salient than language background as a predictor of success in the labor market. A singular focus on the acquisition of English oral language proficiency as a prerequisite to job training and educational programs merely becomes a gatekeeping mechanism that limits the potential success of those who have greater proficiency in other languages. In other words, educational, social, and other services need to be provided, without discrimination based on language background, because literacy based on primary language provides a foundation for the acquisition of English literacy. For this reason, there is a need for better national data on literacy in languages other than English and finer analyses of existing national data. To undertake these goals, we need to move beyond the narrow ideological focus on oral English and English-only literacy instruction.

References

Berliner, D. (1996). Nowadays, even the illiterates read and write. *Research in the Teaching of English, 30*, 334–351.

Berliner, D. C., & Biddle, B. J. (1996). *The manufactured crisis: Myths, fraud, and the attack on America's public schools.* New York: Perseius-Harper Collins.

Chisman, F. P., Wrigley, H. S., & Ewen, D. T. (1993). *ESL and the American dream.* Washington, DC: Southport Institute for Policy Analysis.

D'Amico, D., & Schnee, E. (1997). "It changed something inside of me": English language learning, structural barriers to employment, and workers' goals in a workplace literacy program. In G. Hull (Ed.), *Changing work, changing workers: Critical perspectives on language, literacy, and skills* (pp. 117–140). Albany, NY: State University of New York Press.

Greenberg, E., Macías, R. F., Rhodes, D., & Chan, T. (2001, August). *English literacy and language minorities in the United States* (NCES 2001-464). Washington, DC: National Center for Education Statistics.

Hunter, C., & Harman, D. (1979). *Adult illiteracy in the United States.* New York: McGraw-Hill.

Kirsch, I. S., Jungeblut, A., Jenkins, L., & Kolstad, A. (1993). *Adult literacy in America: A first look at the results of the National Adult Literacy Survey.* Washington, DC: U.S. Department of Education, Office of Educational Research and Improvement.

Kominski, R. (1989, August 6–11). *How good is "how well"? An examination of the Census English-speaking ability question.* Presented at the 1989 Annual Meeting of the American Statistical Association, Washington, DC.

LeBlanc, R., & Painchaud, G. (1986). Self-assessment as a second language placement instrument. *TESOL Quarterly, 19,* 673–687.

Macías, R. F. (1994). Inheriting sins while seeking absolution: Language diversity and national statistical data sets. In D. Spener (Ed.), *Adult biliteracy in the United States* (pp. 15–45). Washington, DC: Center for Applied Linguistics and Delta Systems.

Mathews, J. (2001, July 22). Landmark illiteracy analysis is flawed, statistics faulty, study director says. *Washington Post,* p. A16. (Reprinted in the *Arizona Republic*).

McArthur, E. K. (1993). *Language characteristics and schooling in the United States, a changing picture: 1979 and 1989* (NCES Report 93-699). Washington, DC: U.S. Department of Education, Office of Educational Research and Improvement, National Center for Education Statistics.

National Center for Education Statistics. (2004). *NAAL assessment design.* Washington, DC: Author. Retrieved December 17, 2004, from http://nces.ed.gov/naal/design/about02.asp

National Center for Education Statistics. (2005, December). *National Assessment of Adult Literacy: A first look at the literacy of America's adults in the 21st century* (NCES 2006470). Washington, DC: Author. Retrieved May 8, 2006, from http://nces.ed.gov/NAAL/PDF/2006470.PDF.

Ovando, C. J., & Wiley, T. G. (2003). Language education in the conflicted United States. In J. Bourne & E. Reid (Eds.), *World yearbook of education 2003: Language education* (pp. 141–155). London: Kogan Page.

Shin, H.B. with Bruno, R. (2003, October). *Language use and English-speaking ability: 2000* (Current Population Reports, P20-535). Washington, DC: U.S. Census Bureau.

U.S. Census Bureau. (2003a). *Census 2000, Table 1. Language use, English ability, and linguistic isolation for the population 5 years and over by state: 2000* (Summary File 3, Tables P19, PCT13, and PCT14; Internet release date: February 25, 2003). Washington, DC: U.S. Census Bureau.

U.S. Census Bureau. (2003b). *Census 2000, Public Use Microdata Sample (PUMS), United States.* Prepared by the U.S. Census Bureau. Washington, DC: U.S. Census Bureau.

U.S. Census Bureau. (2004a). *Language use.* U.S. Census Bureau, Population Division, Education & Social Stratification Branch. Retrieved September 8, 2004, from http://www.census.gov/population/www/socdemo/lang_use.html.

U.S. Census Bureau. (2004b). *Census 2000, Language spoken at home for the United States: 2000* (Special Tabulation 224). Washington, DC: U.S. Census Bureau.

Wiley, T. G. (1996). *Literacy and language diversity in the United States.* Washington, DC: Center for Applied Linguistics and Delta Systems.

Wiley, T. G. (2005). *Literacy and language diversity in the United States* (2nd ed.). Washington, DC: Center for Applied Linguistics and Delta Systems.

Wiley, T. G., & Wright, W. E. (2004). Against the undertow: Language-minority edu-
    cation policy and politics in the "age of accountability." *Educational Policy, 18,*
    142–168.
Wrigley, H. S., Chisman, F. P., & Ewen, D. T. (1993). *Sparks of excellence: Program
    realities and promising practices in adult ESL.* Washington, DC: Southport Insti-
    tute for Policy Analysis.

Photo Essay

Literacy and Biliteracy
Expressions in Environmental Print

Klaudia M. Rivera and Ana Huerta-Macías

Bilingual and multilingual directions for transportation.

Public announcements: bilingual disclosure and rules using translation.

Public announcements: bilingual community advocacy using translation.

Public announcements and marketing using translation.

Bilingual advertising on storefronts and small businesses using translation.

Bilingual advertising: storefronts and small businesses mixing languages.

Catering to different populations using their respective languages.

Mixing languages in advertising.

Creating new words on street signs.

Bilingual advertising: storefronts and small businesses using translations.

Bilingual advertising: billboards mixing languages.

Companies marketing to immigrants in their native language.

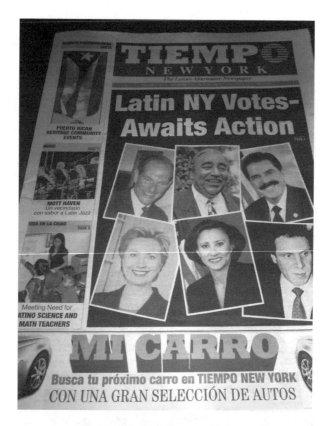

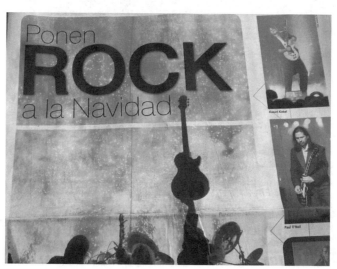

Media and communication: mixing two languages.

Bilingual signs creating new meanings using two languages.

The immigrant labor force: "help needed" signs.

Meeting the civic needs of immigrants in their language.

Immigrant struggles for social justice.

PART II

Adult Biliteracy in Diverse Contexts

3

Adult Biliteracy in Community-Based Organizations

Venues of Participation, Agents of Transformation

Klaudia M. Rivera

Historically, community-based organizations (CBOs) have played an important role in the delivery of adult literacy and English as a Second Language (ESL) services to immigrant learners in the United States. Adult education programs sponsored by CBOs tend to serve students at the most basic levels of literacy and ESL. Because they are usually located in the communities where adults live, work, and conduct their private and public lives, CBOs have an advantage over outside service providers in their ability to tailor services to specific community needs. Their proximity to the community and their immersion in the issues faced by their constituencies allows them to maximize opportunities for the teaching and learning process. This has made them more aware of the bidirectionality of language and literacy learning and the potential of biliteracy.

In the United States, the term *community-based organization* can apply to a number of different programs. While some CBOs are registered nonprofit organizations with the Internal Revenue Service (IRS) and meet the legal requirements to raise funds and create their own governing structures, others are part of larger nongovernmental agencies that cater to a particular population. They range in size from large national or citywide organizations to small grassroots programs. While some CBOs are created by larger institutions and become independent of their parent programs as they develop, others are organized by community members and activists who come together in order to respond to specific community needs.

The particular identity of a CBO may depend on the services it offers and the nature of its constituency. The definition of "community" for these centers therefore varies. Some CBOs define community by the geographical location in which they operate, while others define it by the services they offer. Some are ethnic, gender, religious, or issue based. They may provide services to youth, women, immigrants, the elderly, or may be specifically created to offer adult education services (Eidman-Aadahl, 2002; Honig, Kahne, & McLaughlin, 2001). Some of the principal characteristics of CBOs are having governing boards and staff that represent the community they serve, providing services designed to improve the community and to fill a gap left by the decline of traditional institutions, and running educational programs to foster the empowerment of the participants' personal and social lives (Hill, 2000; Malicky, Katz, Norton, & Norman, 1997).

The missions and goals of CBOs tend to be more diverse and participant centered than those of schools and other governmental institutions. They also tend to offer a variety of programs in order to fulfill diverse needs. CBOs therefore provide a range of services either on-site or by collaborating with other agencies, in order to meet the ever-changing needs of community members. The size and governing structures of CBOs permit them to adapt rapidly to change. This chameleon-like quality allows them to initiate needed programs and end unnecessary ones with less difficulty and better timing than larger outside providers. CBOs thus play an important role in community development by providing the space for community members to remake themselves by achieving their goals and fulfilling their dreams.

The staffing patterns of CBOs tend to be congruent with their missions and often include members of the communities they serve among their paid staff and volunteers. Having staff members who come from the community allows CBOs to be particularly attuned to the individual, educational, and social realities faced by their participants. This in turn has a positive impact on the quality of their services. A number of community-based adult education programs also hire teachers from the group of students they serve. These staff members tend to be knowledgeable of the languages spoken in the community and familiar with students' needs.

Even though CBOs serve a wide variety of clients, depending on the services they offer and the populations they target, this chapter will focus on the role that community-based organizations play in the development of adult biliteracy. Three programs—the Instituto de Educación Popular del Sur de California (IDEPSCA) in Los Angeles County; CASA Latina located in Seattle, Washington; and El Barrio Popular Education Program (EBPEP), which provided services in New York City—will be used to exemplify the various ways in which CBOs have used Spanish and English in instruction.

IDEPSCA began organizing in a public park in Pasadena, California, in 1984 and incorporated in 1997 (IDEPSCA, 2003). It is committed to the creation of a more humane and democratic society through the promotion of self-organizing and self-development programs and the use of popular education. The organization works with low-income Latino immigrants, mostly day laborers, domestic workers, and adult nonreaders, who are identified as the subjects of their formation process (IDEPSCA, 2003). CASA Latina was founded in 1994 by a group of community activists with the goal of improving the lives of Latino workers who were homeless in Seattle (CASA Latina, 2003). Its mission is to empower Latino immigrants through educational and economic opportunities with the vision of their full participation in the democracy and economy of the United States. CASA Latina services to Latinos include comprehensive employment, educational and social services to day laborers, educational leadership for women, and bilingual ESL services in all its programs. New York's EBPEP, which began in 1985 as a research site of the Center for Puerto Rican Studies of the City University of New York with Spanish language literacy classes, became independent from the university in 1991. The goals of the program, which closed in 1997, included the promotion of adult biliteracy for Latinos through the implementations of a philosophy of empowerment and popular education, community leadership and economic development, and the integration of technology in all activities (Rivera, 1997).

This chapter will first examine the role of Spanish language literacy in the United States. It will continue by discussing the role that CBOs play in offering language and literacy services that lead to biliteracy for Latino adults. A description and examples of the shared programmatic characteristics of successful community-based programs promoting biliteracy will follow. Before concluding, the chapter will address some of the challenges faced by CBOs as they strive to provide their services.

Spanish Language Literacy in the United States

The exact levels of Spanish language literacy among Latinos in the United States are not available. The National Adult Literacy Survey (NALS) of 1992 (Kirsch, Jungeblut, Jenkins, & Kolstad, 2002) shed light on the level of English language literacy among adults in the United States, but the survey did not measure literacy in languages other than English. Only estimates from self-reported data on literacy in languages other than English based on a secondary data analysis on the NALS conducted in 2001 by Greenberg, Macías, Rhodes, and Chan are available (see chapter 2, this volume).

The National Assessment of Adult Literacy (NAAL) of 2003 (National Center for Educational Statistics, 2005) included an alternative assessment in which monolingual Spanish-speaking adults were able to participate by responding to questions asked in Spanish (or English) about printed material written in English. However, like the 1992 NALS, the 2003 NAAL, which reports that the average prose and document literacy scores for Hispanics[1] decreased 18 and 14 points, respectively, between 1992 and 2003, only measured literacy in English. Consequently, there are no reliable statistics about the levels of Spanish literacy or its relationship to English literacy among Latino adults in the continental United States.

Greene (1994) states that this lack of knowledge about Spanish language literacy in the United States is not new. He attributes this void to a narrow view of what constitutes literacy and which group's literacy attainment is felt worthy of study. It is worth noting that the first record of Spanish language literacy in what is now the continental United States dates back to 1513, when the Spanish conquistador Ponce de León recorded his arrival in Florida. Other documents include recordings in Spanish of legal events, such as edicts, inventories, and ledgers, also dating back to 1513, and recordings of births, deaths, and marriages to 1565 (Greene, 1994). According to Greene, the earliest documentation of literacy in other colonial languages in the United States is provided by Kaestle, who, citing Lockridge, dated them to 1640, and by Graff, to 1660. This is at least a hundred years after the Spaniards had established schools in Spanish in what are now New Mexico, Florida, and Georgia in the 1500s. The studies by Greene indicate that Spanish language literacy in North America was only predated by literacy in the indigenous languages of the Native American peoples of the United States and Canada and by the Mayas and Aztecs of other parts of North America. Thus, Spanish language literacy antedates English literacy in the United States and other parts of North America.

Literacy and Biliteracy in Community-Based Contexts

Community-based organizations have traditionally offered language and literacy education, including services in languages other than English, to immigrants in the United States. In 1938, the renowned educator Leonard Covello ran the Community Education Adult Program in East Harlem's Benjamin Franklin High School that offered language classes in English, Spanish, and Italian. His school served 1,700 adults in literacy, ESL, citizenship, arts, and high school classes (Perrone, 1998).

Almost 25 years ago, the Information and Resources Center for Educación Liberadora [*sic*] (IRCEL) (1981) published a directory of 28 organizations involved in progressive education for adult Hispanics. Among these organizations there were eight programs that offered Spanish language literacy in the continental United States. These programs defined themselves as community based and offered a variety of services in addition to literacy in the native language. A 1982 study sponsored by Solidaridad Humana and funded by the New York State Education Department to survey adult education programs that offered Spanish language literacy identified 14 community agencies offering these services to approximately 300 adult students (Cook & Quiñones, 1983). By 1991 there were

49 programs offering Spanish language literacy to adults according to a survey conducted by the Center for Applied Linguistics. Almost half of these programs (49%) were housed in a community-based agency (Gillespie, 1994).

A two-year research study conducted by Aguirre International to identify innovative instructional approaches, methods, and technologies providing literacy instruction to adult English language learners recognized that the teaching of native language literacy was a promising approach to the teaching of English literacy to adults who were not literate in their native language. Four of the nine programs studied in detail offered native language literacy in either Spanish or Haitian Creole. A number of these programs implemented a biliteracy approach in their classes (Wrigley & Guth, 1992).

The ways that programs use the native language of the students to teach them to read vary in terms of their educational and linguistic goals and approaches. These differences shape the way the programs teach literacy and English, how and whether the students' native language is developed, and how and when English is introduced. *Transitional* programs are exclusively concerned with English language development and may only utilize the students' mother tongue for a short period and as a tool to teach them English. Some transitional programs may initially offer native language literacy, but once students learn to read and are able to transfer their literate skills to the second language, they continue developing literacy exclusively in English.

Other programs implement a bilingual approach in their instruction. Some of these programs use a *sequential* approach to language and literacy teaching, waiting for students to reach a threshold of literacy in their native language before English is introduced. Other bilingual programs implement a *concurrent* approach in which the students learn to read in their native language while learning English (Rivera, 1999a). In programs where the goal is bilingualism and biliteracy, students develop literacy in their native language and sequentially or concurrently learn English in order to develop literacy in both languages. Education in both languages continues throughout the educational program.

Despite their beliefs about and commitment to teaching their students to read in a language they already know—the native language—many programs are unable to implement an approach that engenders biliteracy. Policy at the federal, state, and city levels (see chapter 2, this volume) and its impact on funding restrict some programs from teaching in the native language. The composition of the student population may also be an impeding factor. Programs with a linguistically heterogeneous student body, where there are not enough students who share a first language, may not be able to offer native language literacy. Other programs serve homogenous language groups, but the speakers come from low-incidence languages in which there is a shortage of teachers and materials that prevent them from teaching literacy in these languages. Constraints notwithstanding, many programs have a commitment to the development of literacy and may teach it in the second language, that is, English.

Characteristics of Successful Community-Based
Biliteracy Programs

Community-based organizations are spaces where traditional notions about literacy have the potential to be transformed. Collectively, these organizations provide significant contexts for literacy work (Eidman-Aadahl, 2002). Their out-of-school location, staffing patterns, and proximity to the communities they serve have enabled CBOs to observe learners performing a variety of community tasks successfully, including using literacy in their everyday lives. Consequently, many CBOs tend to view their participants' linguistic and educational background under a more positive lens than traditional institutions. The result is that the native language and the background and sociocultural knowledge of the participants are more readily included in instruction.

There are a number of characteristics that seem to have a positive impact on the development of adult biliteracy in community-based programs. Among these, the bilingual nature of the pedagogy is of utmost importance. Second is the participatory nature of this pedagogy, which in most cases includes a community organizing component. Other characteristics shared by successful biliteracy programs include hiring staff members from the community of the learners, developing leadership and economic development projects, offering comprehensive services, and contributing to the social and cultural life of the community. While these characteristics are implemented in a multilayered, systemic, and integrated fashion in a particular program—leadership development may take place in the Spanish language literacy classes, for instance—they will be discussed separately using examples from the three programs introduced earlier in the chapter.

Bilingual Pedagogy

Communities are among the richest and most fertile contexts for the development of language and literacy because it is in communities that languages are born, live, struggle for survival, and are utilized in real-life situations. The teaching of English to immigrant students, rather than being a straightforward and unproblematic practice, is a contested one in which there is a struggle about the role and the future of immigrants in our society (Valdés, 2001). Therefore, adult education programs located in community contexts have often viewed their role as much more than teaching reading and writing or English language skills to immigrants. Many programs define themselves as agents of change and understand language and culture to be dynamically connected to real-life situations and projects of transformation. Community-based programs have used the students' native language as a tool to help them achieve their personal and educational goals, improve their lives, challenge oppressive conditions, and contribute to community development.

Furthermore, the use of the students' native language is a fundamental tool in their learning English. As reported by Rivera and Huerta-Macías (chapter 1, this volume), research indicates that native-language literacy provides the foundation for second language learning. Adults, who already have a fully developed language and possess the metalinguistic awareness to use language appropriately and efficiently, can benefit from using this knowledge in their acquisition of English. Furthermore, adults can use what they already know in their first language (their background knowledge) to make meaning and interact with text in the first, second, or both languages.

The use of their native language makes the educational curriculum accessible to students. It allows students to tell their stories, validate their knowledge, and extend it by making it relevant in their education. It also permits them to analyze the social construction of their experience. For example, students can discuss and analyze how their individual stories are related to one another and to larger social movements. During the celebration of *Día de los Muertos*, November 2, at IDEPSCA, participants share and write down their individual immigration stories. These stories are later read out loud in a plenary session to the rest of the participants. The participants' experiences as quasi-invisible immigrants, workers, and impoverished individuals, many of whom have lost relatives crossing the U.S.–Mexican border, are thus critically acknowledged (R. Añorve, personal communication, October 31, 2005). The individual stories become the fabric of a shared history.

Educational program staff benefit by integrating the native language of their students into the classes. This permits them to observe the multiple ways that bilingual and multilingual individuals use literacy in their everyday lives and to pay attention to the bidirectionality of language and literacy learning. That is, by avoiding unnatural boundaries for language use, and by connecting the curriculum to what is happening in the community in meaningful ways, these programs can bridge community and school literacies and create overlapping linguistic contexts for language and literacy learning. They can provide adult students with ample opportunities to use literacy and English in real-life community contexts, such as the workplace, the hospital, the post office, the supermarket, and so forth, rather than teaching students through vicarious and artificial learning exercises, such as language drills. At CASA Latina, day laborers learn English through exercises designed to teach them how to negotiate wages and safety in a job. English is also taught through the language that is used in the different occupations in which the laborers find work, such as in construction, gardening, and carpentry. The day laborers can use what they learn in the ESL class in their work immediately. They can also bring questions to the class that result from their use of English in their everyday lives.

Programs also use the students' native language as a tool for organizing, to help students challenge hegemonic conditions that create social disempowerment, and to reclaim aspects of community that provide them with strengths, such as their culture. IDEPSCA holds public forums in Spanish to address issues of equality and equity in the public schools during local elections. The participants' native language and shared culture are used at critical moments to educate the Latino community on how to ensure fundamental educational rights for their children, and thus to challenge the systematic conditions that produce poor education for Latinos.

The sociocultural and pedagogical reasons given by CBOs to use the native language of their students in the educational program vary and include:

- Allowing students to learn through a language they know and understand
- Giving students access to content knowledge that they can use right away (e.g., to pass the GED, vote, get a job, and use public transportation)
- Including students as active generators of their own education
- Enabling students to produce knowledge
- Publishing students' stories
- Permitting students to use language to connect their past and future
- Enabling students to use what they already know about their native language and the world in their learning English
- Facilitating students' involvement in their children's education
- Connecting the school and community with the larger society
- Giving students access to the curriculum by:
  - Starting from the known, the already lived
  - Including students' view of the world and background knowledge
  - Permitting students to share their stories and personal experiences
  - Allowing students to use the language they know to make sense of the language they are learning

The sociocultural and pedagogical reasons listed above capitalize on the wealth of knowledge that adult students bring into the literacy program and on the ways they use language to actively interact with their social worlds. They build on what students know about their native language to help them learn English. They validate students as the sources of their own curriculum, generators of knowledge, and agents of change. They acknowledge that language and literacy as sociocultural practices relate to the larger cultural and power struggles in society. The native language of the students is used as a resource in their education and as the main vehicle for the analysis and transformation of their reality (Rivera, 1999b).

Participatory Pedagogy/Popular Education

Programs that offer native language literacy tend to favor the implementation of participatory education. Because participatory and popular education coexist in a number of organizations, the shared characteristics as well as differences between participatory and popular education will be discussed together in this section.

For more than two decades, the pedagogy of empowerment developed by the Brazilian educator Paulo Freire has greatly influenced many of the community-based adult education programs serving Latinos in the United States. Virtually all the programs listed in the IRCEL (1981) directory, for example, announced that they were using the philosophy and methods of Paulo Freire and offered "progressive educational programs" for Hispanics (p. i). The study sponsored by Solidaridad Humana found that 4 of the 11 programs they surveyed also implemented the educational philosophy of Paulo Freire (Cook & Quiñones, 1983). Wrigley and Guth (1992) named a participatory methodology as one of the promising practices of the native language programs they studied.

A participatory pedagogy places students' issues at the center of the curriculum and uses dialogue and group-based, learner-centered projects. Participatory education values the participants' daily experience and creates egalitarian relationships in the classroom. The manner in which this pedagogy is implemented includes dialogue, analysis, and *praxis*—action and reflection on the world (Freire, 1970). At the community-based level, this pedagogy has often been tied to issues of liberation and empowerment and to larger commitments for social justice.

The use of the native language allows programs using a participatory approach in their classes to truly engage their adult students in dialogue and analysis and in projects of change. For it is only in their strongest language that adults can engage in complex conversations with one another and collectively question and analyze society and their experiences as immigrants, parents, workers, and citizens in this country. The use of a participatory pedagogy and the learners' mother tongue can therefore provide opportunities for collective action and transformation. It also permits literacy students to recapture the knowledge available in the community and develop new knowledge. For example, the production of texts in the languages of the community can give students voice and develop writers. It can also disseminate students' experiences, written stories, and other forms of cultural capital, such as artistic expressions and artifacts.

Some programs utilizing a native language approach and participatory pedagogy have described themselves as *popular education* programs. See, for example, CASA Latina (n.d.), El Barrio Popular Education Program (Rivera, 1997, 1999c), the Center for Immigrant Families (2004), the Instituto de Educación Popular del Sur de California (1996, 2003), and Mujeres Unidas en Acción (Young & Padilla, 1990). Although participatory and popular education share a number of characteristics, they also have important differences. One of the main differences is that popular educators are prepared to transfer the control of the organizations and their educational projects to community members (Vaccaro, 1990; Rivera, 1997). The transfer to, and the appropriation of, the projects by the participants involves a collaborative process between popular educators and program participants. Through this process the participants learn concepts and knowledge and develop leadership that enable them to take control of the program (Vaccaro, 1990; Rivera, 1997). Seven of the 10 members of IDEPSCA's board of directors are Latinas who have developed their leadership in the organization. Several of their staff members are former day laborers.

Another difference is that while participatory education takes place in a wide variety of programs, from universities to community-based agencies, popular education takes place at the grassroots level and aims at changing oppressive conditions in the lives of the participants and the community. The program's participants who engage in the analysis of their reality are the decision makers and agents of change. IDEPSCA (2003) cautions that

> many privileged individuals are attracted by the [popular education] methodology. … As a consequence, there is much abuse of popular education techniques since many educators focus their pedagogy practice solely on the participatory techniques leaving behind a wealth of analysis generated by engaged participants. (pp. 6–7)

An interesting methodology that has been used to further community empowerment and the social transformation agenda of popular education programs is *popular theater* (Rivera, 1990; Young & Padilla, 1990). According to Boal (1985), theater can be used as a language with which the oppressed can educate themselves and rehearse dramatic scenarios of personal and social change. In Boal's theater, the topics of the plays are based on issues from the participants' lives. The participants become the actors, the protagonists of the play, and as such rehearse different ways of dealing with a particular oppressive situation. Popular theater is process oriented and involves the sharing of stories, reflection, and analysis, and experimenting with change. CASA Latina has used theater to educate day laborers about safe sex, sexual harassment, and how to negotiate wages with potential employers (2002). More recently, popular theater has been used for community building around issues of gender. IDEPSCA has also used popular theater as a way to celebrate and educate the community about the lives of day laborers. In 1998, in the first encounter of laborers from different areas in Southern California, day laborers presented the play *How Many Guys? [¿Cuántos?]* based on their experiences looking for work (IDEPSCA, 1998).

Participatory/popular research has also been used as an educational and organizing tool in adult biliteracy programs. In this type of research, the program participants conduct investigations on the issues that affect their lives, which then become the content of the participatory curriculum (Rivera, 1999c). Through popular research and a bilingual pedagogy, program participants gather information about these issues and inform the community about the results of the investigations. These findings stimulate other investigations and organizing projects. The two languages are used in the ongoing process of learning, investigating, organizing, producing knowledge, and informing the community. The native language can be used to identify and investigate the issues that affect the learners and to organize around these issues. The native language and English can be used to inform the community about the results of these investigations.

In addition, programs can use both languages to further disseminate the results of their curricula though videos, publications, theater presentations, and community forums. At EBPEP, for example, students conducted popular research projects on topics ranging from immigration to the impact that the adults' participation in education had on their children's lives. The research projects were the content of the curriculum. The native language and English were used to gather and analyze data and to reflect on the research findings. Videos were produced by the participants to document and disseminate the findings to the community at large (Rivera, 1999c).

Popular education projects implement a "pedagogy of commitment" because of the establishment of positive relationships between the staff and the program participants and the political commitment to a long-term process of social transformation (Vaccaro, 1990, p. 72). The vision of this transformation is rooted in the participants' reflection on and analysis of their own reality and in their decision to be the agents of its change.

Teachers and Staff from the Community of the Learners

An important programmatic component found in many CBOs implementing a bilingual/biliteracy approach to education is that they hire teachers and other educational personnel from the community of the learners. This practice reflects a commitment to learn from the community, incorporate community issues in the curriculum, and contribute to the development of bilingual teachers who are rooted in community knowledge. The community teachers also facilitate the production of knowledge and enhance the advocacy capacity of the biliteracy programs where they work. Moreover, learners' representation among the staff has shown to be an important factor in students' retention (Briscoe & Ross, 1991).

Having learners represented on the staff provides CBOs with additional tools in the teaching and learning process. These staff members share a language, cultural affiliation, and ethnic background with the students. They also face similar social and educational issues with them, including experiences with immigration, social services, schooling, unstable employment, and a need to learn English.

Including learners as staff enables the CBO to seamlessly learn and draw from community knowledge, skills, values, and practices and include them in the curriculum. Morris (2004) found that one of the positive effects of having African American (AA) educators in schools is that they use their sociocultural capital—that is, their knowledge of AA history and culture—to shape AA children's critical understanding of their history and to make classroom lessons relevant to their everyday experiences. Rivera (1999b, 1999c) also stated the positive effect of hiring teachers from the community of the learners on an adult biliteracy program. She described how popular teachers (students and program graduates who had been trained to teach) enabled the adult biliteracy program to include the stories and social realities of the participants in the curriculum and created classroom environments of collective work and solidarity, leading to high student involvement, participation, and success. The popular teachers also brought to fruition the bidirectionality of education by teaching the academically trained teachers their knowledge of the community and learning formal/academic knowledge from these teachers. In this way, the popular teachers become "learners and teachers in creating and implementing the curriculum" (Rivera, 1999c, p. 492).

Paid personnel, who come from the community of the learners and share the sociocultural capital of the students, make the curriculum more relevant to the lived experiences and needs of adult learners by building on community knowledge and expertise. Many programs, for example, bring community members to speak to students about community history and cultural traditions, thus validating the cultural capital and diverse knowledge housed in the community.

Bilingual programs play an important role in the development of biliterate teachers who are rooted in the culture of the community. At a time of teacher shortages, especially of teachers who come from similar linguistic and cultural backgrounds as their students, the development of these teachers is very important. The manner in which they are trained varies. Gegeo and Watson-Gegeo (2002) argue for teachers to be trained through their engagement in critical pedagogical discussions at the community level. Based on work in the Solomon Islands, they propose a critical pedagogy that creates counterhegemonic teaching practices, one that is inclusive of indigenous epistemology through the incorporation of indigenous language and culture in the curriculum, and that is carried out by the community members themselves. In some programs, teachers are trained on the job through participatory pedagogy, often supplementing their preparation with the support of readings and workshops. At the El Barrio Popular Education Program, teacher training took place during weekly curricular meetings, which included discussions about the issues to be addressed in the curriculum, professional readings, and the participatory philosophy of the program. Popular teachers also worked alongside more experienced teachers before teaching their own classes. Teachers can also be trained by what McCarty (2002) calls "an invested outsider," someone who through many years of educational activism and community collaboration has a commitment to educational social justice (p. 286). In most instances the "invested outsider" comes into the program and works alongside program staff.

CBOs that train and hire teachers and other educational personnel from the community of the learners contribute to community development by highlighting the importance of community knowledge and asserting the value of the native language for instruction. They extend the context for native language use and create the space for critical consciousness raising about the role that traditional schools play in either reaffirming or suppressing the use of the native language in the public sphere. McCarty and Watahomigie (1999) reached similar conclusions in their work with Native American communities. They found that community-based programs that use indigenous languages and community teachers "have created new contexts for Native [*sic*] language literacy, facilitated the credentialing of indigenous teachers, and elevated the moral authority and instrumental value of indigenous languages in communities and schools" (p. 91).

Teachers from the community also become role models and mentors for other students, enabling the program to have a multiplier effect in the community; many community-trained teachers choose to gain teaching credentials, and thus the program can contribute to the long-term alleviation of shortages of culturally competent teachers.

Leadership and Economic Development

As I suggested earlier in this chapter, many CBOs, especially those that define themselves as popular education programs, are committed to the development of leadership at the grassroots level. A number of CBOs also promote entrepreneurship activities to contribute to the economic development of the community and the self-sufficiency of the program and the participants. The leadership and economic development projects are framed within the particular needs of low-income communities and build on the often-overlooked economic expertise of the participants.

Language and literacy classes are not confined to the classrooms. They take place continually as participants engage in organizing around issues that concern their community, implement participatory or popular research projects, and take part in formal leadership development classes. For example, after four years of operation, CASA Latina, an organization initially established to give voice to day laborers in Seattle through literacy and ESL programs, decided that classes were not enough to achieve the organization's mission of providing economic independence to the community. This effort led to organizing a day laborer dispatch center and, in July 1999, resulted in the creation of CASA Latina's Day Workers' Center, a facility where day workers can assemble for dispatch to jobs. The Day Workers' Center offers community literacy workshops in Spanish. Lessons include how to call Metro for bus directions, how to use the phone book, and how to file taxes. The center also offers ESL classes and a Wage Claim Project. Through this project, workers are informed of their rights and assisted in claiming back wages (CASA Latina, n.d.). The Day Workers' Center is staffed by former day laborers who participate in formal and informal leadership development training. Recently one of these staff members and two day laborers were selected by their peers to attend the National Day Laborer Organizing Network's Third National Day Laborer Convention, to represent CASA Latina and participate in additional leadership development (field notes, June 20, 2005).

At El Barrio Popular Education Program, students developed literacy, used English, and applied the math skills they were learning in formal classes by running a food cooperative. They initiated this cooperative as a way to supplement their income after recognizing that the cooking skills they had developed preparing food for large groups were marketable and that there was a need for homemade Latino food in the larger community. The operation of a cooperative demanded that accounts be kept, menus developed and displayed, and the decisions made at meetings be recorded. It also required advertisement and public relations to secure clients. The participants used computers and videos to accomplish these tasks. Participants also took part in formal leadership development training, where they learned about and discussed different leadership styles. Leadership was thereby exercised through collective projects for which they were all responsible. Literacy (in English and Spanish) and technology were used consistently as means to important and concrete ends.

According to R. Añorve, leadership is one of the core activities at IDEPSCA, where participants have developed a number of projects within the organization to address systemic issues of fundamental importance in low-income Latino communities, such as the access to livable wage jobs, culturally based education, affordable housing, health care, gender analysis, and educational equity for public school children (personal communication, October 31, 2005). Leadership development at IDEPSCA is based on two intertwined processes: *capacitación/* training and *formación/*formation. The first process provides skills such as reading and writing, as well as learning about community issues and civic participation. The second process, *formación/*formation, consists of the application of the skills learned in the *capacitación/*training and includes an in-depth analysis of the group's collective practice, or *popular action.* One of the projects developed by IDEPSCA, which combines leadership development and economic opportunities for more than 480 Latinas, is a cooperative called the Domestic Workers Program. Through this project women learn to defend their rights and earn sustainable wages for themselves and their families. Moreover, this cooperative has evolved into another grassroots entrepreneurship project, a Multi-Service Cleaning Cooperative called Magic Cleaners, which is co-owned by six women. In these developments, Spanish has been used consistently from developing the by-laws of the cooperative to establishing agreements and participating in training. All documents are developed in Spanish and translated into English. The use of Spanish, English, or both depends on which language is the most useful and appropriate at a particular moment.

The examples above illustrate that when community-based organizations implement leadership and economic development projects through a bilingual/ biliterate and participatory approach, the borders between classroom and community become blurred. In these programs, language and literacy are used and developed in multiple situational contexts and through different channels and modes (New London Group, 1996). For example, adult students use English, Spanish, or both depending on the demands of the task they are implementing, and use technology (in English, Spanish, or both) to accomplish their goals. Opportunities to learn and opportunities to teach are therefore extended, multiplied, and moved forward, and the walls of the classroom become porous in order to include the different activities that give meaning to the functions of literacy and the uses of English and Spanish in everyday life. Moreover, the bilingual leadership and economic development projects also ensure community involvement in the process of social transformation by preparing community members to take control of the program and to become grassroots organizers.

Comprehensive Services

Since immigrant and minority communities have complex needs, the services offered by CBOs are not offered in a vacuum. These services are defined by the needs of their constituencies. While large organizations are able to deliver comprehensive on-site services, smaller, neighborhood-based organizations create collaborations with other providers in order to offer comprehensive services, often having a strong referral and follow-up component. Some of these collaborations are formal and funded arrangements, while others are informal networks of neighborhood providers. By collaborating with other agencies, CBOs maximize funding and focus on a particular expertise while articulating services more efficiently and effectively for their clients. In addition to ESL and literacy classes, many CBOs offer bilingual GED, citizenship preparation, college articulation classes, and pre-employment and vocational services. They may establish collaborations with social service organizations such as hospitals, legal clinics, homeless shelters, housing assistance, and advocacy services. Bilingual CBOs usually work with local public schools and early childhood centers (day care and Head Start centers) to ensure the appropriate delivery of services to immigrant children. In addition, they may maintain collaborations with colleges, vocational education, and employment agencies. They also serve students who need literacy and ESL services and are referred by the agencies with which they collaborate. All of these services are provided in the native language and in English.

An established referral and follow-up system allows a CBO to respond to the particular and often urgent needs of students in a timely manner. At El Barrio Popular Education Program, for instance, a woman might disclose to a teacher, counselor, or another student that she was in an abusive relationship. After making friends with other women and finding a support system in the program, such a woman would often express a willingness to explore life without the abusive partner. In these instances, the program addressed this need right away through a network of neighborhood agencies. The support systems offered through this network included counseling, transitional shelter, emergency cash assistance, legal services, and permanent housing. The EBPEP also offered on-site training in how to identify and deal with domestic violence. The purpose of this training was to prepare women to provide other women in the community with domestic violence counseling and support. Another example is the wage claim project run by CASA Latina. Through collaboration between CASA Latina and the King

County Bar Association, volunteer lawyers and interns give workshops at the Workers' Center on worker rights and how to file a claim for back wages. They also talk to workers individually about their cases. In 2003, through this collaboration, $21,359 was collected for workers in back wages (CASA Latina, 2003). The ESL classes and health education services at IDEPSCA are based on referrals, collaborations, and partnerships. Since 1997 the organization has also run a Job Placement and Wage Claim program to recover unpaid wages and disability work-related injuries.

In order to meet the long-term educational and employment needs of students, programs also need to articulate services with colleges, vocational education, and employment agencies. This allows providers to make transitions as smoothly as possible for students from a GED program to college, for example. At the same time, it allows the student to continue participating in the programs sponsored by the CBO, including its support systems, while pursuing a college degree or employment training. At EBPEP most of the students who were enrolled in college classes continued attending the program to participate in training workshops in popular education and to teach literacy, computer, and video classes. They also used the program's computer lab and video editing workshop. The program's graduates were role models for other students and served as popular education teachers. Collaborations between CBOs and college-based teacher training programs allow the CBOs to offer their students the possibility of an advanced degree and permit the university to offer ideal placements for their students to acquire firsthand knowledge of and experience with the communities with which they will be working. An important characteristic of successful relationships between two organizations is that they are as egalitarian as possible, especially when those organizations have unequal access to power, which is the case of grassroots CBOs and universities.

Cultural Projects

In addition to the services described above, CBOs implementing biliteracy programs have made important contributions maintaining and promoting the community's cultural and linguistic resources. The use of two languages enables CBOs to include intergenerational activities, storytelling, and the publication of peoples' stories in their curriculum. These activities have resulted in curricula that, drawing from the culture and individual history of the participants, document the collective history of an entire community. At El Barrio Popular Education Program the students published their writing on an ongoing basis. One of these publications, entitled *Historias de la Vida Real: De la Fábrica a la Escuela* [*Stories from Real Life: From the Factory to School*] (EBPEP, 1994), documents the participants' stories as Latinas who had grown up poor, had little formal education, started working at an early age, immigrated to the United States, worked in New York City's garment industry, and were learning to read as adults. Their stories were also documented through videos that the participants researched, edited, and produced. The video *Educación Popular: Un Ejemplo Multiplicador* [*Popular Education: A Multiplier Example*] (EBPEP, 1995) compiles their experiences participating in an adult popular education program.

An important outcome of the CBOs' implementation of biliteracy education, especially popular education programs, is the affirmation of culture as a living entity and a tool to educate and organize. At IDEPSCA, culture is the main vehicle through which participants begin to develop critical consciousness. Culture and its manifestations are examined with a critical eye at IDEPSCA; for example, participants analyze an expression of culture that may be oppressive to a particular group of people. They analyze where the cultural value comes from and when and how it is replicated. This has been done through the use of a *norteña* song, for instance, in which a man treats a woman as an object.

Bilingual CBOs are also sites for celebrations and the promotion of cultural events. One of the four goals of the first encounter among groups of day laborers was "demostrar las habilidades artísticas de los jornaleros a través de la música, poesía y teatro" [to demonstrate the artistic abilities of day laborers through music, poetry, and theater] (IDEPSCA, 1998, p. 1). The musical groups *Los Jornaleros del Norte* and *Los Jornaleros de Hollywood* played at the event, and a theater performance was also presented. Since 2002, IDEPSCA has supported a traveling exhibition of day laborers' art. The celebration of culture also takes place throughout the year by offering programs to commemorate human dignity and democratic practice. One of these occasions is International Literacy Day, September 8, when students reflect on their own education and write and illustrate their stories with drawings or stage them through skits, songs, or other kinds of presentations.

CBOs also play the role of cultural facilitators by opening their doors to community artists and making mainstream cultural institutions, such as museums, accessible to their participants. EBPEP collaborated with the New Museum of Contemporary Art by having an art class taught on-site to the literacy and ESL students. *Nuestras Voces* [*Our Voices*], the limited-edition artist book produced by the participants, was shown at an exhibit at the museum's main site in Manhattan's Soho (New Museum of Contemporary Art, 1993). CASA Latina offers summer ceramic workshops through collaboration with the Seattle Art Museum.

Challenges

While the nongovernmental nature of CBOs gives them the flexibility to offer innovative services in order to meet the changing needs of the communities they serve, it also demands ongoing efforts to secure funds to adequately support these services. Lack of long-term funding threatens their stability and affects the consistency of their programs, including the type of classes, schedules, and social services they offer and the permanency of trained staff. Inadequate funding results in the overextension and exhaustion of teachers, administrators, and support personnel; the organizations' inability to offer stable employment and competitive salaries; and the over-reliance on part-time workers and volunteers, especially teachers, who often lack health and retirement benefits. It also results in long waiting lists for classes and services. Shifting funding priorities, grant sizes, and funding cycles established by private and public donors affect the organizations' long-term planning and growth.

CBOs implementing bilingual and biliteracy programs need also to contend with, and constantly struggle against, funding priorities that enact monolingual policies, call for standardized curricula, and are not inclusive of the diverse needs and strengths of adult literacy and English language learners. Offering bilingual, biliteracy, and bicultural programs while keeping the organization viable and solvent may be a CBO's greatest challenge. McCarty (2002) mentions in her description of the native language literacy program at Rough Rock, an indigenous reservation, "the hardships of financial insolvency, chronic teacher turnover and curriculum instability" that can be traced to institutional arrangements that make the school "dependent on fluctuating federal programs, policies, and funds" (p. 292).

In addition to having to write grants, many CBOs need to sponsor fundraising events such as dances, dinners, auctions, and mailings, to keep them afloat. CASA Latina runs an auction and dinner to fund its programs and operating expenses, and sponsors dances to support its ESL evening classes. These events require human resources and sophisticated public relations, which small grassroots programs do not have and can contribute to overburdening the staff. They also call for members of the organization's board of directors to be knowledgeable fund-raisers. Since the board of directors is responsible for the development and implementation of policy, this is a controversial issue in community-based programs in which students are prepared to be the leaders of the organization. These CBOs struggle to strike a balance between board members with corporate and governmental contacts to secure the financial viability of the organization, and members with community knowledge and expertise to ensure the mission of the organization and the true representation of its members on the board.

Conclusion

Community-based organizations have effectively met the basic education needs of traditionally underserved populations, including undocumented workers, women, and adults who, in addition to literacy and ESL classes, also need an array of support and services due to the precarious social and economic conditions under which they live. CBOs have also become successful providers of educational services that lead to biliteracy for adults.

Adult biliteracy programs located in community-based organizations serve students at the most basic levels of literacy and ESL through well-integrated educational programs that build on the wealth of knowledge and expertise housed in the communities of the learners. By allowing their students to build on the knowledge acquired in their primary language, CBOs have created contexts for language and literacy learning. These contexts are the realities—the everyday lives—of the learners who, through the analysis of their lives, engage in projects of transformation. They have been leaders in the implementation of participatory and popular education and in developing leadership among their students. The integrated programs through which they develop leadership and income-generating activities can lead to the transference of the programs to, and the appropriation of the programs by, the adult participants. Income-generating activities contribute to community development and the self-sufficiency of the students. CBOs have also been successful providers of multilayered comprehensive services and promoters of culture through their programs.

Community-based programs have the potential to make the vision of biliterate citizenship—a biliterate community of citizens who are knowledgeable about their rights and responsibilities—a reality. For this vision to become reality, CBOs need to be equal partners in the delivery of educational services to the multiethnic, multilingual communities in which they operate. CBOs must continue to offer an alternative education system for adults, a system that stretches the notions of what education is and where learning takes place. They must be equal partners in the development and implementation of educational policies that are rooted in the linguistic strengths of communities and that address community needs. They must also have access to funding that is congruent with their mission and allows them to implement transformative programs, that is, bilingual programs that lead to biliteracy and the active participation of immigrants in the design of a more inclusive and equitable society.

Endnotes

1. The term *Hispanic* is used when it appears in the original. Otherwise, *Latino* is preferred.

References

Boal, A. (1985). *Theater of the oppressed*. New York: Theater Communications Group.

Briscoe, D., & Ross, J. (1991). Racial and ethnic minorities and adult education. In S. Merriam & E. Cunningham (Eds.), *Handbook of adult and continuing education* (pp. 583–598). San Francisco: Jossey-Bass.

CASA Latina. (n.d.). *A community program giving voice to Latino immigrant workers*. Retrieved October 27, 2004, from http://www.casa-latina.org

CASA Latina. (2002). *A brief history*. Seattle: Author.

CASA Latina. (2003). *Annual report*. Seattle: Author.

Center for Immigrant Families. (2004). *Segregated and unequal: The public elementary schools in District 3 in New York City*. New York: Author.

Cook, J., & Quiñones, A. (1983). *Spanish literacy investigation project.* New York: Solidaridad Humana.

Eidman-Aadahl, E. (2002). Got some time, got a place, got the word. In G. Hull & K. Schultz (Eds.), *School's out! Bridging out-of-school literacies with classroom practice* (pp. 241–260). New York: Teachers College Press.

El Barrio Popular Education Program. (1994). *Historias de la Vida Real: De la Fábrica a la Escuela* [*Stories from real life: From the factory to school*]. New York: Author.

El Barrio Popular Education Program. (1995). *Educación popular: Un ejemplo multiplicador.* [*Popular education: A multiplier example*] [videotape]. New York: Author.

Freire, P. (1970). *Pedagogy of the oppressed* (26th ed.). New York: Continuum.

Gegeo, D. W., & Watson-Gegeo, K. A. (2002). The critical villager: Transforming language and education in the Solomon Islands. In J. W. Tollefson (Ed.), *Language policies in education* (pp. 303–325). Mahwah, NJ: Lawrence Erlbaum Associates.

Gillespie, M. K. (1994). *Native language literacy instruction for adults.* Washington, DC: National Clearinghouse for ESL Literacy Education.

Greenberg, E., Macías, R. F., Rhodes, D., & Chan, T. (2001, August). *English literacy and language minorities in the United States* (NCES 2001-464). Washington, DC: National Center for Education Statistics.

Greene, J. C. (1994). Misperspectives on literacy: A critique of an Anglocentric bias in histories of American literacy. *Written Communication, 11,* 251–269.

Hill, S. (2000). A tale from the youth field: Using stories to understand community-based youth programs. *Afterschool Matters, 1,* 4–11.

Honig, M. I., Kahne, J., & McLaughlin, M. W. (2001). School-community connections: Strengthening opportunity to learn and opportunity to teach. In V. Richardson (Ed.), *Handbook of research on teaching* (4th ed., pp. 998–1028). Washington, DC: American Educational Research.

Information and Resources Center for Educación Liberadora (IRCEL). (1981). *Descriptive directory of projects.* Reston, VA: Author.

Instituto de Educación Popular del Sur de California (IDEPSCA). (1996). *Del olvido a la esperanza.* Los Angeles: Author.

Instituto de Educación Popular del Sur de California (IDEPSCA). (1998). *De esperanzas a realidades.* Los Angeles: Author.

Instituto de Educación Popular del Sur de California (IDEPSCA). (2003). *Five-year strategic plan: A vision of a grassroots popular education organization.* Los Angeles: Author.

Kirsch, I. S., Jungeblut, A., Jenkins, L., & Kolstad, A. (2002). *Adult literacy in America: A first look at the findings of the National Adult Literacy Survey* (3rd ed., NCES 1993-275). Washington, DC: U.S. Department of Education. Retrieved December 5, 2005, from http://nces.ed.gov/pubs93/93275.pdf

Malicky, G. V., Katz, C. H., Norton, M., & Norman, C. A. (1997). Literacy learning in community-based programs. *Adult Basic Education, 7,* 84–103.

McCarty, T. L. (2002). Between possibility and constraint: Indigenous language education, planning and policy in the United States. In J. W. Tollefson (Ed.), *Language policies in education: Critical issues* (pp. 285–307). Mahwah, NJ: Lawrence Erlbaum Associates.

McCarty, T. L., & Watahomigie, L. J. (1999). Indigenous community-based language education in the USA. In S. May (Ed.), *Indigenous community-based education* (pp. 79–94). Clevedon, UK: Multilingual Matters.

Morris, J. E. (2004). Can anything good come from Nazareth? Race, class, and African American schooling and community in the urban south and midwest. *American Educational Research Journal, 41*, 69–112.

National Center for Education Statistics. (2005, December). *National Assessment of Adult Literacy: A first look at the literacy of America's adults in the 21st century* (NCES 2006-470). Retrieved January 14, 2006, from http://nces. ed.gov/NAAL/pdf/2006470_1.PDF

New London Group. (1996). A pedagogy of multiliteracies: Designing social futures. *Harvard Educational Review, 66*, 60–92.

New Museum of Contemporary Art. (1993). *Testimonio: September 10, 1993–January 2, 1994* [Brochure]. New York: Author.

Perrone, V. (1998). *Teacher with a heart: Reflections on Leonard Covello and community.* New York: Teachers College Press.

Rivera, K. M. (1990). *Popular theater as a discourse for liberation in an adult, native language, literacy class* (University Microfilm 9283). Unpublished doctoral dissertation, Teachers College, Columbia University, New York.

Rivera, K. (1997). El Barrio Popular Education Program. In D. Taylor (Ed.), *Many families, many literacies: An international declaration of principles* (pp. 128–133). Portsmouth, NH: Heinemann.

Rivera, K. (1999a). Native language literacy and adult ESL instruction. *ERIC Digest* (EDO-LE-99-04). Washington, DC: National Clearinghouse for ESL Literacy Education.

Rivera, K. M. (1999b). From developing one's voice to making oneself heard: Affecting language policy from the bottom up. In T. Huebner & K. A. Davis (Eds.), *Sociopolitical perspectives on language policy and planning in the USA* (pp. 333–346). Amsterdam: John Benjamins.

Rivera, K. M. (1999c). Popular research and social transformation: A community-based approach to critical pedagogy. *TESOL Quarterly, 33*, 485–500.

Vaccaro, L. (1990). Transference and appropriation in popular education interventions: A framework for analysis. *Harvard Educational Review, 60*, 62–78.

Valdés, G. (2001). *Learning and not learning English: Latino students in American schools.* New York: Teachers College Press.

Wrigley, H. S., & Guth, G. A. (1992). *Bringing literacy to life: Issues and options in adult ESL literacy.* San Mateo, CA: Aguirre Internacional.

Young, E., & Padilla, M. (1990). Mujeres Unidas en Acción: A popular education process. *Harvard Educational Review, 60*, 1–18.

4

Workforce Education for Latinos
A Bilingual Approach

Ana Huerta-Macías

Most of the current research literature on biliteracy has focused on curricular and instructional issues that arise in working with Latino youth. Dual-language bilingual education programs, English as a Second Language (ESL) curricula, and culturally responsive pedagogy are some of the issues that have been discussed at length in the literature. The education of immigrant adults has received relatively little attention, and there has been virtually no attention paid to the educational and linguistic issues facing immigrants in the U.S. labor market. This chapter presents a discussion of the educational and linguistic challenges facing immigrant workers in this country. The focus is on the foreign born, and thereby on Latinos, because they are currently the largest segment of foreign born, or immigrant, workers in the United States. The author first presents a picture of the educational, economical, and linguistic issues facing these workers. The discussion continues by problematizing traditional workforce education programs and by describing a bilingual approach to workforce education for Latinos. The piece concludes with some reflections on workforce education with immigrant workers.

The Landscape of Work, Education, and Latinos

The numbers are undeniable. Education in the United States has historically failed to serve the immigrant populations in this country. Latinos,[1] being the largest ethnic group, have been particularly impacted. A glimpse into the labor market of this country confirms that Latino immigrants have the lowest levels of education, fill the largest percentage of low-wage workers in this country, are more likely to live in poverty, have the highest unemployment rates, and have the lowest English literacy levels. Consider the statistics:

- Nearly half of all immigrant workers earned less than 200% of the minimum wage, as compared to 32% of native workers (Capps, Fix, Passel, Ost, & Perez-Lopez, 2003).
- Hispanics are the only major group of workers to have suffered a two-year decline in wages, and in 2004 they earned 5% less than two years before (Kochhar, 2004); immigrants compose 20% of low-wage workers, while they comprise 11% of all U.S. residents (Capps et al., 2003).
- Immigrants occupy the two least well-paid occupational groups: private household services, with 42%, and farming, forestry, and fishing, with 37% (Capps et al., 2003).
- During the last quarter of 2003, the unemployment rate for Hispanics was 6.6%, compared to 4.4% for Whites (Kochhar, 2004); second-generation Hispanics, who might be expected to fare better, in fact had the highest unemployment rate in the last quarter of 2003, 10%, compared to 5% unemployment for second-generation Whites (Kochhar, 2004).
- Eighteen percent of the immigrant labor force has less than a ninth grade education, and 30% of them have not finished high school, compared to only 8% of native workers without a high school diploma (Capps et al., 2003).

The figures are not surprising if one considers the educational trajectories of Latino adults in the United States who emigrated to the United States in their youth during their school years. Our nation's public schools have allowed them to fall through the cracks. National dropout rates in 2001 were 65.7% for Hispanics, compared to 7.3% for Whites (National Center for Education Statistics [NCES], 2005). The dropout rate for Hispanics is considerably higher in several states. In Texas, for instance, Hispanic students had an attrition[2] rate of 50%, compared to 45% for Blacks and 24% for Whites (Intercultural Development Research Association, 2003). In Arizona, 42.7% of Hispanics were lost from enrollment between their freshman year in 1996–1997 and their senior year (Intercultural Development Research Association, 2000). Cultural and linguistic barriers are often cited as major factors impacting the decision to leave school. This is particularly true for immigrant students who comprise the largest segment of the Hispanic dropout rate. NCES (2002) reports that the dropout rate of 44.2% for Hispanic 16- to 24-year-olds born outside the United States was more than double the rate of 14.6% for U.S. first-generation Hispanic youth and the rate of 15.9% for second-generation Hispanic youth.

Statistics also indicate that students from low-income backgrounds tend to drop out of school at higher rates. In 1998, for instance, young adults in families in the lowest 20% of all family incomes were four times as likely as their peers from families in the top 20% income brackets to drop out of high school (NCES, 1999). This is significant because Hispanic families are three times more likely to be poor than Whites. In 2001, for instance, 24.9% of Hispanics lived in poverty, compared to 23.1% of Blacks and 7.9% of Whites (Poverty Gap, 2004). Change is imperative for a more just and equitable society and for the economic and social well-being of the country as a whole.

Demographic projections, moreover, indicate that the Hispanic population will increase from 35.3 million in 2000 to 60.4 million in 2020. Second-generation Hispanics (born in the United States) are predicted to grow by 119% through 2020 (Suro & Passel, 2003). The Hispanic labor market will increase 37% by 2008, compared to Blacks by 20% and Whites by 10% (Texas Business and Education Coalition, n.d.).

The numbers are revealing. The immigrant population, particularly Hispanics, is dramatically increasing in the United States. Immigrants are the least likely to graduate from high school, the most likely to fill a low-wage occupation, and the most likely to live in poverty. The lack of education is a major barrier to advancement. Another barrier is the lack of English language proficiency, which limits communication and learning when students are placed in mainstream classrooms taught in English. The following statistics highlight these linguistic issues.

- In 2000, first-generation Hispanics (born outside the United States) were 72% Spanish dominant, 4% English dominant, and 24% bilingual (Suro & Passel, 2003).
- The mean English literacy proficiencies of full-time employees were lowest among Hispanics, followed by Blacks, Asians, and Whites (Sum, n.d.).
- Nearly two-thirds of low-wage immigrant workers do not speak English proficiently (Capps et al., 2003).
- Twenty-eight percent of the overall U.S. labor force with less than a high school education is limited English proficient (LEP) (Capps et al., 2003).

Thus, both education and English language development are key areas that must be addressed if immigrant workers in the United States are to advance. Immigrants, who compose an increasingly large share of the labor force, are overrepresented among low-wage and less educated workers. This group can benefit tremendously from workforce education. Yet, most publicly funded worker training programs are geared toward individuals with at least ninth grade literacy and numeracy levels, and they assume that participants have the English language skills needed to follow a curriculum at that level (Capps et al., 2003). An alternate approach to workforce education for Latinos is critical. One alternative is a bilingual approach that would build on the linguistic and educational characteristics of this population. The following presents some historical perspectives on the use of two languages as a medium of instruction for adults, followed by a discussion of a bilingual instructional model for the workforce.

Bilingual Workforce Education: Historical Perspectives

Bilingual instruction for language minority adults in the United States is not a new idea. Adult literacy educators have often used it in the classroom in order to communicate with recent immigrant students—not unlike what K-12 teachers do in the classroom. However, this informal use of the native language is largely undocumented, unsystematic, and relies largely on the instructor's intuition about which language is appropriate at a given moment. More formalized bilingual instruction for adults occurred during the civil rights era in the 1960s because all-English instruction precluded access to vocational coursework by immigrants. The result was a relatively small program called the Bilingual Vocational Training (BVT) model. In this model, students proceeded immediately into occupational training rather than first having to go through English language classes. In the BVT, English language development took place within the context of a specific vocation. Additionally, the native language was gradually decreased while the use of English increased (Gillespie, 1996). The BVT programs were dissolved over the years as the Reagan and Bush administrations increasingly viewed bilingual education programs as detrimental to the development of English language competence in students. Subsequently, during the Clinton administration, welfare reform was passed. The outcomes of this legislation were a "work first" attitude and an emphasis on job placement over education; this, again, undermined the availability of bilingual instruction for the workforce. What little was gained during the BVT era was lost in the 1980s and 1990s. The result of this negative stance toward bilingual instruction was that little or no provision was made to meet the needs of Latino and other immigrant adults who are seeking to further their education.

Currently, there is an increased awareness of the need to serve workers who have been categorized as LEP students. The U.S. Department of Labor, for instance, has implemented several initiatives to better serve workers with little or no English language proficiency. One of these is an LEP Investment Strategy, which funds the development of training and technical assistance tools to address LEP and Hispanic issues; another is a technical assistance Web page that is LEP focused (Shoholm, 2004). In Texas, the U.S. Department of Labor, in collaboration with the Texas Workforce Commission (TWC), has implemented a series of fora that focus on workforce education for LEP workers (Department of Labor Employment and Training Administration, 2004). Likewise, researchers have turned their attention to exploring programmatic, curricular, and instructional approaches that can bridge the language and cultural barriers for workers who lack English language proficiencies (Huerta-Macías, 2002, 2003; Moore, 2003; Tondre-El-Zorkani, 2001; Wrigley, Richer, Martineson, Kubo, & Strawn, 2003). Increased access to job information and services by our linguistically and culturally diverse worker populations has become a critical issue.

On another front, agencies and local service providers are developing innovative practices to help them reach their diverse populations. Moore (2003), for instance, reports that states such as Colorado, California, Illinois, and Minnesota are hiring multilingual job developers, providing translation services, printing forms in Spanish, printing multilingual brochures, and developing computer literacy programs specifically for immigrants. Innovative practices are also occurring within the classroom through a reconceptualization of bilingual education.

Bilingual Models for Workforce Education

Workforce education programs have traditionally been designed for students who are proficient in English. An English-speaking student who is interested in pursuing a license in welding, for example, might follow a program with two basic components: GED, if needed, and welding. On the other hand, students who are not proficient in English wishing to follow a curriculum in welding have been traditionally placed into a program where English as a Second Language (ESL) or Vocational English as a Second Language (VESL) instruction is provided first. The student remains in English development courses for an indefinite period and is not placed into an occupational course until a certain language proficiency is reached in English. GED instruction (in Spanish) may be concurrently provided with English language instruction, or it may follow language instruction. In any case, there is a sequential order to the English language and occupational training component, with English language development being first. The result is that too many workers have been precluded from learning the occupational skills that they need to find jobs with sustainable wages because they languish in English language classes for months and even years. Consequently, because of time and financial constraints, these workers have been unable to complete the programs leading to an occupational credential.

Bilingual programs for workers who do not possess the English language skills to follow occupational curricula in English are of an integrated design. They integrate English language development with occupational instruction. The outcome is that workers begin to learn the skills they will need to find a job without having to wait and use their time and financial resources for stand-alone English language instruction. Additionally, workers utilize the native language skills and background knowledge that they bring with them as a pathway that provides access to new knowledge. The use of the native language and the second language (English) in linguistically homogeneous classrooms is an innovative aspect of these programs. This notion of dual-language use builds on the research literature in K-12 education, but also differentiates bilingual instruction for adults.

The issue of language distribution (i.e., the amount of time that each language is used) within an adult class can be much more fluid than in bilingual education programs in public schooling. The clear boundaries between the languages found in public school instruction may not be beneficial with adult students. Adult students tend to be self-directed and engage in educational activities that are interesting and relevant to their goals (Merriam, 2001). They will exit the class if they perceive that what they are learning is not useful or if they are made to feel childlike by classroom policies or instructor demands. Additionally, adults have a more developed source of native language transferable skills to draw upon in the development of a second language. They also have a much greater storehouse of background knowledge and lived experiences to help them make sense of printed text. Thus, there is little need to establish defined language boundaries that work toward a model of language use where each language is used for a certain percentage of the school day or week. Rather, the idea is to strategically capitalize on the native language resources that the adults bring in order to develop English literacy and other skills.

Sound bilingual workforce instructional models have been addressed by Wrigley et al. (2003), Taggart and Martinez (2003), and Huerta-Macías (2003). Wrigley and her colleagues advocate for approaches for the workforce that combine language education with skills training. Bilingual vocational training is one such approach, where "the native language is used to teach job-specific skills and English is used to teach job-related language skills" (p. 22). One of the examples they provide is a bilingual training program in computer numerically controlled machining and industrial maintenance mechanics, which is run by the HIRE Center in Milwaukee. Here, students engage in classes in Spanish with translation of key terms in English for 16 weeks, and they gain knowledge about math, electronics, power transmission, welding, and other skills. They also attend an occupational ESL course concurrently with the technical training; all course materials are provided in both languages. Taggart and Martinez (2003) propose a model where educators reflect on the content of the curriculum and respond to the following questions in order to make choices about using either the first or the second language during instruction:

- What pieces do students just need to know in order to carry out tasks relating to this theme? **We can teach much of this in the students' native language.**
- What will students need to read, listen to, write, and talk about in English related to those tasks? To whom will they need to speak? **We must teach the English vocabulary and language structures that students need to be able to communicate in work-related contexts.**

- When students engage on the job, what critical issues may arise around this theme? **We can use the students' native language to explore these issues, and then move to English to develop any additional language skills that emerge as a result of these discussions** [*sic*]. (p. 20)

One example provided by the authors is a computer office skills program that includes three components: computer skills training, English for the office environment, and GED test preparation. In a thematic lesson on office supplies, they use Excel spreadsheets and software in English with the support of instructional manuals and oral instructions in Spanish. Students also learn key vocabulary in English. Spanish is used to discuss critical issues, problem solve, make decisions, and discuss the organization of supply catalogs, purchase orders, and do comparison shopping. The lesson ends with a debriefing and reflection using both English and Spanish (Taggart & Martinez, 2003).

Huerta-Macías (2003) proposes a model that hinges on the strategic use of two languages, as opposed to translation or the haphazard use of two languages. This model basically follows two guidelines:

- Use the native language to explain procedural information, for implementing comprehension checks on new material, and for discussion of prior knowledge as relevant to the lesson.
- Use English for delivery of content, for the delivery of job-specific vocabulary, and for communication skills relevant to the occupation studied.

Examples of how this model might be implemented are as follows:

- The native language would be appropriately used to explain or describe the goals of the class, the program philosophy, attendance policies, classroom routines, and the organization of work groups for the course. During instruction, the native language would be used for a brainstorming session on students' background knowledge relevant to the topic of the lesson. During closure, the first language might also be used to reflect on student learning for that day.
- English would be used to explain and discuss the principal ideas or main points of a lesson; to implement any hands-on activities in the lesson, such as role-plays; for word study of occupational jargon; and for multimedia use. English could also be used at the end of the instructional phase of the lesson to summarize new material that was learned; to engage students in a review activity, such as filling out a graphic organizer or flowchart, or writing a brief and simple narrative with main points; and to reinforce new occupationally related vocabulary.

The intent is to capitalize on the linguistic, cognitive, and cultural resources that the students bring in order to more effectively and efficiently develop their English language proficiencies as well as their occupational skills. An example of how a bilingual lesson on safety on the job might be implemented is described below.

Bilingual Lesson: Construction

The following is an outline of a VESL lesson for Latino workers in a construction program who are embarking on a thematic unit about safety standards and procedures on the job (adapted from El Paso Community College Lesson Template, 2004).

Introduction: The instructor begins by introducing the lesson to students in Spanish through the presentation of topics that will be covered during the unit on job safety. The topics that are mentioned, for instance, are electrical safety, toxic substances, poisonous fumes, and evacuation plans. This discussion is brief, as the extensive dialogue and exploration on these topics will comprise the content of subsequent lessons. The instructor ends by focusing on the topic for the day, which will be an introductory lesson on accidents on the job.

Initial brainstorm: The instructor begins the lesson by having the students brainstorm on what they already know about accidents on the job. Generative questions are posed in English that will elicit the students' background knowledge and prior experiences with job-related accidents. Example questions include: What are some physical hazards that you have seen in previous jobs? Were there any accidents caused by these hazards? What happened? Why did it happen? Although the questions are initially posed in English, students may respond in Spanish and the instructor might also respond, elaborate, and pose questions in either language as deemed appropriate, such that the discussion on prior knowledge is actually implemented bilingually. The key is to provide an opportunity for students to express prior knowledge that is relevant to the lesson. It is during this initial phase of the lesson that the instructor also provides vocabulary study within the context of the discussion as appropriate.

Language focus: The instructor uses the context of the initial brainstorm as a springboard for presenting job-related vocabulary and phrases. This part of the lesson is implemented in English. Some of the vocabulary presented, for instance, is *hazardous, danger zone, fumes,* and *evacuate.* The instructor uses pictures, posters, and other visuals and body language to ensure comprehension of the vocabulary. Some of the vocabulary presented will be encountered in a reading assignment later in the lesson.

Integrated language activity: Students work in small groups to write short statements in English describing the accidents and physical hazards discussed during the initial brainstorm. This activity provides an opportunity for students to apply the job-related vocabulary presented earlier, and to use their speaking, reading, and writing skills in an integrated fashion during an authentic communicative activity. An example of a narrative is the following: "The bucket turned over. It spilled water by the exit door. The water made the floor slippery. The office clerk stepped in it and fell. He hurt his back." Other groups focus on construction-related narratives such as: "The ladder was not standing straight. When the roofer was stepping off the ladder, the ladder slipped. He fell to the ground." Once the groups are finished with their narratives, they are posted on flip charts and shared with the whole class. The instructor takes this opportunity to provide mini-lessons on grammar as appropriate, which include very brief and explicit explanations. These mini-grammar lessons are implemented in Spanish and English and draw on students' literacy skills in Spanish. A clarification, for example, is made on the use of *in* versus *on* to express location. Another is on the use of imperatives and exclamations in English. Students do role-plays using phrases such as "Be careful, there is water on the floor!" and "Watch out for the ladder!" The use of exclamation points and how they change the nature of the sentence is discussed.

Reading: Students read a selection titled "Imminent Danger" from their text. The instructor begins this activity with a think-aloud strategy about the reading selection, and this is followed by silent paired reading by students. The main ideas are then discussed in English; here, students have an additional opportunity to practice previously presented vocabulary and phrases. The discussion is extended to accidents at a construction site, such as with improper placement of ladders and spillage of tar.

Evaluation: For this component of the lesson, students are asked to perform three activities: (1) to describe, in written English, common safety hazards; (2) to deliver verbal warnings relating to safety hazards, in English; and (3) to locate specific safety information in a safety manual, in Spanish or English. The first activity focuses on job-related knowledge and English literacy skills; the second focuses on oral language proficiency in English; and the third is procedural knowledge. The instructor takes note of those areas that need improvement so that they may be addressed in following lessons.

Assignment: The instructor explains the home assignment in Spanish. Students are asked to observe their surroundings in different settings: school, work, home, shopping centers, and so forth. They are to write two descriptions in English of hazards that they see.

The bilingual instructional model that is applied in the lesson above is not prescriptive; it is congruent with the guidelines described by Huerta-Macías (2003), Taggart and Martinez (2003), and Wrigley et al. (2003). The model presented above is also pedagogically sound. It integrates and applies to workforce instruction what we have learned from K-12 bilingual education program research. The following are some findings from this research that are particularly relevant to workforce contexts and are applied in the bilingual instructional scenario described above:

- Students learn best when language is taught via content that is of interest and relevant to them (Brown, 1994; Freeman & Freeman, 1998; Haley & Austin, 2004). This is contrary to more traditional paradigms of language teaching that focus on language development as an end in itself. The idea, then, is that language becomes almost a by-product of a content-based lesson, such as the cleanup of chemical spills, for example. In the lesson described above, job-related language is simultaneously taught along with safety and accident prevention.

- Complex subject matter can be understood by English language learners (ELLs) when the instructional delivery is modified, or sheltered, so that it becomes more comprehensible. The use of demonstrations, tables, pictures, realia, and cognitive organizers, for instance, have been shown to greatly enhance learning of abstract and complex content by ELLs (Center for Applied Linguistics, 1998; Echevarria, Vogt, & Short, 2004; Zainuddin, Yahya, Morales-Jones, & Ariza, 2002). In the lesson described above, posters, pictures, role-plays, and other strategies are used in order to make the occupational content more comprehensible.

- English language development is enhanced through mini-lessons when explicit language instruction is provided. This does not imply that lessons should be centered around grammar; however, brief grammatical explanations, or mini-lessons, should be provided within the context of the lesson and as relevant to the types of discourse inherent in the lesson (Díaz-Rico, 2004; Freeman & Freeman, 1998; Zainuddin et al., 2002). The sample lesson described above includes explicit language instruction as relevant to the content of the lesson. The instructor explicitly discusses imperatives as well as punctuation and prepositions to express location.

- The enhancement or development of vocabulary is crucial to English language development, particularly for the literacy skills. Typically, students must know about 19 of 20 words, or 95% of a text, in order for them to successfully use context clues to guess the meaning (Zainuddin et al., 2002). Thus, learning words in isolation is not always an effective strategy. Rather, vocabulary is better learned in context. Explicit word study that will help students expand their vocabulary is essential for ELLs. Bilingual students, moreover, encounter unknown vocabulary in English more frequently than monolingual students (Kucer, 2001). The lesson described above provides explicit vocabulary study on job-related language, such as names of tools, materials, and procedures.

- Background knowledge is crucial to the development of literacy skills in the second language. Studies in reading comprehension have indicated that proficient readers immediately draw on their relevant linguistic and conceptual background knowledge as they begin to read a text in order to make meaning from the print. Research has indicated that ELL students learn when instructors engage the initial understandings of students' background knowledge and experiences as a springboard for teaching new concepts (National Research Council, 2000). The lack of relevant background knowledge—often stemming from different cultural experiences—often precludes ELLs from understanding the text. It is imperative that the instructor help fill in any gaps in background knowledge in order to enhance reading comprehension by ELLs (Kucer, 2001). The lesson described above includes an initial brainstorm where workers discuss their prior experiences in the area of safety and accidents on the job. The instructor uses these discussions as a springboard into the lesson.

- The learning environment for ELLs must be low risk for students. That is, the environment in the classroom should not be anxiety producing, but rather should be motivating and inviting, so that students will feel free to take risks by using their new language without fear of ridicule or embarrassment. The social context in the classroom should not be a threatening one for any student. This is particularly true for adults who have been out of school for many years and who may have had negative schooling experiences in the past. The affective aspects of learning are most significant for those adults with low levels of prior schooling (Brown, 1994). The class should also be socioculturally compatible to the students in that interactional patterns that are familiar to the student are recognized and used. This might include, for example, the use of collaborative learning and hands-on activities (Díaz-Rico, 2004; Freeman & Freeman, 1998; Heath, 1989). The class described above integrates hands-on experiences through demonstrations and group work. However, the learners also engage in the actual building of a home through a course that is taken concurrently with VESL and that is also a component of the instructional program on construction. Additionally, the use of two languages in the classroom greatly enhances the sociocultural compatibility of the class; it lowers anxiety, increases student motivation to participate, and enhances comprehension of the material.

Given what we know from previous research on bilingual education, the issue becomes one of application to the context of workforce education. The issue is development of English language skills as well as occupational knowledge with workers who have low levels of English literacy skills and varying levels of literacy in their native language. A bilingual instructional model can address both English language development and occupational knowledge in a socioculturally competent manner. A high-quality bilingual model will also integrate best practice as described in the findings listed above. Following is an example of a program that follows an integrated design and that utilizes bilingual instruction in the language component of the program—as illustrated in the lesson described earlier.

Motivation Education Training Program

The Motivation Education Training (MET) program is a private nonprofit organization that operates in four states: Texas, Louisiana, North Dakota, and Minnesota. The focus here is on the Texas program, which serves high numbers of Latinos through its 11 field offices and numerous other entry points throughout the state. MET's migrant and seasonal farmworker career development program is funded by the U.S. Department of Labor and has been in operation, in one form or another, since 1967. The mission for MET is "to provide academic and vocational training to migrant and seasonal farmworkers, and their qualified family members, with the objective of furthering economic self-sufficiency" (MET, Inc., n.d., p. 1). To this end, the program also provides support services as needed, such as low-income housing development and rehabilitation, and comprehensive child and family development services for rural residents through Head Start. There are several eligibility requirements for the program. Primary among these are that workers must have earned a minimum of 50% of their income from farmwork, should have earned at least $800.00 from agricultural employment, and worked only periodically throughout the year. Additionally, male participants born after 1960 must be registered with the selective service (MET, Inc., n.d.).

MET offers three basic components in its training system: classroom training, on-the-job training, and work experience. The classroom training part of the system offers ESL, occupational instruction, adult basic education (ABE), GED, postsecondary transition, and an array of other academic programs. The on-the-job training involves agreements that are made with specific companies to train and hire those clients who may already have limited nonagricultural job skills. MET will pay up to one-half of their salary—contingent upon required qualifications. It is expected that the company hire the employee permanently if the training is completed successfully. The work experience component places clients with few or no skills outside of agriculture with employers who will provide workplace skills. MET pays the complete costs for this training in addition to paying for support services that are necessary for the client to complete the program. Transportation assistance, for instance, is provided by MET. The individual components offered by MET can also be combined in order to offer comprehensive services, as needed, to every client. The ultimate goal of MET is to place clients in unsubsidized permanent employment in a job that pays sustainable wages and that provides opportunities for advancement in both earnings and responsibility. A distinguishing characteristic of MET is that the program collaborates very closely with industry for job placement both during and upon completion of the training and provides follow-up services for up to a year after employment to make sure that the transition is successful (G. Flory, personal communication, February 14, 2001).

The El Paso program serves as an example of how MET is implemented with Spanish monolingual populations or with populations that have low levels of English proficiency. This program serves anywhere from 100 to 300 workers per year, and virtually 100% of the clients are Latino. A new class begins about every five months, with the program for any one cohort lasting between five and seven months. Students enrolled in the program enter with diverse literacy and numeracy skills. There is also a marked contrast among the Borderland population in that many more students are identified as having low levels of English proficiency. In El Paso, 83% of students were identified as having limited proficiency in English, compared to 31% statewide.

There are three components to the program: GED (240 hours of instruction), vocational training with a capstone course that simulates the actual job experience (hours vary depending on the area), and VESL instruction (240 hours). A remediation course lasting 96 hours is provided in Spanish prior to beginning GED instruction for students with very low literacy and numeracy skills (V. Urquidi, Client Service Representative, personal communication, February 16, 2004).

The program is bilingual, with all materials available in Spanish and English. GED instruction is generally provided in Spanish and takes place for eight hours a day, five days a week. Upon completion of this program (after approximately seven weeks), students take the GED exam. After taking the exam, the students begin the occupational and English language courses, both of which are integrated. Students who do not pass the GED are referred to another GED preparation course (outside of MET) or are placed in the GED component again after they complete the VESL and construction training so that they can continue studying and retake the exam. In any case, all of the students are allowed to continue with the VESL and occupational part of the program.

The program that is currently being implemented in El Paso, Texas, focuses on construction. Students take the GED course preparation in Spanish, and then concurrently take VESL (with a focus on construction) and the construction course per se, which is taught by a monolingual English speaker. The occupational aspect of the instruction includes the actual building of homes, which are then sold and moved to a designated lot. The VESL component focuses on the language that is used at the work site, including, for example, names of tools, materials, and language related to foundations, roofing, framing, paint and textures, interior finishing, accident prevention at the construction site, and construction cost estimations. The occupational and VESL instructors meet regularly in order to align the curriculum. During a given week, for instance, the construction instructor may be discussing roofing. The VESL instructor covers related language during the same week, such as *ceramic tiles*, *asphalt shingles*, *gutter systems*, *spouts*, and *guards*. They also discuss the issue of language distribution in the curriculum; both courses use varying amounts of Spanish along with English. In the VESL component of the program both instructor and students use both languages; in the occupational (construction) component, the students use both languages as they go about completing their work. The job placement rate upon completion of the program is impressively high. In El Paso, 97.8% of the clients were placed during the most recent year (V. Urquidi, Client Service Representative, personal communication, September 16, 2004).

The MET program exemplifies a bilingual, integrated program where instruction is strategically delivered via two languages. There is thoughtful reflection and collaboration on the language to be used during instruction in both the VESL and the construction components of the program. Students have an opportunity to utilize the language skills that they bring with them in Spanish and their previous knowledge and experiences in construction. They concurrently develop English language and construction skills through both classroom and hands-on experience.

Conclusion

Low-wage, unemployed, and incumbent workers have an urgency of developing skills for job attainment and advancement. Workers with low levels of English language proficiency and literacy skills are doubly challenged, for they must develop not only job-related skills and knowledge, but also a second language. Thus, it makes sense to capitalize on all of the linguistic, cultural, and personal resources that adult students bring with them as they seek to secure jobs that pay sustainable wages within limited amounts of time. This implies that both of a bilingual's two languages might be used in a class for effective instruction. However, this does not mean that language switching should occur randomly in a classroom; it does mean that a bilingual's two languages should be used strategically in order to produce the desired outcome of the acquisition of knowledge and literacy development. The guidelines proposed herein aim to develop a bilingual instructional model for adults that has the advantage of developing language skills while also developing occupational skills.

The bilingual model carries some cautionary notes, however. The first is that the bilingual instructional model has been designed for classes where students speak the same native language. Additionally, the model requires bilingual and biliterate instructors who are also knowledgeable about the career and technical area that they are teaching. Team teaching, however, is an option that could address this issue. In either case, the instructor must be careful not to let students lapse into the native language whenever they experience the least discomfort with English. Rather, scaffolding should be used when students are struggling with the language in order to increase comprehension and English language use. Overuse of the native language to the exclusion of English will be counterproductive; thus, the instructor must be constantly on guard against this. Instructors must also guard against the exclusive use of English, as this may be a barrier to the teaching of occupational knowledge that is cognitively complex (such as the implications of a violation of Occupational Safety and Health Administration [OSHA] regulations). Finally, despite the cautionary notes, the model can be quite effective where there are large numbers of same-language groups, such as Latinos. Such a model would bring positive change to adult education that is not only pedagogically powerful, but also transformationally powerful, in that the model has the potential to greatly enhance student learning, and thus the probability of job attainment and advancement. Foster (1997) notes that students who experience a learning environment that considers subject matter, linguistic, and personal needs are successful because they "are meeting their goals, seeing an immediate application of their learning, and experiencing a validation of their personal abilities" (p. 37). The bilingual instructional model presented here does that and more; it also significantly increases access to education by adults who are not English proficient. In short, bilingual programs bring us a step closer to achieving educational equity for adult immigrant populations who are seeking to advance economically.

Endnotes

1. *Latinos* is used herein as an all-inclusive term to refer to Puerto Ricans, Mexicans, Salvadorans, and all Latin American subgroups. The term *Hispanic* is used interchangeably with *Latino* when discussing research that uses this term. Thus, the term used in a specific study is preserved when reporting on that study.
2. The attrition rate is closely related to the annual dropout rate; however, it allows for increases and decreases in a district's enrollment figures since district enrollment may vary from year to year.

References

Brown, H. D. (1994). *Teaching by principles: An interactive approach to language pedagogy*. Englewood Cliffs, NJ: Prentice-Hall.

Capps, R., Fix, M., Passel, J. S., Ost, J., & Perez-Lopez, D. (2003, November). *A profile of the low-wage immigrant workforce*. Washington, DC: Urban Institute.

Center for Applied Linguistics. (1998). *Enriching content classes for secondary ESOL students*. McHenry, IL: Delta Systems.

Department of Labor Employment and Training Administration. (2004, April 20). Limited English Proficiency Services, Region IV Forum, Dallas, TX.

Díaz-Rico, L. (2004). *Teaching English learners: Strategies and methods*. Boston: Pearson Allyn-Bacon.

Echevarria, J., Vogt, M., & Short, D. J. (2004). *Making content comprehensible for English language learners: The SIOP model*. Boston: Pearson, Allyn & Bacon.

El Paso Community College Lesson Template. (2004). *Sample lesson plan for a thematic unit: Work related safety standards and procedures* [Workforce Development Programs].

Foster, E. (1997). Transformative learning in adult second language learning. In P. Cranton (Ed.), *Transformative learning in action: Insights from practice* (pp. 33–40). New York: Jossey-Bass.

Freeman, D., & Freeman, Y. (1998). *ESL/EFL teaching: Principles for success.* Portsmouth, NH: Heinemann.

Gillespie, M. K. (1996). *Learning to work in a new land: A review and sourcebook for vocational and workplace ESL.* Washington, DC: Center for Applied Linguistics.

Haley, M. H., & Austin, T. Y. (2004). *Content-based second language teaching and learning.* Boston: Pearson Education.

Heath, S. B. (1989). Sociocultural contexts of language development. In *Beyond schooling: Social and cultural factors in schooling language minority students* (pp. 146–186). Los Angeles: Bilingual Education Office, State Department of Education.

Huerta-Macías, A. (2002). *Workforce education for Latinos: Politics, programs, and practice.* Westport, CT: Bergin & Garvey.

Huerta-Macías, A. (2003). Meeting the challenge of adult education: A bilingual approach to literacy and career development. *Journal of Adolescent and Adult Literacy, 47,* 218–226.

Intercultural Development Research Association. (2000). *Statistics and data on dropout prevention.* Retrieved June 2, 2004, from http://www.idra.org/Newslttr/Fieldtrp/2000/Statsoct.htm

Intercultural Development Research Association. (2003). *Attrition and dropout rates in Texas.* Retrieved June 2, 2004, from http://www.idra.org/Research/dout2003.htm#rates

Kochhar, R. (2004, February). *Latino labor report, 2003: Strong but uneven gains in employment* (Appendix, Tables A2–A3). Retrieved November 30, 2005, from http://pewhispanic.org/files/reports/26.1.pdf

Kucer, S. B. (2001). *Dimensions of literacy: A conceptual base for teaching reading and writing in school settings.* Mahwah, NJ: Erlbaum.

Merriam, S. B. (2001). *The new update on adult learning theory.* New York: Jossey-Bass.

MET, Inc. (n.d.). *Motivation, education & training* [program brochure]. El Paso, TX: One-Stop Career Service Center, MET, Inc.

Moore, I. (2003, September). Addressing language barriers: Strategies for serving those with limited English proficiency, *Welfare Information Network: Issue Notes 7* (11), n.p.

National Center for Education Statistics. (1999, November). *Dropout Rates in the United States: 1998.* Washington, DC: U.S. Department of Education, Office of Educational Research and Improvement.

National Center for Education Statistics. (2002). *Dropout rates in the United States: 2000.* Retrieved May 21, 2004, from http://nces.ed.gov/pubs2002/droppub_2001/8.asp?nav=1

National Center for Education Statistics. (2005). *Dropout rates in the United States: 2001* (Table 3). Retrieved November 30, 2005, from http://nces.ed.gov/pubs2005/dropout2001/tab_fig.asp

National Research Council. (2000). *How people learn: Brain, mind, experience, and school.* Washington, DC: National Academy Press.

Poverty gap between whites, blacks, hispanics. (2004). [Fast Facts on Welfare Policy]. Retrieved May 21, 2004, from http://www.urban.org/UploadedPDF/900703.pdf

Shoholm, J. (2004, April 20). *LEP Services in the workforce investment system*. Presentation at Limited English Proficiency Services, Region IV Forum, Austin, TX.

Sum (n.d.) *Exeuctive summary of literacy in the labor force: Results from the National Literacy Survey*. Retrieved June 20, 2004 from http://nces.ed.gov/naal/resources/execsumlabor.asp

Suro, R., & Passel, J. S. (2003, October). *The rise of the second generation: Changing patterns in Hispanic population growth*. Washington, DC: Pew Hispanic Center.

Taggart, K., & Martinez, S. (2003). One classroom, two languages: Adult bilingual curriculum development. *Focus on Basics*, 6, 18–22.

Texas Business and Education Coalition. (n.d.). *Overview of labor projections for the 1998–2008 period*. Retrieved May 22, 2004, from http://www.tbec.org/gearup-guide/overview.htm

Tondre-El-Zorkani, B. (2001, April 20–21). *Adult education and workforce development*. Presentation at Bridging the LEP Gap in Workforce Development, Dallas, TX.

Wrigley, H. S., Richer, E., Martinson, K., Kubo, H., & Strawn, J. (2003 August). *The language of opportunity: Expanding employment prospects for adults with limited English skills*. Washington, DC: Center for Law and Social Policy.

Zainuddin, H., Yahya, N., Morales-Jones, C. A., & Ariza, E. (2002). *Fundamentals of teaching English to speakers of other languages in K-12 mainstream classrooms*. Dubuque, IA: Kendall-Hunt Publishers.

5

A Crossroads
Family Education Programs

ELIZABETH QUINTERO

> To Survive the Borderlands
> *you must live* sin fronteras
> *be a crossroads.*

> **—Anzaldúa, 1987, p. 217**

The poet Anzaldúa spoke of surviving in borderlands, of being a crossroad. In the current world, in which borders are in a state of flux with tenuous peace and governments that come and go, education programs and families become the crossroads. The voices of teachers, students, families, and friends in communities around the world can be voices of possibility if only they can listen and learn from each other. Family education programs provide an arena for these important discussions. Current ideas about family education emphasize the need to make the school-community dynamics bidirectional. Consequently, some family education programs develop the native language of the parents and provide English to speakers of other languages. Programs can create positive educational contexts when the family's home language is valued and encouraged.

In programs where the home language of the family is valued and encouraged, the curricula develop bilingualism and biliteracy not as an end, but as an integral part of the process of bringing about positive change in the lives of families and communities. It sounds complicated, but in fact, what happens is as natural and integrated as the cultural contexts and practices of child rearing and day-to-day community interactions. Family education programs have the potential to develop critical perspectives by engaging learners in discussion and action about issues that are significant in their lives and by utilizing their native language while also developing their English language skills. This combined participatory agenda enhances learners' abilities to advocate for themselves and their families.

Sometimes family education for multilingual learners takes the form of a bilingual family literacy project, sometimes it takes the form of parent support groups, and sometimes it takes the form of parents designing multilingual curricula through art and history to augment a school's standard curriculum. In each case, adults participate in learning communities in which they use their home languages and background knowledge to deliberate and design the transformative actions and to learn English literacy and survival information for the contexts in which they live in the United States.

Family literacy programs can be found in churches, schools, community-based organizations, colleges, universities, and social service agencies across the country. One such program was a family literacy project for Hmong women and their children in Minnesota. A few years ago, in one of the first family literacy classes in this project, the women came to class with a critical question. They asked: "Why doesn't Loveland School [the elementary school their children attended] tell us about parent conferences, send us notification in our language, or provide an interpreter at meetings?" With the aid of an interpreter and the literacy facilitator, the women discussed at length how angry they felt when they heard of the teachers' comments about how the Hmong parents just did not care about their children's education. The staff at the elementary school said this because the Hmong parents never came to parent conferences, PTA meetings, or other school functions. The women commented on how they had been able to be active in Head Start, in part because the staff always made the effort to provide interpreters at meetings, provide information in their home language, and respectfully talked to parents about questions regarding their children. After comparing the two situations (Head Start and the elementary school), they decided to take action. They wrote a letter, in Hmong, to the principal of the school. Their action and the events that followed (explained later) changed the language practices of the school and the community.

Family Education, Critical Literacy, and Native Language Use

Family education programs and family literacy programs serving multilingual families based upon critical literacy get at many important issues in a related way and focus on one of the most important questions in literacy, learning, teaching, education, and living: Whose stories are important? Which stories can educators learn from? Whose background knowledge will be respected and included?

Whose and which knowledge is power? Research documents the importance of students' telling their personal stories and sharing their background knowledge in their native languages (Hakuta, 1986; Hakuta & Garcia, 1989; Hudelson, 1986; Peregoy & Boyle, 2000; Ovando & Collier, 1998).

Critical literacy, as defined by this author, is a process of constructing meaning and critically using language (oral and written) as a means of expression, interpretation, and transformation of our lives and the lives of those around us. Critical literacy combines reflective thinking, information gathering, collaborative decision making, and personal learning choices, and respects and encourages learners using their native language. The critical literacy approach focuses on students expressing their voice in oral and written ways in their home language (Quintero, 2002). Written expression of student voices enhances language development. Kuiken and Vedder (2002) show that a writing task that involves collaboration in any language helps to ensure the language skills are integrated rather than practiced in isolation. The research literature (Freire & Macedo, 1987; Macedo & Bartolomé, 2001; Rivera, 1999) discusses issues of critical literacy and native language use in learning contexts. Additionally, Norton and Toohey (2004) document ways critical approaches to language teaching, which include native language academic work, cause transformations of social relations and issues of equity in schooling.

Some might question the use of the native language in developing proficiency in a second language, such as English. In academic contexts, the notion that the first language (L1) interferes with the learning of a second language (L2) is questionable (Larsen-Freeman & Long, 1991). It is clear that L1 serves a function in second or foreign language development (see chapter 1, this volume), and that it often supports, rather than interferes, with second language development. Ovando and Collier (1998) state the importance of educating school staff and parents on issues of second language acquisition and the importance of biliteracy development. Furthermore, it has been shown that acculturation and language acquisition are impacted by the process of aligning new societal expectations and requirements with previous cultural norms, individual perceptions, and experiences that are preeminent in immigrants' lives. Issues surrounding acculturation are complex and controversial. Yet these urgent issues are often ignored (Ullman, 1997; Zou, 1998).

The most important function of critical, participatory family literacy is that it provides the family participants with information about literacy and codes of power (Delpit, 1988; Quintero, 2003; Reyes, 1992) in the United States. It also provides a context where participants are able to explore the relationship that this information (both the literacy and the political aspects) has on their life. In addition, the participatory critical literacy setting also uses and values the background knowledge of the participants. This knowledge provides teachers and staff with sociocultural and factual information that enhances the dynamics of any educational setting—information that is, to a large degree, not available in books or teacher development class content. Much can be learned, for example, from parents about sleeping routines and family roles as all participants engage in conversations about storytelling and storybook reading at bedtime. The native language of the students can be very useful in these endeavors. It allows for parents to express concepts as well as abstract ideas, and it also allows them to advocate for themselves and their children.

Many family literacy programs strive to promote educational opportunities of eligible families by combining early childhood education and adult education in an integrated program (Van Horn, Weirauch, & Grinder, 2002). Family literacy programs have created opportunities for language minority families in both urban and rural settings, particularly in parts of the United States with rapidly growing immigrant populations. The National Center for ESL Literacy Education (NCLE, 2002) reports that successful programs address the needs of all families and continually strive to be aware of the differences among immigrant families in terms of their strengths, goals, challenges, and past histories. Best practices research (NCLE, 2002) has identified necessary components of successful programs for English language learners. Successful projects include programs of sufficient duration to demonstrate learner progress, programs that address both early childhood learning and older children's needs, programs that build on parents' language and literacy, and programs that respect parents' cultures and ways of knowing.

Most of the information in this chapter is from two family literacy programs. One program was implemented in Spanish and English, and another was implemented in Hmong and English. A few additional examples come from other family education programs (Quintero, 2004) in which critical literacy and native language use were implemented.

These family literacy groups were organized according to a model designed to provide participatory, critical literacy, and biliteracy development opportunities for families in diverse communities (Quintero & Rummel, 2003). The Spanish-English bilingual family literacy program was for Mexican and Mexican American families in El Paso, Texas. The project, named Project FIEL (Family Initiative for English Literacy), brought parents and children together once a week after school for approximately an hour and a half of activities. Project FIEL was funded as a demonstration family literacy project under Title VII, Office of Bilingual Education and Minority Language Affairs (OBEMLA). The goals of the family literacy project were:

1. To enhance the literacy and biliteracy development of the parents and children through a series of participatory intergenerational activities

2. To provide information regarding the literacy development process in children to the parents and to provide a setting for the parents to utilize the information

3. To enhance parents' self-confidence to contribute to their children's literacy development through participatory group interaction

4. To empower the participants to connect the literacy activities to their own social and cultural situations, thus encouraging their use of literacy for personal, familial, and community purposes

The second project discussed is a family literacy education program for immigrant Hmong and Southeast Asian families in Minnesota. The project was implemented through an interagency collaboration and funded through small grants. The adults and their children participated in activities that involved speaking, writing, and reading in both their native languages and English. The goals of this project were the same as those of Project FIEL, with one additional related goal: to provide a collaboration model of professional and paraprofessional staff working with Asian families in education and social services. This goal was devised to more effectively, efficiently, and consistently serve the needs of the Asian families from the time a child is born until the child becomes a high school student.

The following section describes the components of family education programs and provides examples from the Spanish-English bilingual program in the El Paso, Texas, region and other projects that support Spanish native language and literacy development in family education. The discussion will subsequently turn to the Hmong-English project, and the chapter will conclude with implications of the projects and some final reflections.

Successful Components of Family Education Programs

The Adult Education and Family Literacy Act, Title II of the Workforce Investment Act of 1998, combines the dual goals of helping children become successful in school while enhancing the adult family members' literacy skills. The law advocates adults becoming literate and gaining the knowledge and skills necessary for employment and self-sufficiency. The Even Start Family Literacy Program, which began in 1998 as a part of Title I of the Elementary and Secondary Act of 1965, is currently the major family literacy initiative administered by the U.S. Department of Education (2001). Even Start and many other family literacy programs use an education model with four components (U.S. Department of Education, n.d.):

- Intergenerational parent and child literacy activities so that literacy becomes a meaningful part of parent–child relationships and communication
- Adult education and adult literacy so that parents obtain more information about becoming economically self-sufficient
- Parenting education to help parents support the educational growth of their children in the home and at school

- Age-appropriate education for children to prepare them for success in school and life

Each of the components listed above is described in what follows. Examples of how children's literature can be used to develop biliteracy among adults and their children are included.

Even Start legislation was reauthorized in 2000 and 2001, by the Literacy Involves Families Together Act and the No Child Left Behind Act (Rimdzius, 2003). The focus remains on all the previously mentioned components, with an added stronger emphasis on the quality of instructional content. Academic achievement of children and adult participants and instruction based on scientifically researched approaches are also new emphases. The program now includes a requirement for reading-readiness instructional activities to ensure that children enter school ready to learn to read, and there is a requirement for higher staff qualifications. It has been recommended that there be more emphasis on language acquisition activities and activities that promote cognitive reasoning.

The Third National Even Start Evaluation (Rimdzius, 2003) showed mixed results in terms of student achievement, parent education, family participation, and other measures. However, the evaluation showed that when parents and children participated more in terms of hours per week and months of participation, the children did better on literacy-related tasks such as knowledge of the alphabet, numbers, and colors, and that parents read a greater variety of materials to their children and had more books in their home.

Intergenerational Literacy

During intergenerational literacy, parents or guardians work together with their children in family teams. Together, they work on activities of various types. In programs where the native language of the family is included, they often read bilingual storybooks such as *I Love Saturdays y domingos* by Alma Flor Ada (2002), which is a story about how a child has one set of grandparents who speak Spanish and one set of grandparents who speak English. She describes her visits to both families and what they do and what they say, in both Spanish and English. Then the parents and children participate in classroom and out-of-classroom activities. In a lesson using this storybook, the parents and children may choose pictures to make a family collage to represent their family and write a short story together, in Spanish, English, or both, about the family depicted in the collage.

Another set of activities focused on the storybook *Barrio: El barrio de José* [*Barrio: José's Neighborhood*] by G. Ancona (1998). This is a book about the Mission District in San Francisco. It contains photographs and text that discuss the traditions, customs, art, and food of what the locals call "El Barrio." The book does this by following the goings-on of El Barrio through the life of one boy, José, and his elementary school. After reading and discussing the story, the adults and children go on a walk around their neighborhood and draw or write some of the environmental print (signs, murals, and other scripts), in different languages. The parents and children may then write, draw, or audiotape a short report answering the following questions: What can you say about the neighborhood that these photos were taken in? What stories do these murals tell? This report may be in English, Spanish, or both.

Adult Education and Adult Literacy

Family education programs include a component where the adults come together for classes several times a week. In programs that promote bilingualism and biliteracy, most often the classes are for the purposes of developing native language literacy, ESL, or studying for the GED. Some programs provide career guidance and vocational training and referrals for social services. All of these support activities may be conducted in the native language of participants. For many parents with young children, single parents, and recent immigrants, adults with limited English ability and adults with limited schooling, "working" is a barely tolerable situation that is very different from what the adult student aims for. Many adult students, for instance, are working in service jobs or as maids or gardeners or in other dead-end jobs and receive a salary at or even below the minimum wage. They cannot support their families, much less climb up the economic ladder, with those types of jobs. They aspire to obtain jobs that will offer opportunities for advancement and improvement of their lives. Thus, in one family literacy lesson entitled "Working in America," parents can explore possibilities for future work in various professions. Key phrases that are presented and discussed in Spanish include: Do you work? What do you do? Where do you work? Do you like your job? What kind of work do you do at home? What other jobs have you done in the past? What type of work would you like to do in the future? Students read in their native language about skills and knowledge necessary to achieve their desired professional goals. They can make action plans for themselves about acquiring necessary skills and qualifications for the work.

Parent Education

During parent education, the parents gather for discussion sessions on topics of interest to them. They often invite community experts to bilingual sessions about various issues of family relations and child and adolescent development. Examples of parent advocacy growing from family literacy can be seen in the El Paso project. A family literacy lesson was developed on "School and You: Avenues for Advocacy" because several of the parents had inquired or expressed discontent with specific situations in their children's schools that they had encountered and were frustrated with.

The class discussion was implemented bilingually and focused on the different procedures they could use within the school systems to voice their complaints and advocate for change. Some of the guiding questions of the lesson that were presented in English, Spanish, or both were: When you have a question about what is happening in your child's class at school, when and how can you talk to the teacher? If you are not happy with what the teacher tells you or if the teacher won't talk to you, what can you do then? What are all the avenues you can think of to be an advocate for your children?

During the class, one parent talked in Spanish about the situation of her child's teacher. The teacher was treating the child in a disrespectful way that, the parent felt, was damaging the child's self-confidence and inhibiting her learning. Her child had entered kindergarten, after the generally supportive context of Head Start. However, day after day as she struggled with various writing tasks, her kindergarten teacher reprimanded her for poor performance. At one point, she grabbed her paper, crumpled it up, and threw it in the trash in front of all the students. After discussing this situation with other parents in the family literacy class, the parent found other parents outside the class who shared similar stories. They all decided they wanted to meet at the school for a parent discussion group to brainstorm how they could deal with "children's abuse by teachers." The parents began to meet regularly with each other and sometimes with their school administrators. At other times, they attended school board meetings to make their concerns known (Quintero & Huerta-Macías, 1995). They often informed staff about community and family information that the school otherwise would not have known.

As the preceding example illustrates, the parent education component can also be a place for staff and parents to share information about parenting in the home language. There are numerous storybooks available in Spanish or bilingually in Spanish and English that can serve as a catalyst for these discussions. These are available on the Internet, through large publishing companies such as Scholastic, and through smaller companies such as Redleaf Press. Also, many professional organizations are providing information about child development and early childhood education. One example is *El aprendizaje de la lectura y la escritura: Prácticas apropiadas para el desarrollo infantil* by Susan B. Neuman, Carol Copple, and Sue Bredekamp (2000), which is made available by the National Association for the Education of Young Children.

Age-Appropriate Children's Education

Children attending a family literacy program have opportunities to participate in age-appropriate education and can use their native language in the process. The storybook *Sam y el dinero de la suerte/Sam and the Lucky Money* by Karen Chinn (2003) is an example of a book that can be used for this purpose. It is based on thoughts about family influences on our daily lives, and the "bigger picture" idea of thinking about activist ways to be more of a "human family." The story is about a boy in New York City who goes for a walk through Chinatown in search of a special purchase. In his walk he meets a homeless man and his ideas about money, its use, and his participation in the world are changed. The story is read in both English and Spanish, with children listening to the story in both languages regardless of their native language. Students are then asked to share their feelings about Sam's experience and to talk about things they see in their own neighborhood walks. Various math activities around concepts of same and different, number sense, patterns, and estimation may be developed. In addition, the power of story, language and shared meaning, friendship and respect surrounds this set of activities.

An excellent way to lead into a study of famous people from a historical, artistic, and human rights standpoint, as well as a way to use all aspects of balanced literacy, is to begin with either the storybook *Frida* or the storybook *Diego*, both by Jonah Winter (1994, 2002). Children may be asked in their native language or in English to think back and remember an activity they were passionate about. Then they write about how they spent their time doing this activity and include details about the context: How did you learn to do this activity? How did you become good at doing it? Were there other people involved in your learning? If yes, in what ways were they involved? They may discuss what they like to do and how they express themselves. Frida and Diego both expressed themselves through art. How do you express yourself?

Personal Histories Project: Integrating All Four Components

The following section provides an in-depth look at the family education program that was mentioned in the introduction to this chapter and implemented using two languages—Hmong and English—at Poj Niam Thiab Meyuam [The Mother/Child School]. This example shows how one family literacy and parent education project reflects all four components of best practices for family education. In this project, participants were encouraged to use their native language and to learn and practice their new language while participating in intergenerational literacy, adult literacy, parent education, and age-appropriate activities for children. The women processed information and planned activities in small-group discussions and then collaborated on parts of the lessons where they could use English. In their adult literacy class, the women designed and put together a bilingual book that is a collection of stories about their family history, historical tales of Hmong culture from the past 5,000 years, and folk tales. They decided midway through the project to record some of the stories, in both Hmong and English, on audiotapes to go along with the books. They came to this decision because of their worry about their children and grandchildren losing the ability to speak and understand the oral language of their ancestors.

The women ranged in age from 16 years old to the late 50s. They had little or no formal education previous to this project. Some were preliterate. The challenge of the English literacy class was even more interesting than the usual situation of students with varying experiences and levels of ability in the subject matter. This was because the Hmong culture is historically an oral culture; this was the first generation of Hmong who were using printed materials as a way to learn.

The instructor of the Adult Basic Education English as a Second Language class asked the women what personal needs and issues concerned them and what information they would like the class to present (Larson, 2003). After a discussion, they decided to try to record their experiences in their home country of Laos and later in Thailand and now the United States. They thought that to write these experiences in English was a way to preserve and document them for future generations while improving their English. The participants and their facilitator agreed that the related objectives of the class were to:

- Establish camaraderie within the group
- Provide access to group problem-solving skills
- Increase participants' comfort level with American people, culture, and institutions
- Preserve, honor, and respect the Hmong culture
- Preserve the Hmong oral and written language for future generations
- Understand the current generation of children
- Deal effectively with cultural, generational issues

The decision to record their personal experiences was a way to achieve these multiple objectives; therefore, the women decided to spend the year creating their personal histories. The stories began with their earliest memories. Some remembered homes in Laos; others remembered the refugee camps. They chose topics to write about together, and then each woman ended her entry with her hopes for her children and grandchildren. The text was written in both English and Hmong for all the women. By the time they finished collecting and organizing materials, the original objectives changed to become a composite story. This was at the women's request because they wanted what each woman contributed as part of their own collections.

Key to the success of this project was the participation of a group member who could translate and provide a cultural bridge between the Hmong and American cultures. Yee Moua, who agreed to serve in this role, was extraordinarily gifted in her ability to effectively fill this difficult position. The participants were always comfortable bringing up any problem or question because they were free to talk to Yee in Hmong and she then translated or helped communicate the issues in English. With the collaboration of Yee Moua and the permission of each of the participants, the class completed this project with a compilation that provides a contemporary social history of the experience of Hmong women who immigrated to the United States as refugees from the war in Vietnam toward the end of the 20th century. It is a composite story that begins in Laos, travels through the war years, journeys through the refugee camps of Thailand, and ends in the United States. They also included a chapter of traditional folktales. They were able to locate resources to have the folktales written and recorded in Hmong and to get copies of the collection printed for all the participating families and their relatives, in addition to making copies available to local human service providers who served Hmong clients.

Implications

The examples provided herein may be seen as an illustration of how the definition of critical literacy cited earlier (a process of constructing meaning and critically using one or two languages [oral, written, or both] as a means of expression, interpretation, and transformation of our lives and the lives of those around us) can be extended to biliteracy. This expanded definition led to the categorization of findings into three categories: expression, interpretation, and transformation. These three categories can be guides for discussion of learning in a general sense and specifically of biliteracy development.

In terms of expression, by using a theme of personal history narrative, the participants were given an opportunity to be experts in the telling of their stories. By encouraging a critical literacy approach that drew on speech, writing, and reading in the native language and English, all students, regardless of literacy proficiency, were given the opportunity to tell their stories. In most cases, in each of the classes, the students were more expressive in terms of the content and details of their stories when speaking or writing in their native languages.

Parents in family literacy projects do not always plan to be involved in issues of transformation using their native languages. Yet, when they are respected and encouraged to read their "world" (Freire & Macedo, 1987), often their experiences lead to their taking action in various ways that improve their lives in some manner. While many people define *transformative action* in different ways, most would agree that one example is a parent doing something to make a situation better for her child.

As previously explained, a few years ago, the Hmong women in Minnesota, in one of the first family literacy classes, came to class with a critical question: "Why doesn't Loveland School [the elementary school their older children attended] tell us about parent conferences, send us notification in our language, or provide an interpreter at meetings?" The women commented on how they had been able to be active in Head Start, in part because interpreters were provided at meetings. After comparing the two situations (Head Start and the elementary school), they decided to take action. The parents wrote the following letter:

Tus saib xyuas nyob rau hauv tsev kawm ntawv.

Dear Principal,

Peb yog cov ua niam ua txiv muaj me nyuam tuaj kawn ntawv hauv tsev kawn ntawv Lowell School. Peb xav thov kom nej muab cov ntawv xa los tsev txhais ua ntawv Hmoob. Thaum twg nej muaj tej yam uas tseem ceeb nyob rau hauv tsev kawm ntawv los peb thiaj paub tias yog ntawv tseem ceeb thiab.

Ua tsaug ntau koj muab koj lub sij haum los twm peb tsab ntawv no. (Quintero & Rummel, 2003, p. 126)

As can be seen in the letter, the only English used was the principal's name (changed here to protect the individual's privacy). To paraphrase the letter, the parents asked the principal why they were not notified of school information regarding their children in their language. They stated that they are active parents who cared deeply about their children's education, but when information was illegible to them they could not participate.

The principal responded with a letter, written in Hmong, a week later. Interpreters have been provided at all school functions in which the parents participate and school notices have been translated into Hmong ever since this incident. Not surprisingly, participation by the Hmong parents in school activities rose to over 90% (Quintero & Rummel, 2003).

In terms of interpretation, family literacy based on bilingualism and biliteracy gives ample opportunity for the students to reflect upon and discuss with others their interpretations of events of their immigration. In addition, the act of telling the immigration stories they had written to a classmate became a very dynamic biliteracy-building process in that the parents made choices of using either English or the home language in the process. The adult learners participated in activities by relating their own experiences or choosing other aspects related to the topic of study to further their reading, writing, and background knowledge. They reflected upon the community they had entered, and the needs of English language literacy and Hmong maintenance, and they learned important content knowledge required at their particular level of schooling.

The importance of personally meaningful contexts for writing activities for all learners has been argued by many (Fine, 1991; Giroux, 1987; Torres-Guzmán, 1993). In settings where students have been previously unsuccessful in school, the creation of meaningful links between school and community has proven effective (Norton et al., 2004; Reyes, 1992; Trueba, 1991). Evidence shows that the social context of the setting in which problem posing is implemented enhances the opportunity to focus on the often dramatic transitions that the students experience as they move from one sociocultural context to another (Quintero & Rummel, 1998; Rummel & Quintero, 1997; Shor, 1987). Critical literacy with native language use lends itself to focus on events in students' personal lives while they are learning English and other content area subjects.

Through the process of storytelling and the writing and editing of the stories, the teacher could see the women changing their feelings about their culture and themselves as they interacted more with American culture. In the beginning of this project, not a single woman was telling her children about her childhood; later, several of them regularly reported telling their children about the stories they had told in class, and they were always proud when they talked about them. Some of their older children began asking when the next stories would be ready for them to read.

At the beginning stages of the process, the instructor was worried about whether the women would be comfortable sharing stories. She learned, and documented in her journal, that her worries were unfounded:

> The Hmong women have been sharing stories and experiences orally in groups for as long as they have been able to meet together. They settled into a routine that included a snack on storytelling day and complete openness. Stories were audiotaped for reference and the women were free to tell their stories in their native language. (Larson, 2003, p. 158)

Finally, in terms of transformation, in this type of bilingual and biliterate family education program the opportunities are great. Every immigrant and refugee has experienced a transformation by moving from one country and culture to another. Learning to negotiate the new culture and new language provides for daily transformations. And specifically, by attending to their own development of English literacy and academic English, the students are generating more opportunities for further transformation. Activities in which culture, language, prior knowledge, and current dilemmas are addressed are opportunities for transformation to be the greatest. Personal narrative illustrated the voices of the participants in their cultural contexts as they told about their experiences and explained ongoing efforts at improving, or transforming, their lives and those of their families. The use of the native language as well as English was integral to this transformation process.

The implementation of critical literacy and the inclusion of the native language of the families and their home culture can be transformational in both schools and communities. The sharing of local knowledge that is of interest and significance to the learners can be a catalyst to reading and writing in all classrooms and to critical issues that affect Hmong immigrant learners in U.S. schools, Chicanos in California schools, Turkish students in Eastern Europe and Central Asia, Welsh and Irish students in England, Black South Africans in newly created, postapartheid schools, and many other learners. These issues influence how literacy is used, learned, and taught in many languages and in many forms of media. The women in this adult English literacy class exemplify critical literacy development through the use of two languages as one important avenue for social change on the personal level.

Conclusion

In conclusion, it is hoped that these perspectives on bilingual family literacy and family education will add to the field of family education for multilingual learners. The examples provided from the Spanish-English and Hmong-English programs illustrate the endless potential for content learning and English skills development using the native language. The very different examples of learning activities that use the native language further illustrate the different ways in which the native language can be used in literacy lessons in a variety of family education contexts.

There is a need for educators to think about family education as something other than a way to gain parental support for currently existing school curricula and homework tasks. Family education programs can be seen as opportunities to use families' strengths and knowledge to enrich each others' lives, as opportunities for families to determine what knowledge they need and how to get it, and as opportunities for parents to teach educators about knowledge that is not included in textbooks.

The examples provided from the Spanish-English and Hmong-English programs illustrate the endless potential that using the native language of the families provides for content learning and English skills development. There is much that programs that use a bilingual and biliterate approach have to offer to those concerned with the education of multilingual families. We can learn from each other and be energized by hope.

> Wisdom, then, is born of the overlapping of lives, the resonance between stories. … Hope for a sustainable future depends on reshaping the life cycle—not the individual life cycle alone but the overlapping and intersecting cycles of individuals and generations, reaffirming both the past and the future, not only in families but in the institutions we build and share. (Bateson, 2000, pp. 242–243)

There is an urgent need for educators to ask questions that have never before been asked about the intersecting lives, languages, and cultures of students and their families.

References

Ada, A. F. (2002). *I love Saturdays y domingos*. New York: Simon & Schuster.

Ancona, G. (1998). *Barrio: El barrio de José* [*Barrio: José's neighborhood*]. San Diego, CA: Harcourt, Brace, & Company.

Anzaldúa, G. (1987). *Borderlands: The new mestiza: La frontera*. San Francisco: Spinsters/Aunt Lute Press.

Bateson, M. C. (2000). *Full circles, overlapping lives: Culture and generation in transition.* New York: Random House.

Chinn, K. (2003). *Sam y el dinero de la suerte/Sam and the lucky money.* New York: Lee & Low Books.

Delpit, L. (1988). The silenced dialogue: Power and pedagogy in educating other people's children. *Harvard Educational Review, 58,* 280–298.

Freire, P., & Macedo, D. (1987). *Literacy: Reading the word and the world.* South Hadley, MA: Bergin & Garvey.

Fine, M. (1991). *Framing dropouts: Notes on the politics of an urban public high school.* Albany, NY: SUNY Press.

Giroux, H. (1987). *Teachers as intellectuals: Toward a critical pedagogy of learning.* South Hadley, MA: Bergin & Garvey.

Hakuta, K. (1986). *Mirror of language: The debate on bilingualism.* New York: Basic Books.

Hakuta, K., & Garcia, E. (1989). Bilingualism and education. *American Psychologist, 44,* 374–379.

Hudelson, S. (1986). Children's writing and ESL: What we've learned, what we're learning. In P. Riggs & D. S. Enright (Eds.), *Children and ESL: Integrating perspectives* (pp. 23–54). Washington, DC: TESOL.

Kuiken, F., & Vedder, I. (2002). Collaborative writing in L2: The effect of group interaction on text quality. In S. Ransdell & M. Barbier (Eds.), *New directions for research in L2 writing* (pp. 169–188). Amsterdam: Kluwer Academic Publishers.

Larsen-Freeman, D., & Long, M. H. (1991). *An introduction to second language acquisition research.* New York: Longman.

Larson, B. (2003). Hmong roots: Hmong women refugees in Minnesota tell their stories. In E. Quintero & M. K. Rummel (Eds.), *Becoming a teacher in the new society: Bringing communities and classrooms together* (pp. 155–161). New York: Peter Lang Publishers.

Macedo, D., & Bartolomé, L. (2001). *Dancing with bigotry: Beyond the politics of tolerance.* New York: Palgrave Macmillan.

NCLE Fact Sheet. (2002). *Family literacy and adult English language learners.* Retrieved September 6, 2004, from http://www.cal.org/caela/factsheets/family.htm

Neuman, S. B., Copple, C., & Bredekamp, S. (2000). *El aprendizaje de la lectura y la escritura: Prácticas apropiadas para el desarrollo infantil.* Washington, DC: National Association for the Education of Young Children.

Norton, B., & Toohey, K. (Eds.). (2004). *Critical pedagogies and language learning.* Cambridge, MA: Cambridge University Press.

Ovando, C. J., & Collier, V. P. (1998). *Bilingual and ESL classrooms: Teaching in multicultural contexts.* New York: McGraw Hill.

Peregoy, S. F., & Boyle, O. (2000). *Reading, writing and learning in ESL: A resource book for K-12 teachers.* New York: Longman Press.

Quintero, E. P. (2002). A problem-posing approach to using native language writing in English literacy instruction. In S. Ransdell (Ed.), *Psycholinguistic approaches to understanding second language writing* (pp. 231–244). Amsterdam: Kluwer Press.

Quintero, E. P. (2003). Family literacy: Lessons from Hmong and Latino families. In E. P. Quintero & M. K. Rummel (Eds.), *Becoming a teacher in the new society: Bringing communities and classrooms together* (pp. 121–132). New York: Peter Lang Publishers.

Quintero, E. P. (2004). *Problem-posing with multicultural children's literature: Creating integrated early childhood curriculum.* New York: Peter Lang Publishers.

Quintero, E., & Huerta-Macías, A. (1995). To participate, to speak out ...: A story from San Elizario, Texas. In R. Martin (Ed.), *On equal terms: Addressing issues of race, class and gender in higher education* (pp. 143–152). New York: State University of New York.

Quintero, E., & Rummel, M. K. (1998). *American voices: Webs of diversity.* Columbus, OH: Merrill Education.

Quintero, E. P., & Rummel, M. K. (2003). *Becoming a teacher in the new society: Bringing communities and classrooms together.* New York: Peter Lang Publishers.

Reyes, M. (1992). Questioning venerable assumptions: Literacy instruction for linguistically different students. *Harvard Education Review, 2,* 427–444.

Rimdzius, T. (2003). *Third National Even Start Evaluation: Program impacts and implications for improvement: Executive summary.* U.S. Department of Education. Retrieved June 13, 2005, from http://www.ed.gov/rschstat/eval/disadv/evenstart-third/execsum.html

Rivera, K. M. (1999). Popular research and social transformation: A community-based approach to critical pedagogy. *TESOL Quarterly, 33,* 485–500.

Rummel, M. K., & Quintero, E. P. (1997). *Teachers' reading/teachers' lives.* New York: State University of New York Press.

Shor, I. (1987). *Freire for the classroom: A sourcebook for liberatory teaching.* Portsmouth, NH: Boynton/Cook.

Torres-Guzmán, M. E. (1993). Critical pedagogy and bilingual/bicultural education special interest group update. *NABE News, 17,* 14–15.

Trueba, H. T. (1991). From failure to success: The roles of culture and cultural conflict in the academic achievement of Chicano students. In R. R. Valencia (Ed.), *Chicano school failure: An analysis through many windows* (pp. 151–163). London: Falmer Press.

Ullman, C. (1997). Social identity and the adult ESL classroom. *ERIC Digest* (EDO-LE-98-01). Washington, DC: National Clearinghouse on Literacy Education.

U.S. Department of Education. (Compiled 2001, February 22). *The Even Start family literacy programs statute, as of December 31, 2000.* Retrieved September 30, 2004, from http://www.statewide-initiative.rmcres.com/documents/pdf/Auth_Leg_Even_Start_Statute.pdf

U.S. Department of Education. (n.d.). *Programs and responsibilities: Even Start.* Retrieved October 2, 2004, from http://www.ed.gov/offices/OESE/CEP/evenstprogresp.html#leg

Van Horn, B., Weirauch, D., & Grinder, E. (2002). *Pennsylvania's family literacy program: Results of a statewide evaluation 2000–2001.* University Park: Pennsylvania State University, Institute for the Study of Adult Literacy.

Winter, J. (1994). *Diego.* New York: Knopf.

Winter, J. (2002). *Frida.* New York: Levine.

Zou, Y. (1998) Rethinking empowerment: The acquisition of cultural, linguistic and academic knowledge. *TESOL Journal, 7,* 4–9.

6

Academic Biliteracies for Adults in the United States

ELLEN SKILTON-SYLVESTER

This chapter illustrates the ways that biliterate development can be supported within the ivory tower and calls for reconceptualizing what we mean by biliteracy. Utilizing the continua of biliteracy as a critical frame for understanding the experiences of bilingual high school students at the university and of tutors and students in a university writing center, the chapter shows the possibilities that teachers and administrators have to support biliteracy for adults. It also shows the important role of multilingual and multicultural content and of oral language in the development of academic literacies in two languages.

The right to use one's native language in and out of the classroom is often questioned based on definitions of the role of language in the United States. It is common for us to hear debates about bilingual education in relation to compulsory schooling (K-12), but these debates about bilingualism and the role of the native language also take place in adult learning contexts. One adult English as a Second Language (ESL) teacher explained his position on the use of other languages in the classroom in this way:

> Using the native language is forbidden. Forbidden. When they talk to each other, I say, "Don't speak that kind of language." And they all don't do it. ... I want them, even with each other, not to speak their native language. ... I'm not saying that you shouldn't preserve your culture. I'm not saying you shouldn't preserve your language. But to practice, you

must speak English. You must do as the Romans do in Rome. It's that simple. There's no other way. ... Everyone must speak English. This is America after all, the land of the free and the home of English. (Taped interview, October 24, 1994)

In addition to making other languages "illegal" in his classroom, he also told stories of walking up to immigrants on the street or in restaurants and telling them to speak English. Not unlike the notion of a "citizen's arrest," he felt comfortable in the role of "policing" his neighborhood to make sure that English was spoken.

This adult ESL teacher's comments cannot be seen, however, as purely his individual opinion. His views are quite in line with what Schiffman (1996) calls American linguistic culture—the often covert underlying ideas, decisions, and attitudes on which policy decisions are made in the United States. In the United States, the use of multiple languages in education is not a straightforward process. Although there is widespread support of English monolingualism in mainstream discourses about language, equally important is the notion that U.S. linguistic culture cannot be described as a uniform set of beliefs. This is particularly true in addressing the development of academic biliteracies at the postsecondary level.

Even though there are a variety of options for bilingual adults wishing to develop academic literacies, the most common option is to enter a community college or four-year university. Comprehensive data are not available (see Curry, 2004); however, it is clear that the immigrant student population is growing at higher education institutions in the United States. As Curry (2004) suggests,

Contemporary immigrants often see education as a way to move past low-level jobs in service industries, health care, and agriculture. Furthermore, more adult immigrants are seeking higher education and training, as the changing global economy requires greater levels of education in general, and multiple literacies in particular (Hull, 1997). Immigrants often turn to community colleges because of their open-door policies, low cost, proximity, and range of programs. (p. 52)

This chapter will discuss two programs at a large public university in a major U.S. city that serves a significant bilingual student population. This institution, like many public universities, has agreements with community colleges that make admission and transferring of credits automatic if a certain grade point average is maintained at the community college.

Based on the monolingual nature of U.S. linguistic culture, it is perhaps not surprising that the development of academic literacies at the university tends to be focused on the acquisition of standard English literacies. It is, however, a bit surprising that the topic of bilingual higher education is so rarely addressed.

Although the debate about bilingual education is common when discussing K-12 contexts, the idea of offering bilingual courses at the university is almost unheard of. Recently, however, there has been an increased interest in providing academic native language courses for fluent speakers of Spanish (see Hollingsworth, 2005) in high schools, community colleges, and universities as the demand for a bilingual and biliterate workforce increases (see also chapter 4, this volume). For example, the University of Texas at El Paso offers one of the required general education courses for entering first-year students in Spanish. This development is having more of an impact on some languages (e.g., Spanish) than others (e.g., Khmer) as the impetus for the courses comes from demands in the marketplace (Skilton-Sylvester, 2003).

Because of the many independent units involved in language planning in the United States in what Tollefson (1984) has called a "loosely coupled system," and federal laws that encourage rather than mandate solutions (Christian, 1999), there is some room for innovation and contesting commonplace assumptions at the local level (Auerbach, 1993; Cummins, 1986/2001; Corson, 1999; Freeman, 1996; Ricento & Hornberger, 1996). As Christian (1999) explains, "Adult education has experienced a policy orientation similar to that of K-12 education, in that services for LEP [limited English proficient] adults (and use of languages other than English) are allowed but not mandated" (p. 123). Although the policy orientation is similar for both children and adults, there may be even more possibilities for innovation that contests dominant assumptions at the university level, where there is a less organized hierarchy for determining curricular decisions. It is possible to see the ways that challenges to mainstream U.S. linguistic culture's focus on English only are possible—even within the ivory tower. The following section outlines some dominant, often monolingual, assumptions common in the United States that frame societal and educational decisions about biliteracy. Two innovative programs are then highlighted that support biliteracy at the university and contest these dominant assumptions.

Dominant Assumptions About Linguistic
Diversity in and out of the Academy

Although there are many ways to describe the underlying ideologies of language policies and practices in the United States, the literature suggests several key assumptions in the dominant discourse on the learning of English by linguistic minorities (Christian, 1999; Lo Bianco, 1999; Ricento & Burnaby, 1998; Schiffman, 1996; Wiley & Lukes, 1996; chapter 2, this volume). While this is not an exhaustive list, it highlights some of the perspectives in the literature that this chapter addresses and contests:

1. A prevailing *language-as-problem orientation* is widespread and standard English is seen as the solution (Christian, 1999; Lo Bianco, 1999; Ricento & Burnaby, 1998).

2. An emphasis on *subtractive bilingualism* in ideology and in policy (Christian, 1999; Lo Bianco, 1999; Ricento & Burnaby, 1998; Schiffman, 1996).

3. Immigrant and refugee *rights to native languages* are questioned on the basis of their status as newcomers to the United States (Wiley & Lukes, 1996).

4. A narrow view of other languages that includes a belief that they are useful only if they serve *a pragmatic, instrumental function* (Christian, 1999; Lo Bianco, 1999; Ricento & Burnaby, 1998).

Each of these perspectives of U.S. linguistic culture can be found in particular ways within higher education and provide an underlying, often unspoken, justification for policies and procedures that do not support biliteracy. To create policies and practices that support academic biliteracy, these ideologies need to be visible in order to be contested.

Within academia, the language-as-problem orientation can be seen in the widespread belief that students need to be placed in remedial courses if they do not speak and write standard English (Zamel & Spack, 2004; Rodby, 1999). This idea that language needs to be "fixed" before any complex thinking can go on, and that it is not the job of professors outside of language departments to focus on the teaching of writing, illustrates the ways that this orientation is alive and well within higher education contexts. Subtractive bilingualism, or the belief that English can and should become the dominant language, replacing the first language, is underscored in many K-12 and adult education contexts where, if the L1 is used in instruction, it is only in the service of English language development. For example, in Texas, adult education programs can use the native language only in the service of ESL development in government-funded programs (A. Huerta-Macías, personal communication, June 24, 2005). In postsecondary contexts the first language appears much less frequently, and it is also most often viewed primarily as a means toward an end, rather than as something valuable in its own right that should continue to be developed alongside English (Bean et al., 2003; Curry, 2004).

The notion that speakers of languages other than English have rights to native languages is perhaps the most difficult to imagine within U.S. linguistic culture. Evidence of the focus solely on English in thinking about adults' rights can be seen in both the 1991 National Literacy Act and its reauthorization and the Workforce Investment Act of 1998, Title II, Adult Education and Family Literacy Act. In both acts, other languages are not mentioned. Literacy is defined in English, and satisfactory programs are those that allow students to "achieve competence in the English language" (U.S. Department of Education, 1998). The underlying rights given to citizens of the United States, both in and out of educational contexts, do not address the right to the native language. Finally, the notion that other languages are valued only if they serve a pragmatic, instrumental function can be seen quite clearly in discussions of the positive role of bilingualism for those in the service industry working in a global world (Heller, 1999), but it is much less common for languages that are not economically viable to be valued either within or outside of academia.

Supporting Academic Biliteracies at the University: Two Cases

Supporting the development of academic biliteracies in postsecondary contexts requires: (1) a thorough understanding of the dominant ideologies that undermine biliterate development in these contexts, and theoretical rationales and pedagogical practices for contesting these beliefs, and (2) a complex understanding of biliteracy that includes connections to content, context, and oral language and that acknowledges the many cognitive, social, and educational benefits of academic biliteracies. In the previous section, dominant ideologies were discussed and examined in the context of U.S. higher education. In this section, two examples of university programs that support academic biliterate development are discussed as a way to highlight theoretical rationales and pedagogical practices for contesting dominant beliefs and to illustrate biliteracy in practice.

The discussion draws particularly on the continua of biliteracy (Hornberger, 1989, 2003; Hornberger & Skilton-Sylvester, 2000) as a frame for analyzing a critical perspective on biliteracy that highlights both the traditional power weighting of different dimensions of biliteracy and the possibilities for contesting this power weighting. The framework was not developed specifically for thinking about adult academic biliteracies, but provides a useful structure for analyzing the ways that academic biliteracies are supported (and not supported) in particular contexts. This framework addresses four overlapping and intersecting continua: biliterate contexts, content, media, and development. In the examples that follow, some of the continua are more prominent than others. In each case, however, it is possible to see the ways that academic biliteracies can be supported at the university even within institutional contexts where monolingual ideologies are the norm. In particular, support for L1 literacies, use of L1 literacies, and content that addresses the multilingual/multicultural lives of students will be highlighted.

The support of academic biliteracy development needs to address more than language per se since monolingual English-speaking teachers and administrators can also support the development of academic biliteracies—even without speaking their students' native languages. As Cummins (1986/2001) suggests, "Even within a monolingual school context, powerful messages can be communicated to students regarding the validity and advantages of language development" (p.

664). Skilton-Sylvester (1997) has also suggested that meaningful vernacular, minority, and contextualized content can be quite valuable in supporting biliterate development (Hornberger & Skilton-Sylvester, 2000).

Tse's (2001) recent study of the experiences of 10 bilinguals who were born in the United States and have achieved high levels of literacy in both languages is very useful in thinking about what situations support the development of full biliteracy in the United States. She shows that there are two key elements to their ability to resist language shift: (1) language vitality and (2) literacy environment and experiences. The key element of language vitality in higher education contexts has to do with whether educational institutions and the teachers and administrators who work in them value bilingualism and the particular languages of their students. Tse's discussion of the literacy environment and experiences necessary for high levels of biliterate development for adults includes native language instruction. In the cases below, L1 instruction is happening in one context but not the other.

Two cases of biliteracies in postsecondary academic contexts will be described in the following sections. Each case provides an opportunity to see the ways that individual people and programs within larger institutions can be agents for reconfiguring orientations toward academic biliteracies at the university from the bottom up.

Bilingual High School Students at the University

As part of a career ladder grant from the U.S. Department of Education,[1] an urban public university on the East Coast began offering an intensive summer course for students from two local high schools that had significant bilingual student populations. The goal of the course was threefold: (1) to help students experience a bit of college life and think about their own educational choices after high school, (2) to give students opportunities to engage in college-like literacy events, and (3) to bring multilingual content into a college-level course. The high school portion of the program is called Project PATH because it is meant to be a pathway to higher education and to a career in teaching.

Although not explicitly stated in this way, the goals of this program focus on the development of adults who feel at home as bilingual citizens of the United States. Students in this program come from multiple language backgrounds: Spanish, Haitian Creole, Chinese, Vietnamese, Urdu, Russian, and Arabic. They are juniors and seniors at two local high schools that have significant bilingual student populations. They need to be in good academic standing in order to participate in the program, but do not need to be at the top of the class. Their abilities and confidence in both English and their native languages vary considerably, as does their orientation toward postsecondary education. In many ways, this is a typical ESL educational context in the United States, where many languages and levels of English competence are represented. It is the kind of context in which many would say that supporting biliteracy is not possible because the teacher and the students do not share a common native language.

The instructors are all faculty or graduate students at the university. They are primarily from the education department (and, in particular, the TESOL program), but the program also seeks out bilingual faculty from around the university to participate. Having bilingual Spanish-speaking, Korean-speaking, and Arabic-speaking instructors positioned bilingualism as a resource in this context and demonstrated that higher education success and bilingualism can go hand in hand.

Even though the writing that students do for the course is typically in English, students are encouraged to utilize their native languages in discussions and in informal journal responses. What is most significant about this learning context as one that might support biliteracy, however, has to do with the content of the course, the ways in which offering this course at the university has altered students' monolingual perceptions of higher education. Perhaps even more striking are the ways that the content of the course draws on the strengths of students rather than on the traditional canon. Key topics for the course are growing up bilingual, bilingualism and work, and bilingual education. In addition, the students and instructors discuss their views of what it takes to be a good teacher, the benefits of teaching as a career, and the academic skills needed to succeed at the university. In each case, there is an emphasis on the benefits of being bilingual and the ways in which being bilingual is a strength rather than a liability. One year, students wrote their own life histories (after reading examples of immigrants writing about their arrival and adaptation to the United States), and another year, they worked in groups to create a handbook for newcomers to their schools. In each case, bilingualism and student reflections on their own experiences growing up bilingual in the United States were the central content of the course. In the second year, instructors in the course who spoke native languages other than English talked about their experiences of being bilingual and, in particular, the ways in which they learned academic English at the university.

One of the ways to draw on students' own experiences of language as content in the classroom came from their language logs. In these logs, they responded to scenarios about language use in their lives based on queries for reflection in Thomas and Wareing's (1999) *Language, Society and Power.* For example,

> What kind of identity does your name give you? How do you feel if someone uses it wrongly? Think of the different ways people can name you and how these construct different identities for you in different contexts. (p. 138)

When this item was discussed in class, several students talked about choosing an "American name" because their name was hard to pronounce for mainstream Americans. They also talked about the ways that their home languages and identities were welcomed and not welcomed in school. Another query from Thomas & Wareing (1999) that they responded to was:

> Think about your own speech. Have you ever been corrected by some-
> one on your language use? What kinds of things have they objected to?
> They may have objected to features of your pronunciation or they may
> have objected to features of your grammar. Check with the generation
> older and/or younger than you. Were they or are they corrected by other
> people and was it or is it for the same kinds of features that you have
> been corrected for, or for different ones? (p. 157)

This query encouraged students to think not only about their experiences using English, but also about generational differences within their own language group. This invited Spanish-speaking and Haitian Creole-speaking students to think about varieties of Spanish and French spoken by different individuals and groups and the power associated with these varieties.

Excerpts from students' individual reflections on what it means to be bilingual and their advice to newcomers at their high schools offer a window into the power of their voices when they are encouraged to think about the value of bilingualism. From a group poem entitled "Being Bilingual," students wrote:

> I can learn both languages and can write both languages. It's very help-
> ful. To be smart and very cool. ... Being bilingual means something
> that is sweeter than honey. ... It is like a coin with two sides; it is more
> than having a precious stone in my hand. ... It's a freedom to express
> yourself and the way you feel. ... You know both sides of the balance.
> (Group Poem, August 6, 2004)

As seen in the previous examples, Project PATH directly contests the prevailing monolingual assumptions outlined earlier in this chapter. It particularly highlights a belief that newcomers have language rights that should encourage and protect the utilization of their native languages in both public and private contexts, and an additive rather than subtractive view of bilingualism.

The ways in which this program contests dominant assumptions about academic language at the university are based on theoretical and empirical arguments in the language policy and planning literature and studies of bilingualism and second language acquisition. First, there is a growing body of literature that discusses "linguistic rights" (Kontra, Phillipson, Skutnabb-Kangas, & Varady, 1999; Phillipson & Skutnabb-Kangas, 1995). This claim takes the position that much like other basic human rights, bilingual individuals have the right to utilize all of the languages they speak.

In addition to the well-documented claim that literacy in one's native language can provide positive transfer in literacy learning in a second language (Carlo & Skilton-Sylvester, 1996; Hornberger, 1989; Hornberger & Skilton-Sylvester, 2000; Lenters, 2004), Cook's (1992, 1999) work supporting the notion of

multicompetence highlights the ways in which being bi- or multilingual or bi- or multilterate has general cognitive benefits. As Cook explains,

> Multicompetence is indeed a distinct state of mind from monocompetence. The knowledge of the L1 and the L2 are different in L2 users; metalinguistic awareness is improved; cognitive processes are different. Many of these differences are not immediately apparent; nevertheless, they consistently add up to the conclusion that people with multicompetence are not simply equivalent to two monolinguals. (p. 565)

Within a multicompetent view, both languages are always present even if they are not visible. To ignore the native language, in this view, obscures a powerful and productive resource for learning and denies the cognitive benefits of multicompetence. As Cook (1999) suggests, "From a multicompetence perspective, all teaching activities are *cross-lingual* ... the difference among activities is whether the L1 is visible or invisible, not whether it is present or altogether absent" (p. 202).

If one looks at the continua of biliterate contexts and the continua of biliterate content (Hornberger & Skilton-Sylvester, 2000; Hornberger, 2003), as illustrated in Figure 6.1, it is possible to see the ways that this course provided support for biliteracy by contesting the traditional power weighting of academic contexts and content at the university and by highlighting the vitality of students' native languages. The continua of biliterate contexts (illustrated on the left side of the figure) were developed to illustrate the ways that the social context has a profound effect on individual language development, teacher and student biliterate practices, and language policies. These continua of biliterate contexts encourage an analysis of overlapping contexts at several levels, from micro to macro, while highlighting the role of orality and literacy and the ways that the L1 and L2 are used both concurrently and separately. Similarly, the continua of the biliterate content portion of the model (on the right side of the figure) illustrate the power of content in the development of biliteracy. The right side of the continuum encourages an analysis of minority and majority texts, texts that fall at the literary or vernacular ends of the spectrum or somewhere in between, and decontextualized words and sentences, on the one hand, all the way to stories that connect with students' lives and curricular content, on the other. This part

Context of Biliteracy	Content of Biliteracy
micro ↔ macro	minority ↔ majority
oral ↔ literate	vernacular ↔ literary
bi- or multilingual ↔ monolingual	contextualized ↔ decontextualized

Figure 6.1 The continua of biliterate contexts and content. (From Hornberger, N. H. and Skilton-Sylvester, E., *Language and Education: An International Journal, 14*, 96–122, 2000. Printed with permission from Clevedon, UK: Multilingual Matters.)

of the model allows us to look not only at language, but also at the academic and cultural content discussed as a valuable part of understanding biliterate development. The model offers a way of seeing the spaces between the two ends of the continua as important dimensions of understanding biliteracy, rather than focusing solely on the endpoints themselves. As a result, in using this model, one talks about where a particular literacy event, classroom, or policy might fall on a continuum, for example, more or less oral or literate (looking at the left column in Figure 6.1) or including content that is more or less contextualized (looking at the right column in Figure 6.1). Traditionally, the left side of the continua in each column has had less power, while the right side has had more power in society.

Although more power is typically associated with one end of these continua than the other, it is important to note that this model does not embrace a static view of power, but rather one that is dynamic and open to transformation. As Hornberger and Skilton-Sylvester (2000) state:

> We are not suggesting that particular biliterate actors and practices at the traditionally powerful ends of the continua (e.g. policies which promote written, monolingual, decontextualized, standardized texts) are immutably fixed points of power to be accessed or resisted, but rather that though those actors and practices may currently be privileged, they need not be. Indeed, we are suggesting that the very nature and definition of what is powerful biliteracy is open to transformation through what actors—educators, researchers, community members and policy makers—do in their everyday practices. (pp. 99–100)

This perspective on power in relation to biliteracy illustrates the ways that individual people and institutions can contest the traditional power weighting of the continua by valuing, for example, oral, bilingual, minority, vernacular, and contextualized texts alongside written, monolingual, majority, literary, and decontextualized texts that are typically the sole focus in academic contexts where literacy is taught and learned.

Project PATH highlights the micro end of the continua in creating practices at the micro level that support biliteracy even when policies and practices at the macro levels (e.g., the university, the state, and the nation) do not. It is also a context in which both oral language and written language are valued, rather than a context in which written, academic language is privileged at the exclusion of more oral, informal kinds of language. Additionally, many different languages are used at different times, among students, between students and teachers, and among teachers in this context. In these ways, this program contests the traditional emphasis on monolingualism, written language, and dominant forms of literacy in academic contexts.

In looking at the continua of biliterate content, it is also possible to see the ways that content (and not just the language of instruction and interaction) can be bi- or multilingual and bi- or multicultural. While many university-level social

science and humanities courses focus on formal literary texts written by native English-speaking, American-born authors who consider themselves part of the majority and highlight decontextualized skills associated with the use of academic English, this course draws on the less powerful ends of the continua of biliterate content by addressing texts written by bi- or multilingual authors, often considered part of the minority, and invites students to bring in vernacular content—their ways of speaking and writing among peers—and to focus on contextualized meanings rather than on decontextualized skills.

The tension between the power of English and students' desire to be their bilingual and biliterate selves is more evident in their writing about how to survive in high schools. This illustrates the need for more educational contexts where bilingualism and biliteracy are valued and discussed, and where taken-for-granted assumptions about English monolingualism being "better" are interrogated. Project PATH's ability to focus on the less powerful ends of the continua of biliterate contexts and content comes through in the students' creative writing in a powerful way. However, when students do the more expository kind of writing, for example, when giving advice to other newcomers, one sees the power of academic English come through more significantly:

Be yourself and don't try to be something that you're not. Try to study more and more in English ... so you can be the leader for tomorrow. ... Read more books, and listen and look at how they speak carefully and study hard. Start to try to talk to those people who speak your language and English. ... To be brave is the first step. Try to learn English as fast as possible and [you] have to have self-confidence. Every time you are trying the new thing, it will give you more experiences. How difficult life is and how scary people are, but don't worry. You can overcome it. ... Have good behavior in yourself, pay attention, try to make good friends, listen when your teacher explains something, ask questions, take notes, do what they ask you to do and your homework assignments and focus on your future. ... Don't let anyone take your freedom away except your parents. (Advice to Newcomers, August 5, 2004)

This example also illustrates the necessity of not only focusing on the less powerful end of the continuum. Supporting biliteracy at the university is connected to a social justice orientation to teaching immigrant students in the context of widespread economic and academic inequality. If bilingual adults are to participate in powerful roles in U.S. society, they need to speak, read, and write the language of power (Delpit, 1995), which includes finding ways to address the more powerful ends of the continua of biliteracy. Abiding by a social justice orientation in part means helping students to see that the "language of power" is not necessarily monolingual, and that learning a new language does not mean giving up the first. In fact, the language of power is augmented by biliterate development rather than diminished by it. To the extent that academic biliterate develop-

ment can include an understanding of the linguistic rights of bilingual people, illustrate the ways that multicompetence provides new cognitive possibilities, and open up new academic and economic possibilities in the global economy (Heller, 1999; Lo Bianco, 1999; New London Group, 1996/2000; Tse, 2001), it can provide bilingual college students with not only the *language* of power, but also *languages* of power for making their voices heard in an increasingly multilingual, multicultural world.

This case shows how it was possible to create a micro context in which bilingualism was used and valued in spite of an institutional orientation (at the university and at their high schools) toward monolingualism. The case also demonstrates how to value a variety of oral and written discourses that are not typically a part of the academy while at the same time focusing on the academic discourses of bilingual instructors and writers alongside the everyday contextualized ways of speaking and being that the students bring to the course.

In a thoughtful discussion of both autonomous and ideological (Street, 1984) aspects of academic literacies, Curry (2004) raises just once the possibility of the native language as a resource. She lists several possible supports for students: "communicating requirements and expectations clearly, using cooperative learning, teaching contrastive awareness between languages and cultures and between disciplinary discourse conventions, linking ESOL courses and disciplinary content, and creating learning communities" (2004, p. 59). Only when talking about "contrastive awareness" is the value of the first language mentioned. Two suggestions by Steinman (2003) are addressed that incorporate the native language: (1) writing something first in the native language and then writing about the same topic in English and comparing the two texts, or (2) having students discuss what they see as important in their writing in the L1 and how they might be able to include those same characteristics in English. It is notable that this kind of direct mention of the use of L1 in the development of academic literacies is not typical and that the author's study took place within Canadian linguistic culture.

In one of the few articles explicitly written about the possibilities of native language use in the development of academic literacies in U.S. university contexts (see also Quintero, 2002), Bean et al. (2003) try to think complexly about this issue and illustrate the ways that L1 use in a college composition course can be beneficial. They discuss the experiences of Kutz (2003) in ways that mirror some of what this course for high school students did:

> In the end, we find ourselves trying to figure out what would be involved in constructing a *context of respect*—within a larger context of disrespect. ... [Kutz (2003)] ... shows how we can invite students themselves to explore the different discourse contexts in which they participate, and to bring their home languages and dialects into the English writing classroom as part of their study. ... While such work invites students to write *about*, rather than in their home languages and dialects, it can also

make space for students to reflect on how their work in a new discourse can benefit from drawing on the resources of home language or dialect. (pp. 32–33)

The following example shows a more structured use of the L1 in instruction and the ways that another project at the university is contesting the traditional power weighting of the continua of biliteracy by utilizing and valuing students' native languages in the writing process. This next example also illustrates the ways that administrators in the writing center and bilingual writing center tutors are finding to shift the traditional power weighting of the continua of biliterate media (the channels through which languages are learned and expressed) and development (see Figure 6.2).

Development of Biliteracy	**Media of Biliteracy**
reception ↔ production	simultaneous exposure ↔ successive exposure
oral ↔ written	dissimilar structures ↔ similar structures
L1 ↔ L2	divergent scripts ↔ convergent scripts

Figure 6.2 The continua of biliterate development and media. (From Hornberger, N. H. and Skilton-Sylvester, E., *Language and Education: An International Journal, 14,* 96–122, 2000. Reprinted with permission from Clevedon, UK: Multilingual Matters.)

Korean Language Use in a U.S. University's Writing Center

This example illustrates different aspects of the development and support of biliteracy, and like the previous example, it also shows the ways that individuals can create micro contexts within larger institutions in which bilingualism and biliteracy are valued. This case involves the work of Korean graduate students as writing center tutors at the university and the ways that this has opened up the possibilities for conversations in Korean about papers written in English. It illustrates the relationship between oral and written language as well as the relationship between the L1 and the L2. It is important to note that the reason that Korean tutors came to be tutoring in Korean and English in the writing center had to do with a writing center director and co-director, who saw the value of experimenting with bilingual tutoring, even within an academic culture that typically sees the native language as a problem.

This example also illustrates ways that all four of the dominant monolingual ideologies highlighted at the beginning of this chapter can be contested. It illustrates particularly well the possibilities created when moving beyond a language-as-problem orientation and toward a language-as-resource orientation (Ruiz, 1984). It also shows the potential value of looking beyond the purely pragmatic function that being bilingual can play in the social and economic spheres of society. Viewing academic biliteracies from this point of view requires an emphasis not only on social and cultural dimensions of literacy, but also on the

ways that power and inequality are intricately connected to academic literacies. Many have discussed the "social turn" in applied linguistics (Block, 2003;
Lantolf, 2000, McGroaty, 1998; Norton, 2000; Rampton, 1995), which has led
researchers and teachers to think about not only cognitive aspects of teaching
and learning, but also the central ways that the social and cultural context shapes
teaching and learning.

More recently, we have begun to see a critical turn in the field as well that
highlights social and cultural aspects of teaching and learning with an emphasis
on power relations and addressing inequality. This can be seen in the ways that
the continua of biliteracy illustrate the power that different aspects of biliteracy
traditionally have in society, and the ways that individual actors and institutions
can create policies and practices that draw on the traditionally less powerful ends
of the continua. More generally, the special theme issue of *TESOL Quarterly*
on critical approaches (Pennycook, 1999) illustrated the ways that looking at
issues of inequality were central to understanding language learning. Since then,
researchers focusing specifically on teaching writing to bilingual students at the
university have focused on what this critical perspective might mean. Benesch
(2001) has argued for a critical English for Academic Purposes (EAP) that questions the pragmatic and assimilationist focus of much of language learning at the
university (without, however, calling for the use of the native language in university contexts). This chapter extends this argument to include the possibilities
for L1 instruction at the university as a support to biliterate development, even
when the outcome is not purely pragmatic, but rather social, intellectual, and
(potentially) emancipatory.

In their call for a "critical contrastive rhetoric," Kubota and Lehner (2004)
raise the possibility of the productive use of the L1 in university contexts where
the goal is the development of academic literacies. In their view, a critical contrastive rhetoric is one that questions essentializing notions of the relationship
between language and culture and the inherent value and homogeneity of English
rhetorical structures. Within traditional contrastive rhetoric, there is an assumed
direct and static relationship between the language one speaks (e.g., Korean)
and the way one thinks and an underlying assumption that English rhetorical
structures are better, clearer, and more linear. Critical contrastive rhetoric, on the
other hand, draws on poststructuralist, postcolonial, and postmodern perspectives to make the argument that a student's language does not determine his or
her thought patterns, that individual students and students from particular language backgrounds have multiple ways of thinking and writing, and that English
rhetorical structures utilized in academic contexts are not inherently better.

Benesch (2001) and Kubota and Lehner (2004) provide justification for the
support of academic biliteracies in university contexts—in contesting the narrow and unquestioned focus on instrumental purposes for language learning in
traditional EAP and in problematizing easy comparisons of rhetorical structures
across languages that privilege English thought patterns over the rich complexi-

ties of rhetorical structures within and across languages that bilingual students bring to class. These critical approaches provide theoretical and empirical justification for contesting a language-as-problem orientation and a focus on the pragmatic functions of both literacy and biliteracy at the university.

Korean-speaking students offer an interesting example to consider in exploring and supporting adult biliteracies because there are such a range of different circumstances that lead Korean speakers to study at the university. The range includes international students who are often from economically privileged backgrounds, recent immigrant arrivals, and 1.5- or 2nd-generation students who are educated in the United States and who may be more comfortable in English than in Korean. The range of Korean speakers at the university is an illustration of the range of English language learners in higher education contexts, even though the prevailing assumption is that college-level English language learners are primarily international students (Harklau, Siegal, & Losey, 1999). In spite of these differences among Korean speakers at the university, they tend to have more social, educational, and cultural capital than the high school students described in the previous case.

In trying to understand the experiences of the tutors and the students they worked with, the author interviewed the tutors, both doctoral students in TESOL, to hear their thoughts on the experience. In the following excerpt from one of the interviews, one can see the internal and external forces that make utilizing the L1 in a writing center conference not always easy:

Author: Does it feel like a kind of expertise to be able to speak two languages in the writing center?

Tutor: Not always. I had monolingual bias at the beginning. It felt like it was not just a language decision but a pedagogical decision. How would it help for me to use Korean?

Author: Do you feel comfortable speaking Korean in the writing center?

Tutor: It could change, but right now it feels comfortable speaking Korean in the writing center. It could change, though. (Interview, December 6, 2004)

This student talks about her own monolingual bias and her desire to make sure that using Korean would help her students in their writing. Here, she is wrestling with the prevailing orientations toward both languages as problems and bilingualism serving a useful, pragmatic function. It also shows the fragility of this context in which bilingualism is valued at the university in that it could change if those who run the center are not behind it.

This case also shows us the ways that micro contexts can become places where biliteracy is supported, and it illustrates how contesting the traditional power weighting of the continua of biliterate development and media was pos-

sible in the writing center. Figure 6.2 illustrates the dimensions of the continua of biliterate development and the continua of biliterate media. In thinking about development, the model focuses on both the more receptive end of language skills (e.g., listening or reading) and the more productive language skills (e.g., speaking or writing), both the oral and written dimensions of language and their relationships to each other, and the development of the first and second languages as individual languages and in relation to each other. The continua of biliterate media focus on the channels through which languages are learned. They highlight whether the languages were learned more at the same time (simultaneous exposure) or more one after the other (successive exposure), as well as the similarities and differences between the grammars (structures) and writing systems (scripts) of each language. Figure 6.2 shows the ends of the continua that traditionally have less power on the left side of each column, and those that have traditionally had more power on the right side of each column.

The continua of biliterate development, for example, illustrate the ways that producing written language in English and being able to understand oral language in Korean are on two ends of the continua, with written English typically having much more value in academic contexts than being able to understand spoken Korean does. Because language is usually the channel through which power is negotiated (Corson, 1999), a student (or tutor) in the writing center could easily feel as though his or her ability to act is constrained because of linguistic resources. Creating a space where both English and Korean are valued in their oral and written forms provides possibilities for new biliterate learning and for a new sense of agency within a U.S. academic context.

Similarly, analyzing this academic context through the lens of the continua of biliterate media illustrates the ways that academic contexts privilege other languages that are more similar to English in their grammatical structures and writing systems than to those like Korean, which has quite a different grammar and script. However, the academic way that English is typically learned in Korea, where the native language is mastered in oral and written form before English is introduced, can privilege the successive exposure to both languages that international students experience over the language learning experiences of Korean immigrant students who have learned both languages simultaneously and not necessarily in their academic forms. Understanding what has been traditionally valued about the development and media of biliteracy in postsecondary academic contexts[2] provides a helpful lens in thinking about the ways that utilizing Korean in writing conferences draws on multiple ends of these continua—both those that are traditionally powerful and those that are traditionally less powerful—in ways that are the foundation for a powerful voice in participating in academic discourses at the university and that can productively lead to the development of academic biliteracies.

In thinking about the development of biliteracy, the bilingual tutoring happening in this context focuses not only on productive language skills like writ-

ing and speaking (on the part of the student), but also on receptive skills such as listening (in the L1) and reading (and students' comprehension of what they have read and are trying to write about). Even more striking, perhaps, are the ways in which a writing conference allows for a focus on oral language as well as written language. This is a site for facilitating the development of oral skills not only for talking about writing in English, but also for the ability to talk coherently in any language about one's writing. In this case, being able to choose the language in which one can do this very important kind of academic talking is quite powerful in terms of academic biliterate development. This means that this context focuses not only on the development of the second language (L2), but also on the ongoing development of the first language (L1) in a new context for new biliterate purposes.

In the tutoring situations described above, oral discussion in the L1 was not only allowed, but also encouraged as a way of moving toward a written product in the L2. As in most writing conferences, it was not just what students could produce, but their ability to use their receptive abilities in both Korean and English to understand the feedback given. By being able to use the L1 and L2 in this context, all ends of the continua of biliterate development were drawn on.

In thinking about the media of biliteracy (see Figure 6.2), it is valuable to think about the pathways to biliteracy these students have had. That is, did they learn both languages at the same time (simultaneously) or first one and then the other (successively) or somewhere in between? Although the graduate students' exposure was primarily successive (at the more powerful end of this continua), many of their undergraduate tutees had a much more simultaneous and uneven exposure to both languages. This is particularly true for the 1.5- and 2nd-generation students who went to U.S. high schools and who often speak Korean only at home. In thinking about the Korean script and structure in relation to the English script and structure, there are also interesting issues to consider that influence students' academic biliterate development in this context.

A central and perhaps obvious component of this initiative is these tutors' abilities to speak well in both English and Korean. In some cases, this was a preference of the student tutored, but in some cases, particularly for 1.5- and 2nd-generation students, their simultaneous exposure to both English and Korean has left them English dominant. This is a relatively common scenario for students growing up in the English-oriented United States. As Harklau et al. (1999) state, "Second-generation students may see themselves as bilingual although they have little productive command of a non-English language or designate themselves as native speakers of English when English is their second language" (p. 5). These students may prefer to speak in English or may be able to utilize their oral Korean skills with the tutors even if their written Korean has not been fully developed (see also Burt, Peyton, & Adams, 2003; Chiang & Schmida, 1999).

It is particularly interesting to think about the transfer that might be possible in noncognate languages like English and Korean. Both the grammar and the

scripts are quite different from each other. However, by allowing oral discussion in Korean, students are able to capture some of their "richest thinking and strongest voice" (Bean et al., 2003) before composing or revising in English. Elbow's (1999) work sheds light on this possibility in showing the ways that we move beyond thinking about translation and toward capturing the unique nature of a bilingual person's thinking and composing processes. In his case, a Spanish-speaking learner first wrote down her ideas in Spanish and then worked on writing in English:

> When she translated from her Spanish, she ran into the obvious problems of false cognates and inappropriate syntax for English. But when she put her Spanish text completely aside (after looking it over) and set herself the task of revising or rewriting—*composing explicitly in English* on the basis of it—she was able to call on the richer thinking and subtler distinctions she had produced thanks to her home language. (Bean et al., 2003, p. 35)

The richness of thinking captured by this student is also possible in a bilingual writing center conference. Even though the languages differ significantly more than English and Spanish, adult learners are still able to draw on their thinking and talking in the L1 in order to write in the L2.

One of the things that came up strongly in both interviews was the fact that their choices about utilizing Korean for conversations about writing had to do with context and with the particular people they were tutoring. One tutor told a story about a student who only speaks English with her, but only speaks Korean with the other tutor. Another key element that needs to be brought out is the crucial role of talk in the development of academic literacies and the ways that one's first language is often the language that one has the easiest time thinking through thoughts and ideas. All the studies that were reviewed about the use of the L1 at the university focused on whether to have students write in their native languages, but did not talk about the potential benefits of being able to talk about ideas and about their writing in their first languages (see chapter 4, this volume, for an application of this notion in workforce education, where the students use the native language to develop their critical thinking skills).

Bean et al. (2003) talk about finding ways for students to be able to capture their "richest thinking and strongest voice" (p. 33). In much of what these tutors said, it seemed that being able to talk in Korean, or to talk to someone who understood Korean and what it meant to be Korean in a U.S. context, led them to be able to capture some of their "richest thinking and strongest voice." In part this had to do with their own thinking processes, and in part it had to do with the ways in which they felt that monolingual English tutors only focused on surface-level errors and language usage rather than on the content. The other tutor I interviewed said:

One of my students said, "American tutors don't look at my content. The session is only about the linguistic level. American tutors don't look at my paper. They say it's OK but I know it's not OK. You corrected me but not the American tutors. They say, 'It's OK. It's OK'." ESL students really want to talk and try to develop ideas with the tutor. When I speak Korean to them, they speak more. But even if we don't communicate in Korean, my students say they are more comfortable talking with me *because* I am Korean. (Interview, December 19, 2004)

The benefits of working with a bilingual Korean tutor were not just in the language per se, but in the understandings the student and tutor had of each other. The other tutor also talked about this:

According to my students, they could pick up terms and vocabulary during the session. ... One student said that even when he heard them produced by his instructors, they were not in his productive vocabulary. But when I produced them, who is an L2 user, it was easy for him to pick them up. (Interview, December 6, 2004)

Being able to tutor other bilingual Korean students assisted both students and tutors in important ways with their processes of becoming biliterate and in contesting dominant ideologies about bilingualism and biliteracy. The tutoring enabled them to have academic conversations about their writing in their first language and to understand and learn new vocabulary.

Conclusions

Both of the examples described above provide opportunities to reflect on the possibilities for developing adult academic biliteracies at the university, even in the context of a U.S. linguistic culture and in an American higher education context that is overwhelmingly monolingual in English. The benefits of bilingualism and biliteracy are clear. The development of academic biliteracies at the university provides the students with new cognitive possibilities and economic opportunities while interrogating U.S. monolingual ideologies and shifting power relations at the classroom and institutional levels.

However, these examples also show that more work needs to be done in order to capitalize on the possibilities for academic biliterate development and to dispel myths about the inherent value of one language over another. As Dell Hymes (1992) has stated in talking about language and inequality and the role of language professionals in dispelling myths about language:

[The first aspect of inequality] has to do with something we know, but may forget ... assumptions and knowledge that linguists tend to take for granted—that all languages, and varieties of language, are (potentially)

equal. That users of any language have a right to life, liberty (autonomy) and the pursuit of meaning. We so take this for granted within linguistics now that we may forget to teach it. ... The truth is that we must never take for granted that what we take for granted is known to others. Elementary assumptions of linguistics can be liberating for those to whom they are unknown. The task of confronting misconceptions about the status of languages, as languages, may never be over. (pp. 2, 3, as cited in Hornberger, 2004)

The examples highlighted in this chapter show how segments of the university found ways to contest dominant ideologies about academic biliteracy in ways that had a profound effect on individual students, but also, in smaller ways, on the larger institution. These small legitimizations of biliteracy—the value of all languages—in this higher education context have led to an increased emphasis on linguistic diversity in all teacher education classes at the university and a university-wide committee to look at the particular needs and assets of bilingual students.

We also have much work to do in holding on to the possibilities and potentials of education to address inequalities—linguistic and otherwise. Like Benesch (2001), I am encouraged by Freire's emphasis on hope in thinking about education. As she states,

Freire (1994) insists that education is a struggle to improve human existence, not a set of techniques to carry out institutional goals. Unjust and dehumanizing situations offer opportunities to either accept current conditions or challenge them, guided by hope that equitable social arrangements can be achieved. [As Freire says], "Though I know that things can get worse, I also know that I am able to intervene to improve them." (Freire, as cited in Benesch, 2001, p. 50)

In fact, one of the most striking things about both of these cases is the ways in which individual actors were able to create "contexts of respect" where students developing bilingualism and biliteracy were valued within academic institutions. If, as Ricento and Hornberger (1996) suggest, bottom-up change is the most likely place for change to start, this is indeed a hopeful sign for academic biliteracy development for adults in the United States.

Endnotes

1. This five-year grant directed by Aida Névarez-LaTorre, Career Advancement for Paraprofessionals in Education, or Project CAPE, focused primarily on providing funding and academic support for bilingual paraprofessionals wishing to become certified teachers. Two secondary goals were to infuse undergraduate teacher education with issues of linguistic diversity and to interest bilingual high school students in college and, particularly, in careers in education.

2. Written academic English (L2) as opposed to oral Korean (L1); full academic bilingualism and biliteracy in both the English language and one that is quite similar to English in terms of structure and writing system, as opposed to partial development of the English language and one that is quite different from English and without significant global usage

References

Auerbach, E. (1993). Reexamining English only in the ESL classroom. *TESOL Quarterly, 27*, 9–32.

Bean, J., Cucchiara, M., Eddy, R., Elbow, P., Grego, R., Haswell, R., Irvine, P., Kennedy, E., Kutz, E., Lehner, A., & Matsuda, P. K. (2003). Should we invite students to write in home languages? Complicating the yes/no debate. *Composition Studies, 31*, 25–42.

Benesch, S. (2001). *Critical English for academic purposes.* Mahwah, NJ: Lawrence Erlbaum Associates.

Block, D. (2003). *The social turn in second language acquisition.* Washington, DC: Georgetown University Press.

Burt, M., Peyton, J. K., & Adams, R. (2003). *Reading and adult English language learners: A review of the research.* Washington, DC: National Center for ESL Literacy Education & Center for Applied Linguistics.

Carlo, M. S., & Skilton-Sylvester, E. (1996). *Adult second-language reading research: How might it inform assessment and instruction?* (NCAL Report TR96-08). Philadelphia: National Center on Adult Literacy.

Chiang, Y. D., & Schmida, M. (1999). Language identity and language ownership: Linguistic conflicts of first-year university writing students (pp. 81–96). In L. Harklau, K. M. Losey, & M. Siegal (Eds.), *Generation 1.5 meets college composition: Issues in the teaching of writing to U.S. educated learners of ESL.* Mahwah, NJ: Lawrence Erlbaum Associates.

Christian, D. (1999). Looking at federal education legislation from a language policy/planning perspective. In T. Huebner & K. Davis (Eds.), *Sociopolitical perspectives on language policy and planning in the USA* (pp. 117–130). Philadelphia: John Benjamins.

Cook, V. (1992). Evidence for multicompetence. *Language Learning, 42*, 557–591.

Cook, V. (1999). Going beyond the native speaker in language teaching. *TESOL Quarterly, 33*, 185–209.

Corson, D. (1999). *Language policy in schools: A resource for teachers and administrators.* Mahwah, NJ: Lawrence Erlbaum Associates.

Cummins, J. (2001). Empowering minority students: A framework for intervention. *Harvard Educational Review, 71*, 649–675. (Original work published 1986)

Curry, M. J. (2004). UCLA Community College review: Academic English for English language learners. *Community College Review, 32*, 51–68.

Delpit, L. (1995). *Other people's children: Cultural conflict in the classroom.* New York: The New Press.

Elbow, P. (1999). Inviting the mother tongue: Beyond "mistakes," "bad English," and "wrong language." *JAC: A Journal of Composition Theory, 19*, 359–388.

Freeman, R. (1996). Dual-language planning at Oyster Bilingual School: "It's much more than language." *TESOL Quarterly, 30*, 557–582.

Freire, P. (1994). *Pedagogy of hope: Reliving pedagogy of the oppressed.* New York: Continuum.

Harklau, L., Siegal, M., & Losey, K. M. (1999). Linguistically diverse students and college writing: What is equitable and appropriate? In L. Harklau, K. M. Losey, & M. Siegal (Eds.), *Generation 1.5 meets college composition: Issues in the teaching of writing to U.S. educated learners of ESL* (pp. 1–16). Mahwah, NJ: Lawrence Erlbaum Associates.

Heller, M. (1999). *Linguistic minorities and modernity: A sociolinguistic ethnography.* London: Longman.

Hollingsworth, H. (2005, April 23). *Many employers clamor for biliterate, bilingual workers.* Retrieved April, 28, 2005, from http://www.boston.com/news/nation/articles/2005/04/23/writing_classes_for_spanish_speakers

Hornberger, N. H. (1989). The continua of biliteracy. *Review of Educational Research, 59,* 271–296.

Hornberger, N. H. (Ed.). (2003). *The continua of biliteracy: An ecological framework for educational policy, research and practice in multilingual settings.* Clevedon, UK: Multilingual Matters.

Hornberger, N. H. (2004, October). *Nichols to NCLB: Local and global perspectives on U.S. language education policy.* Paper presented at the 14th Annual Nessa Wolfson Colloquium, Graduate School of Education, University of Pennsylvania, Philadelphia.

Hornberger, N. H., & Skilton-Sylvester, E. (2000). Revisiting the continua of biliteracy: International and critical perspectives. *Language and Education: An International Journal, 14,* 96–122.

Hull, G. (Ed.). (1997). *Changing work, changing workers: Critical perspectives on language, literacy and skills.* Albany: State University of New York Press.

Hymes, D. H. (1992). Inequality in language: Taking for granted. *Penn Working Papers in Educational Linguistics, 8,* 1–30.

Kontra, M., Phillipson, R., Skutnabb-Kangas, T., & Varady, T. (Eds.). (1999). *Language: A right and a resource.* Budapest: Central European University Press.

Kubota, R., & Lehner, A. (2004). Toward critical contrastive rhetoric. *Journal of Second Language Writing, 13,* 7–27.

Kutz, E. (2003). From outsider to insider: Studying academic discourse communities across the curriculum. In R. Spack & V. Zamel (Eds.), *Crossing the Curriculum* (pp. 75–94). Mahwah, NJ: Lawrence Erlbaum Associates.

Lantolf, J. P. (Ed.). (2000). *Sociocultural theory and second language learning.* Oxford: Oxford University Press.

Lenters, K. (2004). No half measures: Reading instruction for young second-language learners. *Reading Teacher, 58,* 328–336.

Lo Bianco, J. (1999). The language of policy: What sort of policy making is the officialization of English in the United States? In T. Huebner & K. Davis (Eds.), *Sociopolitical perspectives on language policy and planning in the USA* (pp. 38–65). Philadelphia: John Benjamins.

McGroaty, M. (1998). Constructive and constructivist challenges for applied linguistics. *Language Learning, 48,* 591–622.

New London Group. (2000). A pedagogy of multiliteracies: Designing social futures. *Harvard Educational Review, 66,* 60–92. (Original work published 1996)

Norton, B. (2000). *Identity and language learning: Gender, ethnicity, and educational change.* New York: Longman.

Pennycook, A. (1999). Introduction. Critical approaches to TESOL. *TESOL Quarterly, 33,* 329–348.

Phillipson, R., & Skutnabb-Kangas, T. (1995). Linguistic rights and wrongs. *Applied Linguistics, 16*, 483–504.

Quintero, E. (2002). A problem-posing approach to using native language writing in English literacy instruction. In S. Ransdell & M. L. Barbier (Eds.), *New directions for research in L2 writing* (pp. 231–244). Dordrecht, the Netherlands: Kluwer Academic Publishers.

Rampton, B. (1995). *Crossing: Language and ethnicity among adolescents.* London: Longman.

Ricento, T., & Burnaby, B. (Eds.). (1998). *Language and politics in the United States and Canada: Myths and realities.* Mahwah, NJ: Lawrence Erlbaum Associates.

Ricento, T. K., & Hornberger, N. H. (1996). Unpeeling the onion: Language planning and policy and the ELT professional. *TESOL Quarterly, 30*, 401–428.

Rodby, J. (1999). Contingent literacy: The social construction of writing for nonnative English-speaking college freshman. In L. Harklau, K. M. Losey, & M. Siegal (Eds.), *Generation 1.5 meets college composition: Issues in the teaching of writing to U.S. educated learners of ESL* (pp. 61–80). Mahwah, NJ: Lawrence Erlbaum Associates.

Ruiz, R. (1984). Orientation in language planning. *NABE Journal, 8*, 15–24.

Schiffman, H. (1996). *Linguistic culture and language policy.* New York: Routledge.

Skilton-Sylvester, E. (1997). *Inside, outside and in-between: Identities, literacies, and educational policies in the lives of Cambodian women and girls in Philadelphia.* Unpublished doctoral dissertation, School of Education, University of Pennsylvania, Philadelphia.

Skilton-Sylvester, E. (2003). Legal discourse and decisions, teacher policymaking and the multilingual classroom: Constraining and supporting Khmer/English biliteracy in the United States. *International Journal of Bilingual Education and Bilingualism, 6*, 168–184.

Steinman, L. (2003). Cultural collisions in L2 academic writing. *TESL Canada Journal* [*Revue TESL du Canada*], *20*, 80–91.

Street, B. (1984). *Literacy in theory and practice.* New York: Cambridge University Press.

Thomas, L., & Wareing, S. (1999). *Language, society and power: An introduction.* New York: Routledge.

Tollefson, J. (1984). Centralized and decentralized language planning. *Language Problems and Language Planning, 5*, 175–188.

Tse, L. (2001). Resisting and reversing language shift: Heritage-language resilience among U.S. native biliterates. *Harvard Educational Review, 71*, 476–708.

U.S. Department of Education. (1998). *Adult education.* Retrieved May 27, 2005, from www.itan.us/webfarm/stateplan/natlitact.html.

Wiley, T. G., & Lukes, M. (1996). English-only and standard language ideologies in the U.S. *TESOL Quarterly, 30*, 511–535.

Zamel, V., & Spack, R. (Eds.). (2004). *Crossing the curriculum: Multilingual learners in college classrooms.* Mahwah, NJ: Lawrence Erlbaum Associates.

7

Civics Education and Adult Biliteracy

James S. Powrie

English literacy and civics education has in one form or another been a part of the U.S. landscape for more than a hundred years. Although today's federal initiative promoting integrated civics and English literacy instruction (EL/Civics) is relatively new (since 1999), the practice of combining English instruction with civics education is not. From the settlement houses in the early 1900s to today's adult education programs, many millions of new immigrants have participated in classes that teach English, civic responsibility, and preparation for the U.S. citizenship test—often sequentially, at times combined. The desire for citizenship, economic security, and social acceptance has been and continues to be a strong incentive for immigrants wanting to learn English. How best to facilitate accomplishment of the individual immigrant goals of security and improved quality of life, and the societal goals of integration and stability, as well as determining what role bilingualism and biliteracy might play in the process are topics of ongoing debate.

Throughout the history of immigrant education, civic education programs have followed a dual direction. On the one hand, "top down" programs have emphasized the need to help immigrants become "Americans" (acculturate into the existing social order); on the other, there have been "bottom up" efforts to help immigrants see how they can challenge the status quo and work together for social justice in an effort to create a better life for themselves, their families, and their communities. A review of popular textbooks and existing curricula indicates that the former approach emphasizing acculturation that focused on knowledge of history and government (required for the citizenship test) predominates.

The language focus of civics and citizenship has shifted over the past hundred years. In the early years of the resettlement efforts, bilingualism and biliteracy played significant roles as mutual help organizations run by immigrants provided information on American culture in the native language. Foreign language newspapers and radio stations also provided information in the native languages of the early settlers, most notably in German (Kloss, 1998). Today, ethnic media use print materials, videos, and audiotapes in the native language to help newcomers understand English and prepare for citizenship. However, official government-sanctioned efforts to encourage a bilingual and biliterate citizenry are limited. While some states, such as Texas, support bilingual education for their younger immigrants, state monies are generally not available to teach civics and citizenship education to adults in the native language. Federal efforts focus largely on English as a means to promote immigrant integration into the larger society.

Civics is not just another context in which to teach English. At the core of any nation is a set of shared beliefs, values, and ways of being. In an immigrant nation, such as the United States, decreasing the social distance among different groups, identifying shared values, and finding a common ground among diverse cultures are matters of national concern. Federal and state policy makers grapple with a wide range of issues related to the integration of immigrants into the broader society and provide guidance and funding for those who might implement their policies. In the case of English literacy and civics education, it is the adult education programs (implemented by colleges, school districts, and community-based organizations) that must take tangible steps to realize broad policy goals. There is often a significant gap between the visions of policy makers and the capacities and orientations of service providers. However, in the case of EL/Civics, there has been a fairly coherent implementation of program strategies that reflect the intention of the policy makers, the capabilities of the service providers, and the desire of immigrants and refugees to understand and be part of the country that is their new home.

The implementation of today's EL/Civics program has been more evolutionary than revolutionary. The federal program as implemented by states has allowed for the development of a variety of promising approaches to language instruction and civics education that will likely have long-term impacts on English for Speakers of Other Languages (ESOL) instruction. Understanding how this process ensued and where it is now, as well as examining practical strategies for implementing EL/Civics programs, can benefit policy makers, administrators, and practitioners alike.

This chapter describes the origins and driving forces behind the contemporary emphasis on EL/Civics education and approaches to instruction. It examines two EL/Civics programs in terms of key implementation strategies, including the use of the participants' native language in instruction, project-based learning, and visual prompts and technology by teachers and students. Finally, this chapter presents a framework for categorizing various types of EL/Civics services and identifies strategies for the classroom that build on and help develop bilingualism and biliteracy.

Origins of the Current EL/Civics Program

Today, there is a broad national interest in English literacy and civics education that extends well beyond the traditional immigrant destination states (California, Texas, New York, Florida, Illinois). This is in large part because of the rapid expansion of immigrant labor across the United States into states that do not have extensive experience in providing ESOL instruction. To understand the contemporary direction and practice of integrating English literacy instruction and civics education, it is useful to take the investigator's tack: "Follow the money." Implementation of the EL/Civics program is driven directly by funding priorities of the U.S. Department of Education.

As part of the Adult Education and Family Literacy Act of 1998, in November 1999, the U.S. Department of Education announced the availability of English Literacy and Civics Education Demonstration Grants (Federal Register, 1999). These grants were "to support projects that demonstrate effective practices in providing, and increasing access to, English literacy programs linked to civics education" (Federal Register, 1999, p. 62920). EL/Civics was defined as "an education program that emphasizes contextualized instruction on the rights and responsibilities of citizenship, naturalization procedures, civic participation, and U.S. history and government to help students acquire the skills and knowledge to become active and informed parents, workers, and community members" (Federal Register, 1999, p. 62920).

The solicitation outlined a compelling social need for assisting immigrants "to become full participants in American life," and stated that significant portions of the non- and limited-English-speaking population had little or no civics education. It further indicated that as of 1999, the education delivery system was inadequate to meet the need for appropriate educational services. While acknowledging that federal and state grants provided funding for English literacy programs and citizenship classes, the solicitation identified the need for a more "integrated and coordinated program for individuals of limited English proficiency" (Federal Register, 1999, p. 62920). The solicitation did not address issues related to biliteracy in instruction, but left the door open for a wide variety of teaching methods and activities "that meet the language, literacy, and cultural needs of students" (Federal Register, 1999, p. 62920).

Twelve Demonstration Grants Lead the Way

Based on the 1999 solicitation, in May 2000, the U.S. Department of Education awarded 12 grants under the English Literacy and Civics Education Demonstration Grants Program. These grants, totaling $6.9 million, funded a range of program models consistent with the intention of the EL/Civics initiative. Most of the projects emphasized the development of products that could be used by the adult education field. In this way, the Department of Education sought to kick-start the EL/Civics initiative by providing effective models and resources for practitioners. Information about the 12 demonstration projects is available on the U.S. Department of Education Web site (http://www.ed.gov/programs/elcivics/elcivgrant2.html). Two of these projects are described in this chapter.

In addition to the demonstration grants, Congress authorized formula grants to states to provide EL/Civics instruction under the Workforce Investment Act of 1998. In fiscal year 2000, $25.5 million of formula funds was awarded. Only 31 states and the District of Columbia were included. Half of the money was allocated to states with the largest need for funding; the other half went to states with the largest recent growth in the need for services. Reauthorization for 2001 increased formula funding to states, and all states were included in the allocation. Continuation funding for existing grant recipients was made available through June 30, 2005. No matter what happens with federal and state funding for EL/Civics programs in the future, it is likely that programs that combine English literacy instruction with civics education will continue as an integral part of adult education for some time to come.

From Citizenship to Civics

Before the current EL/Civics initiative, most information about U.S. government and civic institutions was taught to immigrants at intermediate or advanced English levels who participated in citizenship classes. A key aspect of EL/Civics services is that it extends civics education to low- and intermediate-level English learners who are relatively new to English and may or may not be interested in gaining citizenship. This includes the majority of immigrants who, because of limited opportunities for schooling in their home countries, need additional time to develop their English language skills along with their literacy skills. Previous efforts to broaden civics curricula to include issues related to civic involvement on a more personal level were often unsuccessful because participants came with a narrow focus: to prepare an acceptable citizenship application, study the 100 questions about history and government, pass the civics exam, and raise their English up to a level where they could converse with the examiner to pass the English language interview. Students often resisted broader discussions or activities focused on civic engagement since any activity not clearly linked to passing the test was seen by many students as wasting time better spent on developing the skills and strategies needed to pass the exam (Wrigley, 2004a).

The EL/Civics initiative allows programs to open classes for students whose skills are too low to apply for citizenship and for those who want to take English to help them navigate daily life in their communities. As with any ESOL program, creating effective strategies that build knowledge and skills with low level learners is a significant challenge, particularly in areas that are linguistically isolated and where English is not required as the lingua franca of daily life (such as in El Paso, Texas, and smaller communities along the U.S.–Mexico border, as well as ethnic enclaves in large cities such as Chicago, Los Angeles, and New York). The EL/Civics initiative, however, offers sufficient latitude to allow education providers to develop flexible and innovative approaches to both language development in bilingual communities and civic involvement that is responsive to the needs and interests of newcomers with little experience in civic participation.

EL/Civics and Dual-Language Use

Although EL/Civics classes are clearly designed for immigrants and refugees who are new (or relatively new) to English, issues related to civic participation in a language other than English are not addressed in legislation, regulations, or guidelines. Neither is there guidance on the role that the native language might play in helping students understand key concepts related to civics or in discussing issues that affect civic life, such as bilingual education or raising children in bilingual environments. There is also no mention of issues related to navigating life in families where older generations are monolingual in their native language and younger generations are moving toward monolingualism in English. This is often a key motivator for parents and grandparents to learn English. Because the U.S. Department of Education and the states provide little or no guidance when it comes to the use of native language in civic education, teachers may use adult bilingual models as long as they help adult immigrants and refugees acquire the English skills necessary for participation in the larger U.S. society. The challenge for instructors is to implement effective educational strategies that allow students to activate background knowledge for the understanding of key concepts related to civic participation, and promote the acquisition of English communication and literacy skills—all aspects of the EL/Civics initiative.

Relying almost exclusively on English to help immigrants at beginning or intermediate levels of English to gain knowledge of U.S. history, government, and community issues can retard efforts at language acquisition. It is extremely difficult to understand the often complex concepts and principles of government if they are explained in a language one does not fully understand. Similarly, exploration of how one's community functions and the roles that different groups can play to strengthen neighborhoods and cities is limited if only English language teaching materials are used.

Attempts to remain in an English-only learning environment while teaching complex content tend to yield more frustration than understanding. In contrast, providing complex information in a language that adult students speak fluently can facilitate the acquisition of knowledge of history and government that is required for U.S. citizenship. Encouraging students to read and discuss historical information in the native language can deepen such knowledge and accelerate understanding of democratic values and principles that goes well beyond what individuals are able to grasp in a language they do not yet understand. Having learners explore their community and conduct inquiries into political processes or social inequities that shape their lives will be limited to surface details if using English only is required. In contrast, using the native language to discuss issues based on information provided by the print, radio, and TV ethnic media and other native language materials can promote much greater insights. Using dual-language approaches to teach specific content and discuss complex issues can facilitate English language acquisition and promote biliteracy. Specific strategies for fostering bilingualism and biliteracy in the classroom are presented later in this chapter.

Two Model EL/Civics Programs: Promising Practices in Action

The following describes two EL/Civics programs that grew out of the federal EL/Civics initiative. The students entering these two programs, like the majority of new immigrants participating in EL/Civics programs, spoke little or no English, and most had limited schooling in their home countries. In each program the low- and intermediate-level learners showed clear gains in English communication and literacy skills and substantially broadened their understanding about and engagement with civic life. The programs shared some of the same approaches to instruction; however, they faced different challenges, including different language configurations and the necessity to use English to conduct daily life. Each program implemented different strategies to deal with those challenges. Looking at the similarities and differences between these programs can help illuminate key issues with which most EL/Civics programs must contend.

EL/Civics on the Border: Socorro Independent School District

The Socorro Family Literacy and Adult ESL Program (part of the Socorro Independent School District (ISD)) is located in a low-income, semirural suburb of El Paso, Texas. It serves primarily Spanish-speaking immigrants from Mexico. The program has two components, a family literacy component funded through Even Start and an adult ESL component funded partially through North Amiercan Free Trade Agreement (NAFTA) funds and serving low literacy workers who lost their jobs due to plant closings in El Paso.

In 2001, Socorro ISD successfully competed for a grant from the Texas Educational Agency (TEA) to operate a demonstration EL/Civics project. This Border Civics Project included curriculum and instructional materials development, teacher training, and publishing of reports and materials on the Web for others to use. It also included daily classes for students and sufficient resources to purchase and use technology with both teachers and students. The program has full-time teachers who have access to paid staff development (fairly unusual in adult literacy programs). Most of the teachers are bilingual to some extent, some minimally proficient in Spanish, having studied it in school or college; others grew up in households where parents spoke Spanish, but the language among the siblings was often English; while still others are fully bilingual and use both languages on a regular basis.

In El Paso (even more so in Socorro) it can be quite difficult to find someone who speaks only English. Spanish is the primary language for most area residents, particularly in the neighborhoods where the students live, shop, and attend classes. Consequently, even when students do try to converse in English with a shopkeeper, for example, the person will invariably answer back in Spanish. Spanish-speaking immigrants in El Paso have little difficulty conducting day-to-day activities, shopping, or even working on jobs that generally have Spanish-speaking supervisors and customers.

Although one can get by in Spanish, there are many reasons to learn English along the border. Being able to help their children with homework is one reason students indicate they want to speak English. Talking with health care professionals and the teachers of their children is another. The changing job market in the El Paso area is also an increasing incentive for learning English. The old manufacturing jobs, where thousands of non-English-speaking adults were employed, are no more. The demand occupations today are in health care, education, and call centers that require English fluency and literacy. Another motivator for learning English is to be able to move away from the border for better jobs. Only in a narrow strip along the border can people manage a somewhat normal life being literate only in Spanish. One travels a hundred miles north and it is a different story.

There are many reasons to learn English on the border. Participating in civic life, however, is not one of the reasons that are often mentioned by students. This may be in part because immigrants from Mexico are not used to the democratic practices in the United States and may have little experience in getting civil institutions to meet their needs. It is also likely that for some, their lack of legal status inhibits their involvement in civic processes. Nevertheless, students indicate a strong desire to see their communities improved, including more and better parks, accessibility to water and sewage systems, roads without potholes, and schools without violence.

As mentioned earlier, most of the students enrolled in family literacy programs in Socorro are low-level English learners. Based on the skill levels of the students and their expressed interests, the EL/Civics program in Socorro focuses on the building of essential skills, such as teamwork, decision making, completing projects on time, and presenting results to an audience. The teachers in Socorro often use Spanish to explain complex concepts related to U.S. history and culture as well as the use of technology, but emphasize the use of English in general classroom discussions and presentations. The program also incorporates personal reflections and writing about home and community (in both Spanish and English) as well as exploration of community issues and basic civic action. For example, students in the EL/Civics class videotaped cars navigating a badly potholed road and then showed their video to the person in the city who was responsible for fixing the roads. The whole process (including the meeting with the city official) was documented and edited into a video that was presented at an exhibit of work.

The EL/Civics program in Socorro embraces the principles of project-based learning (Wrigley, 2004b). Students are encouraged to experiment, take control of their own work, and negotiate among themselves what needs to be done. Surveys and interviews are used to encourage students to use English to collect data from family members and strangers and to get to know their fellow classmates. Visual information is often incorporated by teachers and students in lessons and projects. Combining pictures with personal writings helps students connect with and communicate more complex ideas and feelings. Using sequential images with text in a storyboard promotes thinking through processes, such as in cookbooks and how-to manuals.

Technology, team-based projects, and presentations before peers and strangers also play a major role in the Border Civics Project. Each classroom has several computers connected to the Internet. Digital still cameras and video cameras are used in the completion of projects. Technology is used as a tool for communication (e-mail, online chats), collaboration (virtual visits, projects), application of skills (creating products), and basic skills practice. Students practice communication skills and cognitive skills by problem posing and problem solving based on scenarios of everyday life and community issues. By conducting research on their community and Web searches for background information on cultural, historical, and contemporary issues, the students build background knowledge and analytical skills. Students create a wide range of products, including personal books, posters, calendars, brochures based on field trips, maps of places of interest in the community, inquiry maps, and multimedia projects on hot topics such as domestic violence, diabetes, and the rights of the undocumented.

Information about the project and resources can be found online at http://www.bordercivics.org

Bright Ideas: Coalition of Limited English Speaking Elderly

The Bright Ideas Program, operated by the Coalition of Limited English Speaking Elderly (CLESE) in Chicago, was one of the original 12 demonstration projects funded under the U.S. Department of Education's English Literacy and Civics Education Demonstration Grants Program. CLESE is a small organization that works with over 16 different ethnic community-based organizations to coordinate citizenship and ESOL activities. The organization was well aware of the challenges elder immigrants and refugees faced in making a new life in the United States. They also had observed that older students with low English literacy skills participating in traditional ESOL programs showed little progress over many months of participation and would be unlikely to pass the Immigration and Naturalization Service (INS) citizenship test, a critical issue since these individuals were in danger of losing their Social Security Income (SSI) benefits unless they became citizens. CLESE wanted to see if they could change this dynamic for students and teachers by collaborating with an outside research and development team with experience in adult immigrant education. The team helped them to design a teaching model and professional development strategy that would extend the capacity of their member organizations to provide quality EL/Civics instruction.

Although the learners were generally much older and constituted a more diverse set of cultures and languages, they had a number of things in common with the Socorro students. They represented a significantly underserved group with little or no proficiency in English and often had low literacy skills in their home language. The students tended to live in language enclaves where they could generally get by without English, although these were the size of neighborhoods, not entire communities. Unlike the Socorro teachers, none of the Chicago teachers had any formal preparation for instructing students with such limited skills. This is common in community-based programs that often provide ESOL and citizenship instruction for low-level learners; their teachers are often biliterate and bicultural, but do not have formal training in the kinds of language teaching strategies that lead to important learning gains.

The instructional program and staff development efforts at CLESE were designed to meet the specific needs of the community-based programs and the elder clients they served, although the underlying approaches and principles could be applied in a variety of settings with different client groups, as illustrated in the Socorro example. Four community-based agencies in Chicago participated in the demonstration project. Three served single populations (Bosnian, Assyrian, and Chinese), while the fourth served a mixed-language group made up of refugees from Bosnia-Herzegovina, Macedonia, and Romania, as well as a sprinkling of immigrants from the Philippines. These organizations were primarily social service agencies with some experience in teaching ESL, but they had limited or no experience in providing ESL or civics instruction to the elderly. Most offered a broad range of services to members of their ethnic group, of whom the elderly were only a part. Existing teachers were part-time and generally paid a low hourly rate. The Assyrian teacher, who had taught English as a foreign language to university students in the Middle East, and the Bosnian teacher, who had an elementary school credential from Bosnia, were bilingual. The teacher of the group from China spoke some Chinese as a result of missionary work, and the teacher of the mixed group was a young refugee from the Ukraine who used only

English with his group. As with the teachers in Socorro, the bilingual teachers often explained complex issues in the native language, but used English as much as possible.

All the students were older (55 to 87) and spoke little or no English. The majority of the students fell into Student Performance Levels 0 to 1 on the Basic English Skills Test (BEST). Many had only limited formal education in their home countries, and some, particularly those from rural areas, had no literacy skills in their home language. Almost all of the refugees and immigrants lived in small ethnic enclaves in Chicago that were linguistically isolated. Many of the students were homebound since they had difficulty walking and did not drive. Their sons and daughters typically worked, and while they had some friends from the home country, they were isolated from other groups, immigrant as well as U.S. born. All had expressed a desire to learn English and make friends. Many reported not being able to communicate with doctors, pharmacists, and social service providers outside the resettlement agency. Sadly, many also reported that they were not able to talk to and share stories with their grandchildren since they themselves did not speak English and their grandchildren, who went to U.S. schools, were not proficient in the home language. Wong Fillmore (1991) and Weinstein-Shr (1995) have reported similar language loss among immigrants and refugee children. Many of the students believed they were too old to learn, although they very much wanted to learn English and be able to communicate with others outside their ethnic communities. In addition, like all elderly, they faced a range of physical barriers: disabilities, problems with vision and hearing, and other health problems. For most of these students, citizenship was not the most immediate objective, although they were aware that their benefits were threatened. Given the needs and interests of these students, the research and development team worked with agency administrators and instructors to develop teaching strategies and learning opportunities that would give the elderly a chance to learn the kind of English they could use for their everyday lives. Finding ways to decrease their social isolation, a first step in civic engagement with the broader community, was also a high priority.

To make a difference in the lives of teachers and students, the program designed an instructional approach to make English accessible to adults with little experience in schooling, promote interaction with other language groups, and connect classrooms with community. Since written texts presented a problem for the students (and they expressed much more interest in oral communication skills), the project needed to create a curriculum that took advantage of visual information and real-life experiences, while at the same time building on practices found to be effective with adult literacy learners. To that end, the research and development team built on previous research conducted by Johnston (1999) for the Adult Literacy Media Alliance (ALMA), producers of the award-winning adult literacy television series, TV 411, which showed that video segments that focused on learner stories acted as a strong motivator to learning. It was also recognized that in order for students to improve their oral communication skills, they needed to use English both inside and outside of the classroom. Early findings of a national study of adult ESL literacy students (Condelli, Wrigley, Yoon, Cronen, & Seburn, 2003) supported this contention. To this end, field trips were integrated into the curriculum.

As with the Socorro program, the Bright Ideas Program design incorporated a strong emphasis on using visual materials (videos and pictures) as prompts for vocabulary development and language acquisition. However, the use of project-based learning and technology was minimal. Other activities, such as scenarios, problem solving, and discussions about family and current events, were included in order to encourage discussions in English. Students also participated in field trips and "walkabouts" in the local neighborhoods, where they were encouraged to ask vendors simple questions in English, such as "When does your store close?" or "Excuse me, how much are the tomatoes?" A further and highly effective strategy for encouraging interactions in English was to hold annual get-togethers of all the classes where English was the only shared language. To help students grapple with their own issues and concerns, the research and development team wrote a set of scenarios based on situations the students had suggested. These scenarios included: the lonely neighbor, the lost wallet, and the eviction notice. They gave students a chance to use English in open-ended conversations as they tried to understand a situation, consider options, and discuss how a situation might be handled. In the classes where students spoke little English, the teacher or other students acted as translators to explain the situation; students used the native language to brainstorm ideas. They then either reported their suggestions in English or worked with the larger group and the teacher to generate ideas in English. The mixed group had enough English to grapple with the scenarios in English from the start. Other groups with a common language and limited English discussed the scenarios first in their native language and then worked on the necessary vocabulary in English. This bilingual and biliterate approach to instruction is consistent with the practices in the Socorro program. A discussion of the scenarios by one group of students was videotaped, and their interactions served as an example of cognitive apprenticeship (Rogoff, 1990) for the other groups. This video, as well as other examples of teaching strategies, is available on the agency's Web site: www.clese.org

Common Approaches to EL/Civics

The approaches allowed under EL/Civics guidelines are characterized by different underlying beliefs about what counts in learning and by the emphasis placed on skills development and knowledge acquisition (Eisner, 1994; Demetrion, 2005; Wrigley, 2004a). Common orientations that shape EL/Civics curricula and teaching are (1) social and economic adaptation, (2) learning how to learn, (3) basic skills and a common educational core, (4) personal and cultural relevance, and (5) social justice and social change.

Social and Economic Adaptation Orientation

Programs that seek to build knowledge and skills leading to personal and family self-sufficiency fall under this approach. Many popular curricula and most commercial EL/Civics textbooks reflect this model in their English language component, stressing life skills, such as making appointments at a clinic, filling out application forms, reading a paycheck, getting a driver's license, or memorizing one's social security number. Focused largely on functional literacy, these approaches see civics as a way of helping students to get help (calling emergency numbers), be safe (reading warning labels or the importance of using child car seats), and stay out of trouble (financial literacy). In some cases, information about community resources (libraries, parks, fire departments, social services) is included. Issues or problems are not raised, and the negative sides of community life (fear of violence, inadequate services, labor exploitation, drug and alcohol problems, unequal treatment by police) are not usually addressed. One reason why this orientation predominates might lie in the desire of newcomers for basic English communication skills and their need to find their bearings in a new community before they are ready to take on (or even discuss) broader and more complex issues of civic life. A second reason identified by teachers is that poorer immigrants often see the United States as a place of opportunity and are reluctant to talk about the negative aspects of their communities, lest they appear unappreciative. Avoiding negative aspects of life in the United States, however, can lead to a sterile and unengaging class, not to mention one that fails to address the many challenges immigrants face. A few simple activities can enrich the learners' experience beyond basic life skills and can lead to greater civic engagement. An activity that has worked to allow thoughts and feelings to emerge honestly without overpowering students at the Socorro program has been the use of poems that list the pros and cons of living in a particular community. Writing a piece on "Five Great Things About Living on the Border and Five Not so Great" provided a starting point for learners and teachers in Socorro. Students functioning at the beginner level wrote their poems in Spanish and then translated them into English. This was the case with the following poem:

El Paso and Juárez: My Two Homes

I love Juárez because I was born there
I remembered the mellow times when I was a child
and I could feel the tranquility of my border
At that time the people walked safely on the streets
and the children had fun wholesomely
and their innocence wasn't interrupted

> I am sad because nowadays all things have changed in my loved border
> Now we live a fast out of control life as a river overflowing or as a horse
> without reins

The student was videotaped by other students as she read her poem. The video and poem were then added by the students into a PowerPoint presentation that was later posted to the Internet. (This poem can be seen at http://www.bordercivics.org/Products/Lesson_Plans/Border_Poems_Desc_Table.htm)

As the poem was shared with other classes, it led to further discussions by students in other places. Even a civics class that focuses primarily on life skills and basic information about communities can provide an entry point into exploration of civic life in a particular region. Exploration of life on the border, where communication in two languages is the order of the day, invites the use of biliteracy in creative expression. As needed, Spanish is encouraged while students are developing materials. Since the school's focus is primarily on the development of English skills, English is used in the presentation of materials. Dual language use is encouraged and is a means of exploring how expressions and images differ from language to language and how poetic thoughts might be articulated in both languages.

Learning How to Learn Orientation

This approach emphasizes the development of cognitive process skills and understanding rather than specific content. This is not a common approach taken by teachers of ESOL, probably because project-based learning is generally not included in professional development for ESOL teachers (Wrigley, 2004a). One approach, however, that has resonated with teachers and students is a model that stresses language use outside of the classroom and connects learners to people and places within their community. This approach stresses the importance of structuring activities in such a way that trips to fairs, museums, or local agencies become not only an opportunity for understanding what a place has to offer, but also a way to use English in various community contexts. In an instructional module on how to use field trips to maximize language learning that was used in the Socorro family literacy program, students were shown how to apply cognitive learning strategies such as connecting prior knowledge to new knowledge, predicting (what they may see and hear), generating questions (asking crafts people questions about their products and work), and making connections between various learning events, such as exploring community art (visiting murals, outdoor sculptures, local galleries, and museums). These strategies for making connections and seeing commonalities and differences (key features in cognitive development and comprehension) are then further highlighted in the family literacy program where discussions with parents, who are eager to help their children be successful in their academic work, provide opportunities to explore how these strategies can be used in the native language (see chapter 1, this volume). The program stresses that in helping children succeed, English is not the only (and often not the most important) language to consider. Parents learn about research that shows that parents can support their children's school achievement by discussing with them ideas that matter (cause and effect, science concepts, exploration of the natural world) and that such academic success is fostered even if the language of the home and the language of the school are different (Snow, Burns, & Griffin, 1998; see chapter 1, this volume).

Basic Skills and Common Educational Core Orientation

This approach emphasizes not only the acquisition of a standard set of structural skills (phonemic awareness, vocabulary, grammar) related to language and literacy development, but also the learning of core concepts related to American history and government. The belief underlying this orientation stresses the need for strong foundation skills in language and literacy to be explicitly taught along with basic aspects of U.S. government and history. These often include key concepts, structures, and institutions (innocent until proven guilty, three branches of government, Supreme Court); important events (American Revolution, Civil War); and people who made a difference (George Washington, Abraham Lincoln, Martin Luther King). In its strong form, this orientation stresses the need for teaching complex values, such as unexamined patriotism ("the greatest country on earth," "my country, love it or leave it"), while weaker forms may seek to problematize some of these issues (the United States has separation of church and state, yet our money says "in God we trust," balancing majority rule with minority rights). Immigrant students are often quite eager to learn more about the United States and enjoy reading about historical figures and events. Feedback from teachers indicates that students like feeling and becoming "educated" and sharing in the kind of knowledge that is common among people who have gone to school in the United States. In the Socorro program, students were introduced to people and events that reflect American values, such as freedom of speech and the right to organize, while exploring biographies of people such as Dolores Huerta and Cesar Chavez.

Since most, if not all, of the instructional materials in the Socorro program were in English, teaching the official version of U.S. history presented in Immigration and Naturalization Service (INS) textbooks, with its emphasis on the Revolution, the Declaration of Independence, the Constitution, the Civil War, and the various presidents, was not attempted for the lower levels. Complex concepts, such as the tripartite powers and the branches of government, along with language, such as "we hold these truths to be self-evident" and "unalienable rights," cannot easily be explained in simple English, even to English-speaking students. Spanish-speaking students who had had limited opportunities for schooling in Mexico and whose literacy skills in Spanish were not fully developed would likely have had difficulty even if these concepts were translated, since their abstract nature makes them difficult to understand. This is especially true for students who do not have experience discussing government structures and processes.

Discussions and explorations of the key values of the United States, such as tolerance, civil rights, acceptance of diversity, religious freedom, and the separation of church and state, would be much easier to explain and discuss in the native language. The use of bilingual and biliterate approaches to these issues becomes even more critical as the United States prepares for a new citizenship exam. The new test (currently under development) will move away from allowing applicants to memorize 100 questions related to history and government toward a new construct designed to present and assess a more meaningful understanding of history and government. This approach requires a great deal more literacy as well as familiarity with multiple-choice formats. The potential that less educated immigrants might fail at a higher rate than is presently the case is a concern. In its response to the government's effort to change the citizenship exam, the National Academy of Sciences suggested that testing knowledge of history and government in the native language be considered, since the statute governing U.S. citizenship testing requires only knowledge of ordinary English. Whether the U.S. Citizenship and Immigration Service (USCIS), an office of the Department of Homeland Security and the agency that replaced the INS, will go along with this suggestion is somewhat doubtful, although the agency does plan to publish study guides in the major languages.

Personal and Cultural Relevance Orientation

This orientation emphasizes language development through the expression of personal feelings and thoughts and links cultural expressions with civic pride. It also seeks to maintain cultures and traditions within the context of an immigrant nation like the United States. This orientation assumes that adults are capable of assessing their learning needs and setting appropriate goals, and that doing so will increase their engagement with learning. Project-based learning is an approach capable of combining personal and cultural relevance through the identification of issues that have meaning to learners. The Socorro EL/Civics project is informed by both the tenets of engaged learning (emphasizing active learning and the creation of knowledge by learners) and Rogoff's (1990) model of cognitive apprenticeship and his work on the three planes of interaction: cognitive/individualistic, social and collaborative, and cultural. The project seeks to connect values and ideas from the immigrant culture with concepts and norms of the dominant culture through a special focus on issues related to diversity, multiculturalism, bilingualism, and biliteracy. The teachers and students address the quandary that immigrant families often face in wanting to raise children who are fluent in English, will be successful in U.S. schools, and can navigate American culture, but who will also honor traditional values associated with home and family. Since both English and Spanish are important to the Socorro students, they explore topics in both languages, publish their projects in English (being able to demonstrate their skills in English is very important to them), and present their projects in Spanish and English to other students (in Spanish for lower-level students and in English for more proficient groups). The projects that students have chosen include issues-oriented projects (domestic violence) as well as community awareness projects (community maps, a newscast focusing on issues related to family literacy, the local water shortage, and the success of an all-girl soccer team). Most popular by far, however, have been cultural projects, including alphabet books for adults focusing on the special features of the region (*c* is for Chile), and activities that focus on cultural artifacts (students wrote directions for making tortillas the old-fashioned way using a wooden tortilla press). Entry points into larger collaborative projects have been personal reflections of their experiences as new immigrants, the telling of family stories, and the creating of memory books for their children.

The groups chose to explore dual-language issues, bilingual education, and multiculturalism head-on as parents increasingly seek guidance on how to support their children's language development in both English and the home language, Spanish. To this end, parents explored their own early experiences with schooling in Mexico and now in a family literacy program in the United States. They mapped how family members negotiated between languages and cultures. Readings introduced them to the art and science of learning another language, and they conducted interviews with bilingual staff and other parents to help them see the role of bilingualism and biliteracy in the lives of individuals and communities on the border. Other options included creating a bilingual video with tips and hints for parents of bilingual children and a Q&A sheet to help parents maximize their own English language learning in a community that is largely Spanish speaking. These projects build on the parents' knowledge and interests, allowing them to move beyond being "learners" to becoming "creators" of knowledge that is shared with others.

Social Change Orientation

At the heart of civics education is the concept of civic responsibility and the assumption that one person working alone or in concert with others can make a difference. Literacy combined with civic action promotes empowerment in a way that memorization of how Congress works cannot (Mezirow, 1997). However, students who are new to the United States and have little experience with personal or civic empowerment and are often burdened by everyday survival may find it overwhelming to participate in broad-based social change activities. Moreover, with little understanding of how civic institutions operate in the United States, students engaged in civic action generally have to follow the leadership of a more knowledgeable and experienced person, such as their teacher or other person associated with the sponsoring organization. Even if the teacher embraces the action from a learning perspective, asking students to follow the leadership of another person (in participating in a demonstration designed to impact social policy, for example) may contribute little to self-empowerment or the acquisition of English. This is particularly true for immigrants and refugees who are relatively new to English, new to the concept of large-scale civic participation focused on social change, and new to the United States. Small, limited, and low-threat engagements in civic action, such as organizing a neighborhood cleanup activity, or even requesting from the city council a stop sign at a dangerous intersection, however, can fit neatly into an EL/Civics program. As illustrated in the Socorro students' advocacy project to fix potholes, civic action projects tend to be more engaging to students when they are generated by the students themselves.

Teachers in Socorro reported some success as a result of introducing scenarios that are based on issues that immigrant students have faced, such as an employer collaborating with the INS to turn over unsuspecting undocumented workers, and not being able to get a driver's license because social security numbers were required. Students have discussed these issues and brainstormed solutions, but neither students nor teachers were motivated to dig deeper in analyzing local inequities. Notions related to participatory education and a social justice orientation, however, came to life when discussions around unfairness were brought to the table by individual students who talked about their experiences and asked the group for help.

A session with elderly immigrants and refugees in the Chicago program started with everyday scenarios related to students' lives and ended with one man telling the story of how Public Aid was threatening to pull his support payments because he had recently turned over his house in Manila to his daughter. He talked of his concerns for his health (without support he would not be able to afford the many medications he had to take) and shared his unhappiness about no longer being able to work. In response, the class brainstormed ideas that ranged from talking to public officials and "doing a demonstration" (a woman from Romania suggested he write a sign that said "I have heart problems, please help me" and parade in front of the state house in Springfield) to finding support through a local mutual assistance agency. In the end, someone shared her way of dealing with problems, saying, "I pray, I sing," and then started to sing "Amazing Grace." Spontaneously, the other students joined in singing or just humming along—an experience that was quite moving to all. At the end of the session the old man who had shared his problem was in tears, thanking his fellow students by saying, "I love you and I know you love me. God bless you"—a clear expression of what education related to civic action can achieve for new immigrants not ready to take on the larger system but ready to consider smaller steps to help themselves and others confront barriers. By providing the student with an opportunity to share his concern and be heard, and by offering love and support, the class ended up as a strong community comprised of diverse cultures ready to help each other. This aspect of adult learning where students express their emotional needs and strive to be authentic with each other has been elaborated by Dirkx (1997).

Most ESOL programs incorporate several of the orientations listed here, which are appropriate to meet the varying needs of students and communities. However, teachers and administrators must be careful in how they combine program elements. An overly aggressive eclecticism can result in a hodgepodge of approaches that are confusing to students. Similarly, issues related to bilingualism and biliteracy need to be carefully considered both to promote the learning of English and to provide sufficient opportunities for more in-depth understanding of U.S. culture, history, and institutions, as well as expression and advocacy in the languages that make up the civic life of a community.

Strategies for Using Bilingualism and Biliteracy in the Classroom

In both training and teaching, it is necessary to address the dual-language needs of learners in ways that are systematic, coherent, and educationally sound. The native language of the learners can be used to enhance learning, give them immediate access to background knowledge, and make complex concepts and ideas understandable (see chapter 1, this volume). At the same time, programs must meet the need that adults have for learning English. Policy and funding priorities play an important role in how languages are used in the educational program (see chapter 2, this volume). For instance, both components of the program in Socorro are funded as an adult ESL program by the U.S. Department of Education (ED). While the U.S. Department of Labor (DOL) recognizes bilingual vocational education for adults as a viable instructional model, the Office of Adult and Vocational Education (part of ED) insists that both the language of the instruction and the goal of the program be English. This requirement includes instruction of preschool children in family literacy programs who only speak Spanish. This means that while Spanish is the dominant language of the individuals and the local community, the need for education in both languages is not officially recognized. The Socorro program was recently told that federal funds cannot be used to support classes leading to the GED in Spanish. This is despite the fact that many employers in El Paso require the GED and accept the certificate based on passing the test in either language. Nevertheless, in the ESL program in Socorro, both languages are used regularly by teachers and students alike.

To address these issues and build on research regarding the role of the native language in second language acquisition and the development of biliteracy (see chapter 1, this volume), programs must recognize the need that learners have to learn and live in two languages and help them use learning strategies that allow them to take advantage of what they know and can do. To that end, the teacher training conducted at the Socorro program introduced a multilayered approach that included discussion with students as to when, where, and how Spanish and English should be used in the ESL classroom. This included a preview/review model of instruction designed to take advantage of the bilingual nature of teaching and learning, and strategies for negotiating between languages when complex issues needed to be discussed in a language that students understood and felt comfortable with. The training also included short readings and discussions on how to raise bilingual children (many of the parents had their children in English immersion classes) and offered ideas for interview projects with teachers, staff, and fellow students to explore attitudes and values related to bilingualism and biliteracy in the Socorro community. Strategies for using both languages in teaching and learning are described below:

- Introduce class topics in terms of both content and process in Spanish to activate students' background knowledge and preview lesson.

  Concept vocabulary is explained in both languages, while everyday expressions are explained in English. Teachers then provide opportunities for hearing and using English that are well structured so that students can succeed. Instead of translation, teachers use modeling and realia to demonstrate a task. Students are asked to "give English a chance" and trust their ability to understand and use English even if they have only minimal English language skills to start. Time is then set aside to answer questions that students might have about the task, topic, or language. The discussion may be in English, Spanish, or both. Teachers then provide graphic organizers (such as concept maps or flowcharts) so that students can see and understand relationships between ideas without getting mired in words. The teachers may also use this opportunity to explain how English works, highlighting patterns in English (grammar, phonology, morphology) and engaging students in analysis, contrasting key differences between English and Spanish. More tasks that require use of English might follow. Finally, at the end of the session, the teacher reviews what has been learned in Spanish and then provides a synopsis in English to reinforce learning.

- Extend students' knowledge in English and Spanish through the use of homework and in-class assignments.

  Homework assignments are used to maximize exposure to English since most students at the beginning levels never use English outside of the classroom. Students may be asked to watch the local news first in Spanish and then in English and then compare which stories were highlighted or discuss the approaches to the news that the different stations (El Paso in Texas and Juarez in Chihuahua, Mexico) provide. Students are invited to write down two or three words that they understood in the English broadcast (most students are beginning English language learners) and some words that they somewhat understood but wondered about. Students discuss what they think were hot topics, often organizing their thoughts into what, where, who, how, and why, and then report their findings to the rest of the class. They then may look over newspaper articles that deal with a related topic, adding further depth to their knowledge and breadth to their language (proficiency). In the end, they may present the information in the form of the "weekly news" either orally in class or in writing. In many cases, students work in small groups to discuss topics in Spanish first, but then work together to present their ideas in English to the class as a whole. Projects that the students design and showcase follow a similar pattern: Students decide on a topic using both English and Spanish to discuss ideas; they then research the topic using resources such as the Internet or encyclopedias in English and Spanish, and finally create and present materials either in two languages or in English. One group of students created a video entitled "The Socorro News" that included sections in both English and Spanish. Another group had written stories they had heard as children in both English and Spanish ("La Llorona" was a favorite among the group members).

- Use formal presentations geared to specific audiences to challenge and reinforce students' learning.

The notion of the functions of literacy as cultural practice, as described by Sparks (2002), was exemplified in Socorro. Presenting their projects (live skits, PowerPoint presentations, videos) to a larger audience of teachers and students in El Paso was both a major challenge and a major success for the students in the program. Doing so almost entirely in English was a greater accomplishment still; students spent many hours negotiating between English and Spanish to capture the right ideas and get the language just right. Doing the hard work and getting large amounts of positive feedback helped to increase both the competence and the confidence of the students who had never used English in a public forum. Yet, all classes realized the importance of also presenting their research and cultural projects in Spanish, both to reinforce the connection between the two languages and to make the information accessible to other classmates, spouses, children, and other family members. Each year, the students in the family literacy component of the Socorro program present their projects in Spanish at the different schools in the area (Even Start classes are spread throughout the community) at smaller showcases. While the projects themselves remain in English, discussions on why the projects were chosen, how they were developed, and what results were achieved take place in the language the group prefers (most often in Spanish). Thus, Spanish acts as a way to hold the groups together, while English serves to further increase language learning.

- Build in opportunities for students to explore culture and history to foster their engagement in their learning.

   Exploration of local culture and history is an integral part of adult
learning (Amstutz, 1999; Talmadge, 1999) in the EL/Civics projects in
Socorro. Students visited the El Paso Museum of Art, went to a local
artist's gallery, toured murals in El Paso, and interviewed staff at a local
bakery. The inclusion of culture and history in the adult education program seems to be a characteristic shared by many community-based
bilingual programs (see chapter 1, this volume). Since civics education
involves both strengthening community connections and building the
background knowledge of students new to the United States, the project
has developed materials around people and events that serve as a starting point to explore ideas and make connections between past, present,
and future. One set of lessons contains a set of quotes by famous artists; students are invited to discuss the quote and make connections to
both their own lives and current events. Quotes can be in either English
or Spanish. One set of quotes in Spanish included political statements
by Emilliano Zapata ("Es mejor morir de pie que vivir de rodillas" [It
is better to die standing up than to live kneeling down]) and Martin
Luther King ("We should never forget that everything Adolf Hitler did
in Germany was legal and everything the Hungarian Freedom Fighters
did was illegal") to tie together various civil rights movements. Students
also read a statement on relationships by Frida Kahlo, "I suffered two
grave accidents in my life. One in which a streetcar knocked me down.
The other accident is Diego." A quote by Cesar Chavez combined the
personal and the political: "You are never strong enough that you don't
need help."

   Students then engage in further exploration of the cultural or political contexts on either side of the border that gave shape to these statements. For example, individuals may choose a quote and a person to explore via Web Quests that
list Web addresses for both English and Spanish language Web sites. Students
then delve further into historical events, reading and discussing materials such as
"I Have a Dream" in English and Spanish and comparing two translations in the
process, one generated by a computer and the other written by a person, which
leads to a great deal of discussion around language competence and what it takes
to capture the meaning of a piece in translation. Readings may include a short
background piece on the Bracero program and its contribution to the working
conditions of Mexican farmworkers in the United States. Again, Web sites written in both English and Spanish serve to encourage students to dig deeper and
follow their interests. Students often listen to music as part of the exploration of
a topic. One example has been songs inspired by the plane crash at Los Gatos,
California, an event in which a crew of farmworkers being sent home was killed.
The names of the workers were never mentioned, and they were simply listed in

the papers as "deportees." Students listen to various versions of the "Deportee" song written by Woodie Guthrie and compare different interpretations sung by Arlo Guthrie, Joan Baez, and Peter, Paul and Mary. Teachers also introduce modern artists who speak to the same cultural and political issues, such as the songs by Lila Downs, who recorded both "El Bracero Fracasado" [The Failed Bracero] and "This Land Is Your Land (It Used to Be Our Land)," a comment on the historical dealings related to the Treaty of Guadalupe and the Gadsden Purchase, both of which shaped the lives of people and the conditions of the border communities in which students now live.

Conclusion

It is by no means clear what will happen to the federally funded EL/Civics program in the future. The program is burdened with the politics of what it means to be American and what are perceived as acceptable strategies for integrating new immigrants into the mainstream of American culture. But as it stands, with its open mandate and lack of specificity of approach, the EL/Civics program allows for the development of learning strategies largely based on the immigrants' strengths and needs. This includes helping them to develop the knowledge, skills, and strategies they need to successfully navigate systems, meet their own potential, and make their voices heard as members of both immigrant communities and U.S. society at large. By developing ways to connect learners to both their immigrant community and the wider community, EL/Civics programs can help language minorities find grounding in their own culture while feeling connected to other groups. In sharing their stories and their work with others, adult learners can feel welcomed, affirmed, respected, and valued, and can in turn extend these feelings to other groups different from themselves. In making issues around language use and language values explicit, and by inviting learners to explore what it means to become and remain biliterate, these programs can help strengthen the language resources of families, communities, and the nation.

References

Amstutz, D. (1999). Adult learning: Moving towards more inclusive practices. In C. G. Talmadge (Ed.), *Providing culturally relevant adult education: A challenge for the twenty-first century* (pp. 19–32, New Directions for Continuing Education Series). San Francisco: Jossey-Bass.

Condelli, L., Wrigley, H. S., Yoon, K., Cronen, S., & Seburn, M. (2003). *What works study for adult ESL literacy students* (Final Report). Washington DC: U.S. Department of Education, Office of the Under Secretary.

Demetrion, G. (2005). *Conflicting paradigms in adult literacy education: In quest of a U.S. democratic politics of literacy.* Mahwah, NJ: Lawrence Erlbaum Associates.

Dirkx, J. M. (1997). Nurturing the soul in adult learning. In P. Cranton (Ed.), *Transformative learning in action: Insights from practice* (pp. 79–88, New Directions for Continuing Education Series). San Francisco: Jossey-Bass.

Eisner, E. W. (1994). *The educational imagination: On the design and evaluation of school programs* (3rd ed.). New York: Maxwell Macmillan International.

Federal Register. (1999, November 17). Vol. 64, No. 221. U.S. Government Printing Office. Retrieved May 1, 2006, from http://www.ed.gov/legislation/FedRegister/announcements/1999-4/111799b.html

Johnston, J. (1999). *Enhancing adult literacy instruction with video.* Unpublished manuscript, University of Michigan, Ann Arbor.

Kloss, H. (1998). *The American bilingual tradition.* Washington DC: Center for Applied Linguistics and Delta Systems.

Mezirow, J. (1997). Transformative learning: Theory to practice. In P. Cranton (Ed.), *Transformative learning in action: Insights from practice* (pp. 5–12, New Directions for Continuing Education Series). San Francisco: Jossey-Bass.

Rogoff, B. (1990). *Apprenticeship in thinking: Cognitive development in social context.* New York: Oxford University Press.

Snow, C. E., Burns, M. S., & Griffin, P. (Eds.). (1998). *Preventing reading difficulties in young children.* Washington, DC: National Academy Press.

Sparks, B. (2002). Adult literacy as cultural practice. In M. V. Alfred (Ed.), *Learning & sociocultural contexts: Implications for adults, community, and workplace education* (pp. 59–68, New Directions for Continuing Education Series). San Francisco: Jossey-Bass.

Talmadge, C. G. (1999). Culture as context for adult education: The need for culturally relevant adult education. In C. G. Talmadge (Ed.), *Providing culturally relevant adult education: A challenge for the twenty-first century* (pp. 5–18, New Directions for Continuing Education Series). San Francisco: Jossey-Bass.

U.S. Department of Education. (1999). *English literacy and demonstration grants program, archived information.* Retrieved May 1, 2006, from http://www.ed.gov/programs/elcivics/elcivgrant2.html.

Weinstein-Shr, G. (1995). Learning from uprooted families. In G. Weinstein-Shr and E. Quintero (Eds.), *Immigrant learners and their families: Literacy to connect the generations.* Washington, DC: Center for Applied Linguistics and Delta Systems.

Wong Fillmore, L. (1991). When learning a second language means losing the first. *Early Childhood Research Quarterly, 6,* 323–347.

Wrigley, H. (2004a). We are the world: Serving language minority adults in family literacy programs. In B. H. Wasik (Ed.), *Handbook on family literacy: Research and services* (pp. 449–466). Mahwah, NJ: Lawrence Erlbaum Associates.

Wrigley, H. (2004b, June). Research in action: Teachers, projects, and technology. *Literacy Links, 8.* Texas Center for the Advancement of Literacy and Learning, College Station, Texas A&M University.

PART III
Themes, Issues, Challenges

8

Capturing What Counts

Language and Literacy Assessments for Bilingual Adults

Heide Spruck Wrigley

> *Not everything that counts can be tested and not everything that's tested counts.*
>
> **—Attributed to Albert Einstein**

Learner assessment is one of the most contested issues in learning and teaching, and the field of language learning and biliteracy development is no exception. In fact, the arguments for and against different types of assessments become even more contentious as dual-language issues are taken into account. Since bilingual learners, by definition, need to negotiate between what they know in the native language and what they are trying to learn in the new language, effective assessments should be able to capture what students know and are able to do in two languages.

Currently, teachers and programs serving bilingual adults are caught between having to use standardized tests to meet accountability requirements—tests that often fail to capture the full range of learning gains that literacy students are able to make—and having to find or create alternative assessments that provide more meaningful insights into who is learning what, how, and why. Assessing the strengths and challenges faced by adult bilingual learners is complicated by the fact that tests that consider the dual nature of language proficiency in adults are hard to find. Similarly, notions of biliteracy are noticeably absent from discussions of adult tests and testing practices.

This chapter will address some of the complexities that surround assessments for language minority adults. It will start with a brief overview of the advantages and shortcomings of standardized tests and will move on to discuss options for alternative program-based assessments. Finally, the chapter will offer descriptions and examples of different types of alternative assessments that are more likely to provide a rich portrait of what bilingual adults can do as they seek to make meaning and express ideas in one or more languages.

The Complexity of Assessing Language and Literacy

Assessing literacy in any language is a complicated undertaking made so by the fact that language and literacy are extremely complex processes as yet not fully understood (Alderson, 2000; Bachman, 1990; Ellis, 1997; Grabe, 2004). Since literacy cannot be separated from language, and language is central to cognition, communication, and culture, selecting or creating assessments that capture all the essential aspects of literacy provides a significant challenge, one that must entail making decisions about which domains to test explicitly and which domains to deemphasize. When we consider that proficiency in any language is multidimensional, encompassing not only literacy skills related to reading and writing, but also oral communication skills associated with speaking and listening, in addition to the sociocultural and pragmatic skills concerned with the appropriateness of oral and written discourse, the enormity of any testing endeavor is evident. If we add to the functional aspects of language (i.e., being able to communicate effectively) the structural components of language, such as morphology (word endings and their meanings), syntax (sentence structure and tenses), phonology (sound system), and vocabulary, it becomes clear that no one type of test can come close to addressing all the essential elements of proficiency. By necessity, tests are only able to capture a subset of elements of language. As a result, the knowledge and skills assessed by any given test may not be those considered most important by students, teachers, administrators, or even funders. In the end, what is tested is what can be tested efficiently, and the complex nature of language tends to pose too much of a challenge to be captured easily.

For bilingual adults and those on their way to becoming biliterate, the elements of language that must be learned exist in two languages, and the processes by which they interact and either support each other or provide barriers are not yet fully understood. The minds of bilingual adults acquiring another language constantly negotiate two language systems, and effective assessments must take into account the degree of bilingualism and biliteracy an individual possesses. For example, second language learners may or may not have high levels of literacy in the native language, may or may not have had the experience of participating in formal schooling, and may or may not be able to read and write in English at the same level that they can communicate ideas orally. All of these factors influence how quickly or how well a learner is able to acquire and use language skills, and sound assessments that address proficiency both in the native language (L1) and in the target language (L2) are needed to help practitioners, administrators, and policy makers make informed decisions.

To capture what bilingual adults know and are able to do in two languages is a complicated endeavor, although these notions are seldom considered when tests in adult English as a Second Language (ESL) programs are selected or administered. Instead, current assessments for adults are almost solely focused on capturing what students can do in English. Students whose assessments show that they understand and speak no or little English are commonly placed into a single class, with the result that individuals who may never have gone to school at all and who have minimal literacy skills in any language are expected to learn at the same rate as adults who have graduated from high school and have strong reading and writing skills in the first language. The implications of relying solely on an English assessment are cause for concern: neither programs nor teachers have the information necessary to design differentiated learning experiences that support those who are learning to read for the first time and, at the same time, provide appropriate challenges for those who can easily transfer reading skills from L1 to English.

To remedy this situation, a more nuanced approach of assessing bilingual adults is required, an approach that takes into account the four key elements of biliteracy: the level of literacy in the native language (L1) and the level of literacy in the new language (L2), along with the levels of oral proficiency in both L1 and L2.[1]

Approaches to Literacy Assessment

Given the many perspectives on the roles, functions, and uses of literacy, it is not surprising that approaches to literacy assessment vary widely. Some programs select tests that focus on evaluating overall communicative competence through integrated tasks, while others focus on one or more particular skill areas, such as reading, writing, speaking, and listening. As the emphasis on basic reading continues—reinforced by the No Child Left Behind Act—tests that focus on the components or subskills of reading are finding their way into adult literacy (see Davidson and Strucker, 2002). Developers of component assessments are less interested in test results that indicate how well students navigate the print demands of daily life (e.g., getting information from the newspaper, writing a note to a child's teacher, finding the best price for tomatoes based on a supermarket flyer) and are more concerned about the underlying skills that make reading comprehension possible (e.g., phonemic awareness, fluency, decoding, vocabulary).

Most of the adult language tests currently in use—life skills oriented or component oriented—rely on a narrow set of skills. Students may be asked to identify a correct response from a set of multiple-choice answers, read a series of words or sentences to demonstrate skills associated with fluency and decoding, or respond to an oral prompt (e.g., "Tell me about this picture"). While results on these tests provide an indicator of general competence in a language—more proficient students tend to score higher than less proficient students—they often lack face validity in the eyes of learners and teachers. That is, they do not represent the broader language challenges that students face outside of the classroom—challenges that come into play when disputing a traffic ticket, negotiating an eviction notice, or trying to understand breaking news on the radio.

Efforts are now under way in the United States to develop standardized assessments that capture a broader scope of proficiency-related skills through performance-based assessments that mirror literacy tasks reflective of real-life demands. Among the major assessments of this kind is a Reading Demonstration, first developed for the national *What Works Study for Adult ESL Literacy Students* (Condelli and Wrigley, 2006). The Reading Demonstration is a functional literacy assessment that asks beginning readers to name everyday items that they recognize (chosen from such common items as a Coca-Cola can, a McDonald's bag, a lottery ticket, a grocery store insert, or an electric bill). Students are asked to select an item that they can recognize and read as much as they can as the assessor expresses encouragement and asks follow-up questions.[2] The assessment has been successfully used by teachers in adult ESL programs in an effort to assess English literacy skills of students who are unable to demonstrate what they can do with literacy on a pencil-and-paper test. Programs serving nontraditional language learners, such as the elderly, farmworkers, or others who have not had the opportunity to develop school-based literacy skills, are especially well served by an assessment of this kind, one that asks adults to identify what they know, recognize, and can read, thus allowing them to demonstrate competence, rather than ignorance.

The Reading Demonstration has been adapted by the U.S. Center for Educational Statistics for use in the National Assessment of Adult Literacy (NAAL)[3] in the form of ALSA, the Adult Literacy Supplemental Assessment. ALSA is designed to give low literacy adults who cannot complete the main NAAL items a chance to demonstrate what they can do with print (e.g., identify key words on a food package, point to a key message in a simple announcement, or determine the cost of an item on a supermarket flyer). Since the test uses actual items that respondents might use or see as part of their daily lives, test takers can use visual clues such as logos, pictures, or charts.

The ALSA contains features that are quite unusual for a national literacy assessment used in the United States. Examiners are bilingual, and respondents may choose either English or Spanish as the language they want to hear when directions are given or tasks are clarified (the items themselves are written in

English). Background questions that probe employment status, family circumstances, and educational backgrounds are asked in Spanish as well, if the respondent requests that language.

The ALSA portion of the National Assessment of Adult Literacy contains other innovative features. For example, test takers:

- Have the opportunity to work with materials they are likely to recognize and that appear in their authentic form rather than on photocopied pages, as is the case in almost all other standardized literacy assessments
- Sit across from a person rather than look at a test booklet or a computer screen
- Do not have to struggle with reading directions since the questions and prompts are presented orally in either English or Spanish
- Get a chance to hear questions and directions in a language they understand

While ALSA is only available as a national assessment and not as a program assessment—there are no pre- and post-test versions of the assessment—it nevertheless points the way toward more authentic assessments that allow low literacy Spanish-speaking respondents to demonstrate what they can do with literacy. By making L1 support an option, the ALSA moves language and literacy assessments for bilingual adults ahead a step or two. The door of assessing literacy bilingually has now been opened,[5] and the United States has the opportunity to extend language support beyond Spanish. In fact, a report by the National Academy of Sciences (NAS) has recommended that efforts should be made to include speakers of languages other than Spanish so that a fuller national picture of what adults know and are able to do with literacy can emerge.

Currently under development on a national level are other large-scale performance-based assessments that have greater content validity than pencil-and-paper tests. Equipped for the Future (EFF), a national initiative started by the National Institute for Literacy, is developing authentic assessment tasks as part of their learning, teaching, and assessment system. The language and literacy tasks being created are meant to reflect the challenges that adults face every day as they interact with print, try to understand what others are saying, or attempt to get their point across in spoken or written language (Stein, 2000). Although not developed specifically for bilingual adults, the EFF performance-based assessment system shows promise in moving the field away from pencil-and-paper-based tests toward assessments that allow learners to demonstrate competence on tasks that reflect real-life challenges.

Types of Tests Commonly Used in the Field

Currently, a range of assessments are used by programs serving language minority adults. Most states now require a standardized test for accountability and leave it up to individual programs to create and use alternatives. As a result, programs may use a patchwork of assessments that are not always linked through a coherent framework. Following a taxonomy developed by Lytle and Wolfe (1989), the assessments used by programs can be divided into four main types:

- Standardized test, which may be either norm referenced (students are compared to each other, most often across programs) or criterion referenced (student achievement is compared to an externally derived standard)
- Materials-based assessment, in which assessment is based on a particular set of teaching materials, often commercially packaged and sold
- Competency-based assessment, in which learner performance is compared to pre-established competencies that need to be achieved
- Participatory assessment, in which learners play a significant role in deciding both the content and process of assessment

For program purposes, we can combine these four assessment areas into two broad categories:

- Formal assessments, such as standardized tests, that are designed to measure achievement, knowledge, and skills of large groups of students across programs. The standardized tests selected by states are said to have "content validity" (they measure components related to language and literacy development). Since they are used across states and curricula differ a great deal from site to site and program to program, standardized tests do not reflect what individual teachers teach. Nor are they related to the goals that propel immigrants to participate in programs. These tests do, however, reflect the larger goals of the system, namely, to improve the language and literacy skills of adults (as defined by the tests) who are not yet proficient in English. Almost none of the formal assessments used in programs seek to capture what students can do in the native language. Rather, they focus solely on English proficiency skills of various kinds.
- Program-based assessments that reflect the educational approach and literacy curriculum of a particular program. These assessments seek to capture what students know and what they want to know, and they tend to take a broader view of literacy, encompassing not only basic skills, but also skills and strategies related to literacy behaviors used across cultures and languages. Some programs, most notably those serving youth, may include knowledge, skills, and understanding related to affective factors and social and emotional development (Wrigley, 2003). While programs have a great deal of leeway in selecting or creating assessments designed to capture levels of native language literacy, few have the expertise or the resources to do so.

Standardized Testing

When it comes to systematic assessment across programs, standardized tests dominate adult education. This is true for second language learning, adult literacy, and ESL literacy. One reason for the popularity of standardized assessments may lie in the history of testing in the United States, and the recent mandates of the National Reporting System, which has emphasized the need for program accountability and sees program quality largely in terms of increases in test scores and less in data that demonstrate that education meets the needs, desires, and interests of the adults for whom the system is designed (Merrifield, 1998).

Standardized tests are also used in large-scale research and evaluation studies that seek to determine to what extent one approach might be more effective than another in increasing the English literacy skills of adults on their way to becoming bilingual. Following the maxim that no single test can provide sufficient information to make high-stakes decisions (Brown, 2001), national studies tend to combine various assessments, selecting separate tests to capture the different skills associated with language proficiency. For example, now under way in the United States is a large-scale five-year evaluation designed to determine the effectiveness of a life skills curriculum that is enhanced through the explicit teaching of English literacy to adults who have only limited literacy in the native language. The National Impact Evaluation of Adult ESL Literacy, carried out by the American Institutes for Research and funded by the Institute for Education Studies (IES) branch of the Department of Education, is expected to combine component testing focused on fluency and decoding with an assessment that captures reading comprehension skills and English communication skills. Since most English literacy learners are Spanish speakers, the study is likely to include a Spanish language assessment designed to capture the relative levels of Spanish literacy that a study participant might possess so that relationships between Spanish literacy and gains in English literacy can be established. While studies of this sort rely heavily on standardized tests, using them as the center part of their assessment efforts, they nevertheless recognize that a single test is not likely to capture all or even most key skills that make up the language proficiency of a bilingual adult. Rather, these national evaluations employ a battery of tests, each designed to capture a different element of language competence. This notion, that no one test can do justice to the complexity of dual-language proficiency has strong implications for both program practice and program accountability where currently a one-dimensional view of what it means to be competent in a language prevails.

Advantages of Standardized Tests

Standardized tests are popular because they offer certain advantages: (1) their construct validity and scoring reliability have been tested, (2) they are cost effective and do not require a great deal of training to administer, (3) funding sources accept them as part of the documentation of program accountability, (4) they allow for comparisons of learner progress across programs, and (5) they give learners a sense of where they stand compared to students in other programs (see also Brindley, 1989).

Shortcomings of Standardized Tests

In spite of their apparent advantages, standardized tests have a number of disadvantages. These are most evident in the standardized tests commonly in use in adult literacy, that is, pencil-and-paper tests that use a multiple-choice format. In general, these types of standardized tests:

- Fail to distinguish among language, literacy, and culture. In other words, they do not tell us whether a learner has trouble with an item because he or she (1) is unfamiliar with the cultural notion underlying the task, (2) lacks the requisite knowledge of English vocabulary or sentence structure, or (3) does not have enough experience with reading and writing to complete the task.
- Reduce the complexity of language and literacy learning to a discrete set of skills, ignoring the integrative nature of language.
- Do not reflect what has been taught or capture all the learning that has taken place.
- Do not capture changes in language use and literacy practices beyond the classroom.
- Do not provide data on the sociolinguistic and affective dimensions of language and literacy.
- Do not discriminate well at the lower end of literacy achievement, failing to capture experience with environmental print or provide information on the different levels of initial literacy, such as being able to write the names of one's children but not those of strangers.
- Focus on print-based tasks, the very things that literacy students have trouble with.
- Do not provide opportunities for literacy students to show what they can do in "real life."

Standardized Tests and English Language Learning Adults

While these shortcomings hold true for any standardized test, there are additional concerns if these instruments are used to assess the literacy levels of adult English language learners who face literacy challenges.

ESL literacy learners may not be familiar with the cultural conventions underlying these tests. For example, one ESL test asks students to read a label on a piece of prepackaged meat, listing weight, price per pound, and total price.

Students who are not used to buying their meat prepackaged may have difficulty understanding the underlying concept, even though they might be able to read the individual words (see Weinstein-Shr, 1988). Standardized tests, in an effort to be "fair" to all, either discount the unique background knowledge that learners bring to school or assume that cultural conventions are universal and shared across the countries of origins of the students.

Standardized tests often fail to distinguish between language problems, in which the learner is unfamiliar with the language or concepts of the test item, and literacy problems, in which the learner lacks the requisite reading and writing skills but could easily respond to similar items presented as part of a conversation.

Standardized tests treat language and literacy as isolated from the social context of the learner. Students are assessed individually, and no help may be given or received. ESL literacy students, as a rule, work together to help each other solve problems that require English or reading and writing and often develop strong coping skills and social networks that allow them to deal with problems that require literacy. By disallowing access to resources, peer assistance, or group work, standardized tests fail to measure the very strengths that many bilingual adults bring to class, the ability and willingness to work together and solve problems collaboratively.

In addition, most standardized tests fail to take into account the wide range of literacy practices in which learners engage in their mother tongues. By disregarding the biliteracy aspect of ESL literacy, they give the impression that literacy in English is the only literacy that counts (Macías, 1990; Wiley, 1996). As such, they fail to provide valuable information about learners' past and current experiences with literacy in two languages (see chapter 1, this volume). In cases where assessments are available in both English and Spanish, they often represent parallel tests that test either or both languages, but do not reflect the thinking or language use of bilingual adults living in dual-language environments. These adults do not use one language or the other, but rather use both, and quite often combine knowledge of L1 in efforts to explain or deal with tasks in L2, in the process of being able to demonstrate what they know, get a point across to monolingual English speakers, and communicate comfortably with other bilingual adults. When assessed, these adults may use L1 phonology to demonstrate fluency in English and in the process give the impression that they do not have decoding skills when in fact their decoding skills are quite strong, but may be covered by pronunciation difficulties. Similarly, when bilingual adults are given word lists to read, they might move back and forth between phonological systems, pronouncing words that could belong to either language sometimes in the home language and sometimes in English (e.g., *come* could be either an English or Spanish word). Similarly, bilingual adults may code switch between languages in speaking, reading aloud, or writing, a mode quite natural for this group, but a process not easily captured as an example of positive use across languages (see also Escamilla's [2000] work with bilingual children). Unless test designers and assessors are aware of these tendencies, second language speakers being tested might be diagnosed and labeled as deficient in either language, rather than as readers and writers capable of drawing upon two systems simultaneously.

Program-Based Assessments

In an effort to make assessments more responsive to the concerns of learners and teachers, many programs are developing and using alternatives to standardized tests (see Wrigley, 2000). These assessments are meant to influence teaching and learning; that is, they are expected to have "consequential validity" and serve as a tool for continuous monitoring so that instruction that meets learners where they are can be planned and executed. Among the advantages of program-based alternative assessments are that they:

- Reflect the local curriculum and provide information that is helpful to the program.
- Are developed by the individual program, sometimes with the help of evaluators or other researchers, and thus are responsive to the program context.
- Focus on learning processes, not just outcomes, allowing for trial and error instead of giving learners just one chance to answer each question; they do not insist on a "cold start" response.
- Actively involve learners by giving them the opportunity to (1) discuss their goals and interests in literacy, (2) choose the kind of reading and writing they want to be evaluated on, and (3) talk about what they have learned. In other words, they are part of a process in which assessment is done with adults, not to them.

Most importantly, perhaps, alternative assessments go beyond conventional skills-based notions of language and literacy. When carried out as part of an initial intake process and repeated at regular intervals during the teaching cycle, they can provide information that can be used for curriculum development.

Increasingly, alternative assessments also focus on nonlinguistic factors, such as learners' changing perceptions of what it means to be literate, how to help one's children to enjoy literacy, increased confidence in one's ability to deal with tasks that require literacy, and a stronger voice in presenting one's own ideas. In addition, assessments that capture turbulent issues (such as illness, unemployment, etc.) and other factors that shape opportunities to learn and succeed are finding their way into programs serving adult English language learners and their families.

What Should Be Assessed?

Given the multidimensional nature of language and literacy learning (Kucer, 2001) and the integral relationship between first and second language literacies, decisions regarding what should be assessed and how remain significant challenges. However, since the needs and interests of adults participating in programs go beyond the acquisition of basic skills, it seems worthwhile to assess knowledge, skills, and strategies in a number of domains and consider progress and success in at least two areas: those related to language and literacy development and those related to nonlinguistic aspects. Nonlinguistic domains may relate to broader aspects of learning, such as increased civic engagement, along with greater confidence and competence, which may translate into increased abilities to take advantage of existing opportunities and create new opportunities for oneself and others.

Evidence of success in language and literacy development may include the following:

- Increases in English proficiency, including gains in strategic, sociolinguistic, grammatical, and rhetorical competence
- Progress in reading, including increased use of reading and writing strategies; systematic use of verbal and nonverbal clues to access print, predict meaning, and confirm predictions; a broader range of reading materials selected and read; and more sustained reading
- Progress in literacy development, including greater ability to express thoughts, ideas, and feelings in print; developing a sense of voice; and demonstrating style and creativity
- Greater approximation to standard English writing conventions; increased ability to self-edit
- Greater ability to use literacy in efforts to link personal experience with the experiences of others and with writings from the larger community, society, and the world
- Greater sense of "critical literacy," using language to connect personal and collective experiences and to examine the circumstances of one's life
- A broader range of literacy practices in the classroom, at home, in the community, and at work
- Increased engagement with print in both languages
- A deeper awareness of the role that literacy and biliteracy can play in one's life and in the life of the community

Evidence of success in nonlinguistic domains may include the following:

- Increased participation in a language and literacy program
- Greater confidence in one's ability to handle challenges, a feeling of greater independence, and pride in one's accomplishments

- Increased opportunities for job placement or advancement, admission to vocational or training programs, and transition to mainstream ESL or academic classes
- Increases in civic engagement and greater involvement in community activities or in efforts to advocate for oneself and others
- Greater confidence in one's own abilities and increased self-efficacy
- Greater social and emotional maturity (particularly for populations labeled "at risk")

Assessment at Different Stages of a Program

Assessments have multiple functions and uses. They (1) provide information on the context in which literacy occurs (workplace, family, school, community); (2) serve as initial assessments of the strengths that learners bring to the program and of the challenges they face; (3) indicate the levels of proficiency learners have attained in language and literacy; (4) help document the needs, goals, and interests of the learners; (5) document the progress learners are making and the changes that occur in their lives; and (6) provide evidence of program success and show where a learner may need additional development or support.

Different forms of assessments serve different functions, and different types of assessments are used at various stages of a program. These types include community needs assessments, intake assessments, initial assessments, progress assessments, and performance reviews.

Community Needs Assessments   Community needs assessments are designed to identify the needs and goals of potential participants. Information may include demographic data, information on employment patterns in the community, and the availability of child care or transportation services. Needs assessment information is often used to decide on scheduling, class sites, and the kinds of ancillary services that will be provided. At the work site, the needs assessment often takes the form of a situational analysis, which describes the context in which the workplace literacy program takes place. Since the goal of these assessments is to gather information, it is important to ask questions in a language that potential participants can understand (quite often this cannot be English) and allow for plenty of opportunities to discuss, clarify, ask questions, and make recommendations. For programs intended to serve beginning English learners, these conversations have to be held in the native language if they are to have any validity.

Intake Assessments   Intake assessments are designed to elicit information regarding learners' needs, goals, and prior educational backgrounds, including previous experience with both schooling and literacy, whether in English or in the mother tongue. Intake increasingly includes information on how, where, and why learners are using English and literacy in their daily lives, such as at home, in the community, at work, or in their interactions with the school system. Some intake assessments also try to probe the perceptions of literacy that learners bring to class and the expectations that learners bring to the program. Again, bilingual assessors are needed to offer non-English speakers the opportunity to tell their stories in a language they can handle and with which they are comfortable.

Initial Assessments   Initial assessments are designed to gauge how proficient a learner is in English and may also measure what levels of biliteracy he or she possesses. Used as diagnostic tests for placement, for development of a learning plan, or as a baseline against which progress can be measured, initial assessments now frequently include learner self-assessment and, in some cases, peer assessment.

Progress Assessments   Progress assessments are designed to show changes in the ways students are interpreting print and using literacy. While these assessments have traditionally been dependent on how well students can do pencil-and-paper tests, we now increasingly find assessments that look beyond the test and seek information on how learners use literacy and English to explore and express ideas, solve problems, or effect changes in their lives. Progress assessments are often used in formative evaluations designed to provide feedback to learners and teachers and improve program services and literacy classes.

Documenting Social Contexts as Part of Assessment   ESL programs that are part of comprehensive social service models, most often those that are part of community-based organizations, often take a broader view of what it takes for adults to succeed. They may see success in language and literacy development connected to the larger social, economic, and cultural factors that shape learners' lives and may seek to work together with the adults they serve to address challenges, improve individual circumstances, and advocate for social change (see Rivera, this volume). In these programs, documenting challenges and barriers to both individual learning and social well-being provides a basis for understanding the lives of learners and a starting point for advocacy.

Gaining a broader sense of students' lives beyond the classroom also provides insights to teachers and counselors who may wonder why some students are angry and hostile while others may appear quiet and subdued, but may nevertheless be alienated from their peers and disengaged from school-based learning. These profiles are common in inner-city programs that serve immigrant youth who may be foreign born but whose schooling has taken place largely in the United States and may be part of the 1.5 generation[6] or women who are mandated to improve their work-related language skills in order to not lose government support.

One assessment that looks at social context is the Family and Community Development Matrix, a tool used by a number of community action groups in California and elsewhere serving farmworkers, as well as by the Youth Literacy Demonstration Program in British Columbia, Canada. As used in the youth project (see Wrigley, 2003), the matrix provides a framework for capturing information that students and parents and other caretakers share in interviews and through conversations. All private information remains confidential and is shared in aggregate form only. The matrix helps capture where families see themselves on a continuum from in crisis to thriving, along a range of social indicators such as health, family relationships, employment, and safety. This information can then be used for various purposes: to capture social concerns and document the work done (or not done) by social service agencies, to gain insights into student needs so that appropriate support can be developed, and to document the number of families in crisis. Assessments of this sort can be used to document both needs and gaps in services and to advocate for better support and increased funding.

Major Challenges and Promising Practices

Alternative assessments are not without their shortcomings. Many teacher-made assessments are ambiguous and home-grown assessments often lack rigor. They can be highly unreliable, and if used unchecked, they may be worse than standardized tests that have undergone a lengthy process of field testing and norming. If alternative assessments are to provide more than insights to a single teacher, practitioners must be trained in creating and implementing assessments and in analyzing and interpreting results. Additionally, teachers working with bilingual students must also understand the complexities of second language development. Since most adult literacy teachers are already underpaid and overworked, asking individual teachers to take on the task of designing tests is not likely to yield instruments capable of capturing data that are meaningful beyond the classroom setting. If program-based assessments are to be trustworthy and capture how well students can express and understand ideas, they must be created by educators who have been trained in developing assessments so that information about student progress and achievement can be considered valid and reliable. Given the knowledge, time, and financial resources necessary to develop assessments that meet even basic testing standards, it may seem unrealistic to expect teachers to develop assessments that can meet the accountability requirements of funding agencies that demand pre- and post-test data on student learning across classrooms. This, however, does not mean that programs should be discouraged from constructing assessments that inform program development and help teachers make decisions about instruction.

Locally developed assessments are particularly important in bilingual settings since instruments that capture the needs, abilities, and progress made by bilingual adults are often not available. The following section presents a case in point that illustrates the collaboration between teachers and educators with deep knowledge of both bilingual learners and assessment methods.

A Framework for Assessment of Bilingual Learners in El Paso

Several years ago, the Small Group Instruction Project at El Paso Community College used a curriculum that was based on generative themes important to the students (see Huerta-Macías and Quintero, 1992). For several years, the El Paso program developed a framework that assessed the various areas of language and literacy that bilingual learners, teachers, and coordinators considered significant. In trying to evaluate learner progress, the program developed a framework that included the following three assessment tools:

1. A literacy behavior profile that identifies classroom interactions and includes questions such as: Does this student "attend regularly," "participate verbally in class," "use English in class," and "display critical thinking"?

2. A reading inventory that includes a description of readings the student has mastered, along with a checklist for indicating evidence that the student has understood the materials. Checklist categories include "oral response to affective questions in Spanish (or English)," creative writing response, informal discussion with friends and classmates, and "use of knowledge gained from readings outside of classroom."

3. A student writing evaluation included:
   - Strengths and limitations in writing behaviors. Descriptors may include phrases such as "writes independently but asks for constant assistance from tutor," "asks tutor for spelling of individual words," and "asks tutor for spelling of entire sentences."
   - Mechanical/kinetic skills, such as "writes on lines," "leaves spaces between words," and "forms letters of uniform size."
   - Sentence structure skills such as "the student uses adjectives/ adverbs/pronouns correctly" and "the student uses complete sentences."
   - Affective dimensions of writing. Here categories include student "writes from personal experience," "expresses emotions in writing," "shows pride in work," and "will read aloud to tutor (classmate)."
   - Links between classroom work and outside literacy. Teachers are asked to provide examples to items such as: "Has this student approached you to initiate literacy use? Describe" or "Has the student given you an indication that he/she is using the literacy skills used in your group outside of class? Describe."

The information gathered on these questionnaires about behaviors, skills, and strategies was rated on a 1 to 3 scale (never, sometimes, often) and recorded during the second week of class, at mid-cycle, and at the end of a cycle. During that time, teachers also collected three writing samples to evaluate. In addition to marking quantitative information on the assessment form, teachers wrote a short paragraph outlining the progress that a particular student made during the cycle. For several years, the assessment process was continuously examined and refined to reflect new insights.[7] This type of assessment is promising for learners who are developing bilingual and biliteracy skills. The value lies in its ability to capture progress in underlying literacy behaviors and skills, irrespective of the language in which they are expressed.

Alternative assessments for bilingual adults are relatively new and are threatened by the predominance of standardized testing done to meet accountability requirements. However, a number of programs are now adapting assessments originally designed for literacy programs serving monolingual English speakers in K-12 contexts. Although these assessments are sometimes time consuming to develop, the insights they provide can serve to strengthen both teaching and learning. By examining and adapting assessments such as checklists to capture a range of literacy levels (moving from an emergent literacy level to a proficient level), rubrics to assess changes in writing, or portfolio assessments designed to capture changes in performance (e.g., projects and other work samples, interviews or role-plays, form completion), adult educators get the opportunity to consider how language develops, both in the native language and in the target language, and focus on critical aspects of language development for adults.

Promising Assessment Practices

While the El Paso family literacy program represents a coherent system for assessing students, it is also possible to supplement existing tests with additional evaluation tools that link teaching, learning, and student assessment. The following practices, focusing on both literacy and language, can be implemented either in English or in the home language, and also lend themselves to measuring proficiency across languages.

Student–Teacher Interviews and Conferences   Student–teacher interviews and conferences involve discussions between teachers and individual learners. Such conferences may focus on particular pieces of reading and writing that learners are working on, or they may try to document changes that are occurring over time. Some conferences focus on whether learners have (1) made changes in literacy practices (when, where, and how they read); (2) increased the range of literacy materials they use (movie guides, newspapers, letters); (3) made changes in the support systems they use or the support they provide to others (spouses, kids, neighbors); and (4) changed the way they use literacy in their family (listening to children's stories, writing notes to the teacher, taking kids to cultural events). Interviews and conferences are particularly appropriate for bilingual learners since they allow for a choice of language. Interviews allow adult learners to use the language in which they are most comfortable or code switch between languages to express ideas in ways that feel most comfortable to them.

Reading Profiles   Profiles not only assess language and literacy skills that learners have, but also focus on the strategies they use in reading both in the native language and in English. To develop a profile, a teacher or aide may sit down with an individual student and ask her to read a section aloud together with the teacher and then continue reading silently. The teacher may use a chart that captures reading fluency and comprehension along with competence in subskills related to phonemic awareness, word identification, or understanding of key vocabulary. At higher levels, students can engage in tasks that require them to predict meaning from context, make connections among various sources of texts (TV, magazines, in-school reading), and link what they read to their own lives. Information on how well a student is able to retell or summarize a story should be captured as well as part of the reading profile. Conducting the assessment bilingually offers insights into the dual-language competency of learners acquiring a new language and allows teachers to see whether strategic competence acquired in one language transfers to another. In other words, bilingual learners who learn how to apply comprehension strategies in the new language might try to use similar strategies in their home language even if they have previously not done so.

Reading Files and Free Reading Logs   Reading files and logs record what learners have read and their reaction. In some cases, these files include checklists on what adult learners can read, do read, and would like to read (e.g., the Bible, newspapers, letters from home, TV guides, bills, advertisements, recipes, children's report cards, paychecks). As students engage in various texts, informational as well as narrative, they can be asked to place cards in a box that indicate what they read, when they read it, and how much they liked it.[8] Logs are particularly appropriate for readers developing a new language since they allow students to indicate which texts they have read in what language, how successful they were in gaining meaning from these texts, and how interesting or useful they found the information (Wrigley & Guth, 1992). Since the understanding of language precedes the production of language for all learners, reading logs allow learners to read in the new language while expressing their opinions and insights in the home language.

Writing Portfolios   Portfolios contain samples of learner progress along with comments on the work done. In many cases, learners choose the work they want to see included, such as pieces of other people's writing they have enjoyed reading, their favorite language experience stories, or samples of their best handwriting.

As a rule, teachers help students organize the information and, in collaboration with other teachers, decide on procedures for analyzing and interpreting the data. Writing portfolios may contain pieces of text read in English, but reaction in Spanish, or vice versa, and thus allow learners and teachers to consider the trajectory of biliteracy development, not just the development of English skills. Learners with few years in education in the home country might be inspired to write passages in their native language, a practice they may not have tried before. Engaging in various forms of writing, in an ESL classroom as well as at home, can help adults feel comfortable expressing their ideas in print (often for the first time) and can help them find their voice. Bilingual portfolios that capture what students can write in the home language and in English can provide significant insights not only as to the strengths of a student's writing, but also into motivation to write anything at all. After all, if writing is only assessed in the second language, it is difficult to determine if relative weaknesses are due to a general unwillingness to put ideas on paper, difficulties in writing in any language (in L1 as well as L2), or insufficient knowledge of the linguistic or rhetorical structure of the language to be learned. Looking at L1 and L2 writing side by side, on the other hand, allows the teacher to tailor feedback and support in much more meaningful ways than if only texts written in English were available.

Role-Plays, Case Studies, and Simulations   Through role-plays that surround a literacy event (e.g., an official-looking letter arrives in the mail and the group must respond), teachers can assess the coping skills that students use to deal with everyday literacy materials. These coping skills may include guessing meaning from context, looking up key words, and checking letterhead, logos, or the address of the sender. Asking students what they might do in a particular situation (such as being given a traffic ticket or receiving an eviction notice) can help teachers to identify the level of background knowledge that learners have. Similarly, having someone "play" a mother who has been asked to a conference with the child's teacher about a report card will provide information about the learner's experience and expectations of such literacy events. Repeated several times throughout the semester, reports of role-plays can help document learner progress in oral language and literacy, as well as the development of sociocultural competence across languages, an added dimension of bilingual and biliteracy development. They also link classroom work to real-life situations, as students get a chance to try out potentially intimidating interactions and gain a better sense of how these exchanges can be negotiated even while English skills are still developing. Role-plays and simulations allow those who are new to English to explore survival strategies, such as drawing a picture, using key words and language chunks that have been memorized, and interjecting words in the first language when the word needed in the second language does not come to mind.

Conclusion

Standardized tests using pencil-and-paper-based multiple-choice formats are now well established in adult literacy education. We must assume they are here to stay as accountability requirements become increasingly linked to learner outcome data. Their ease of use, their reputation for high levels of validity and reliability, and their cost effectiveness are likely to outweigh any shortcomings. This is particularly true in instances when large numbers of students need to be assessed and data must be aggregated across sites. However, standardized tests have serious limitations, and it is generally accepted that no single measure should serve as the basis for assessing and evaluating student ability and growth. Alternative assessments can fill many of the gaps left by large-scale standardized tests and provide a much richer picture of what students want to know and how well they are able to negotiate various types of literacy tasks. These assessments, if properly designed and implemented by trained teachers, can measure what is taught and capture a much broader range of skills and strategies associated with language and literacy. Their use in settings where both teachers and learners are bilingual offers opportunities and insights that reflect the realities of adult learners who draw from both the new language and the home language as they read and write, try to understand others, and communicate their ideas. Alternative assessments designed to capture the realities of bilingual communities can open our eyes to the communication and literacy skills that adults possess in the native language and can document the changes that occur as a second language is added to a first.

Endnotes

1. In some areas, assessing literacy skills in the native language is further complicated by the fact that a significant number of bilingual adults speak a language or dialect that is distinct from the national language of their native country, and therefore may not be fully proficient in the language spoken in their community. For example, families from areas such as Chiapas in Mexico may never have gone to school and may speak Miztec at home. As a result, they still struggle with both oral and written Spanish, although their difficulties may not be apparent to teachers who assume that all of their students from Mexico have Spanish as their native language.
2. For a local demonstration of the assessment with a Bosnian woman who is low literate in Serbo-Croation and struggling with English, see "Reading Demonstration" on the Web site for the Coalition of Limited English Speaking Elderly at www.clese.org
3. For details on NAAL and ALSA, see the Fact Sheet created by the National Center for Educational Statistics (NCES), http://nces.ed.gov/NAAL/index.asp?file=Highlights/AdultLiteracyFactSheet.asp&PageId=41
4. NAAL now also includes a fluency assessment in Spanish.
5. The author was a member of the National Academy of Sciences committee that made these recommendations.

6. Students who are part of the 1.5 generation share characteristics of both new immigrants and language minority youth who were born and raised in the United States.
7. The project lost its original funding and no longer assesses a broad range of skills.
8. In some programs, such as the National Adult ESL Lab School in Portland, Oregon, reading logs capture what and how much students read during a period of sustained silent reading and what their responses are to what is being read.

References

Alderson, J. C. (2000). *Assessing reading.* Cambridge, England: Cambridge University Press.

Bachman, L. F. (1990). *Fundamental considerations in language testing.* Oxford: Oxford University Press.

Brindley, G. (1989). *Assessing achievement in the learner-center curriculum.* Sydney: Macquarie University, National Centre for English Language Teaching and Research.

Brown, H. D. (2001). *Teaching by principles: An interactive approach to language pedagogy* (2nd ed.). White Plains, NY: Pearson Education.

Condelli, L., & Wrigley, H. (2006). Instruction, language and literacy: What works study for adult ESL literacy students. In I. van de Craats, J. Kurvers, & M. Young Scholten (Eds.), *Low educated adult second language and literacy acquisition: Proccedings of the inaugural symposium* (pp. 111–133). Utrecht, Netherlands: LOT: Graduate School of Linguistics.

Davidson, R., & Strucker, J. (2002). Patterns of word-recognition errors among adult basic education native and nonnative speakers of English. *Scientific Studies of Reading, 6,* 299–316.

Ellis, R. (1997). *Second language acquisition.* Oxford: Oxford University Press.

Escamilla, K. (2000). *Bilingual means two: Assessment issues, early literacy and Spanish-speaking children.* Washington, DC: U.S. Department of Education. Retrieved May 31, 2006, from http://www.ncela.gwu.edu/pubs/symposia/reading/bilingual5.html

Grabe, W. (2004). Research on teaching reading. *Annual Review of Applied Linguistics, 24,* 44–69. New York: Cambridge University Press.

Huerta-Macías, A., & Quintero, E. (1992). Teaching language and literacy in the context of the family and community. In J. V. Tinajero & A. F. Ada (Eds.), *Literacy and biliteracy for Spanish-speaking children* (pp. 152–157). New York: Macmillan-McGraw Hill.

Kucer, S. B. (2001). *Dimensions of literacy: A conceptual base for teaching reading and writing in school settings.* Mahwah, NJ: Lawrence Erlbaum Associates.

Lytle, S. L., & Wolfe, M. (1989). *Adult literacy education: Program evaluation and learner assessment.* Columbus, OH: ERIC Clearinghouse on Adult, Career, and Vocational Education.

Macías, R. F. (1990). Definitions of literacy: A response. In R. L. Venezky, D. A. Wagner, & B. S. Ciliberti (Eds.), *Toward defining literacy* (pp. 17–23). Newark, DE: International Reading Association.

Merrifield, J. M. (1998). *Contested ground: Performance accountability in adult basic education* (NCSALL Report 1). Boston: National Center for the Study of Adult Learning and Literacy.

Stein, S. (2000). *Equipped for the future content standards: What adults need to know and be able to do in the 21st century.* Washington, DC: National Institute for Literacy.

Weinstein-Shr, G. (1988). *Project LEIF: Learning English through intergenerational friendship: A manual for building community across languages and across cultures.* Philadelphia: Temple University, Center for Intergenerational Learning.

Wiley, T. G. (1996). *Literacy and language diversity in the United States.* McHenry, IL: Delta Systems and Center for Applied Linguistics.

Wrigley, H. S. (2000). Assessing ongoing progress: Are we progressing? In D. Holt & C. Van Duzer (Eds.), *Assessing success in family literacy and adult ESL* (pp. 63–95). Washington, DC: Center for Applied Linguistics.

Wrigley, H. S. (2003, November). Building a proactive and collaborative research and development model: Real world research in the National Youth Literacy Demonstration Project. *Imprints: The Newsletter of Literacy BC, 9* (2). Retrieved May 25, 2006, from http://www2.literacy.bc.ca/pub/NEWSLET/nov03/20.htm

Wrigley, H. S., & Guth, G. J. A. (1992). *Bringing literacy to life: Issues and options in adult ESL literacy.* San Mateo, CA: Aguirre International.

9

Issues and Future Directions

ANA HUERTA-MACÍAS AND KLAUDIA M. RIVERA

There is an absence of sensible policy when it comes to the education of non-English-speaking adult immigrants and other linguistic minorities in the United States. As Castro and Wiley point out in this volume (see chapter 2), despite the fact that the 2000 Census shows the United States to be a multilingual society, it is erroneously assumed to be a monolingual nation. Monolingual ideology, in which language diversity is seen to be a problem, coupled with an absence of reliable data regarding the levels of English proficiency and literacy among language minorities, results in a de facto policy that is primarily shaped by attitudes and beliefs rather than by reliable data and research. This translates into restrictive monolingual instruction in English as a Second Language (ESL) classes, workplace literacy development, and every other context where immigrants and other language minorities should exercise their basic human right to use their native language to communicate, learn, and work. That immigrants and speakers of languages other than English should learn English to partake in the democratic process and prosper in the United States is indisputable. The issue is how to best meet their sociolinguistic and educational needs in a manner that is pedagogically sound while they lead productive and happy lives and learn English.

This volume critically analyzes the assumptions that normalize monolingual and monoliterate approaches to adult education and to the teaching of English to immigrants and other language minorities in the United States. By integrating theoretical principles with their applications, it furthers the discussion of the effects that bilingualism and biliteracy have on adult instruction. Applying research-based theoretical principles to the contexts in which adults learn, work, engage in civic participation, raise their children, and come together in community, this volume sheds light on the multiple ways in which adults use their first and second languages in these same contexts as they carry out their lives.

This concluding chapter will first discuss and summarize some of the most salient theoretical concepts in this volume in the context of their sociocultural and educational settings. It will proceed to highlight recommendations for programs and policy.

Learner Resources in Adult Education

The experiences of the programs described in this volume challenge beliefs about monolingualism and make visible the resources that bilingual individuals, along with the knowledge embedded in bilingual communities, can offer to adult instruction. These resources include background knowledge, native language development, native language literacy, and the ability to transfer learning from one language to another. The authors provide examples of how the first language can be utilized for adults to learn English and apply what they already know to the demands of their new environment. These examples make obvious how the stressing of English as the only language of instruction limits the ways in which adults can actively engage in their education, and prevents them from using all their cognitive resources in the teaching and learning process.

The Role of Background Knowledge

Students developing bilingualism and biliteracy come to the classroom with previously acquired knowledge and strategies that are available to them in the second language as soon as they begin to develop proficiency and are able to express themselves in that language. For adults who are learning English, background knowledge provides the foundation to make sense of the language they are learning and serves as a springboard to the new knowledge they need to grasp. Huerta-Macías in chapter 4, for example, discusses how activating what a student knows about a workplace accident can provide a context for the learning of English through relevant and interesting content. In chapter 3, Rivera describes how day laborers learn English at CASA Latina by applying what they know about construction and gardening to the ESL lesson. Similarly, Powrie (chapter 7, this volume) explains that a student who has learned U.S. history in Spanish would not have to learn this material anew in English. Knowledge about the U.S. Constitution, for instance, might allow the student to better understand what the teacher is explaining in English, thus expediting the student's development of vocabulary in the second language. Background knowledge and the use of the student's strongest language provide a context for the learning of English.

The Role of the Native Language

Adults' first or native language is intrinsically connected to everything they know because it is in and through their native language that they have acquired the knowledge they possess. The use of the adults' first language in education can expedite their understanding of complex concepts. Powrie, for instance, explains how learning the core concepts of American history and government can be facilitated by using the student's native language in civic programs. Complex concepts such as unalienable rights can be more easily understood and learned when they are taught in the language in which students think. Since these concepts are difficult to grasp even for English speakers, teaching them in English to students who are learning the language can be frustrating and unproductive (see chapter 7).

The use of the first language opens the space for adults to share their stories, stories that speak of their past and have the power to connect generations. In the project that Quintero describes in chapter 5, in which Hmong and English were used in the family literacy program, the adults recorded in Hmong their experiences in Laos, their native country, in Thailand, and in the United States, where they now live. The stories were read by their children, who have been raised in the United States, thus providing them with an opportunity to learn about their family background and history. The sharing of stories by adult learners, Rivera argues in chapter 3, allows students to discuss and analyze the social construction of their experiences and to understand their place in history. These stories can also be texts for adults to learn to read, as well as to learn English.

Building intergenerational activities through the use of the native language can strengthen family relations and avoid the deterioration of immigrant families in the ways described by Wong Fillmore (2000). Parents can discuss and read about how to raise bilingual children in the United States without alienating them from their family language and culture. As described by Powrie in chapter 7, parents can understand that in order to help children succeed academically in the United States, English is not the only language to be considered; they can learn that they can discuss ideas and read to their children in their family language, and through such discussions and readings support their children's academic development in two languages. At a time when immigrant and nonimmigrant Latinos are experiencing very high dropout rates in the United States, bilingual family literacy programs can make an important difference. They can contribute to the development of strong foundations for Latino children in both of their languages, teaching them how to use their linguistic repertoire in learning how to learn. Biliteracy can also provide genuine spaces for immigrant parents and other language minorities to be involved in their children's education in ways that go beyond traditional school-defined forms of parental involvement. Bilingual family literacy programs can strengthen family relations and maintain cultural continuity while at the same time facilitating the interactions between schools and parents.

206 Adult Biliteracy: Sociocultural and Programmatic Responses

According to Rivera (chapter 3, this volume), programs that use the native language can bridge school and community literacies by creating overlapping linguistic contexts for language and literacy learning, and providing adult students with ample opportunities to use literacy and English in real-life contexts, rather than teaching them through artificial language exercises such as drills. Programs that use the students' native language can also organically connect the curriculum to what is happening in the community and respond to community and student needs right away. Day laborers, for example, can read Occupational Safety and Health Administration (OSHA) regulations and discuss their application in the workplace in Spanish while they also learn how to negotiate safety rules on the job with their employers in English.

The community-based programs described by Rivera combine the use of the native language with a participatory pedagogy that places students' issues at the center of the curriculum. Through the use of the students' native language and a participatory pedagogy, students can engage in dialogue, social analysis, and projects of change. The use of the native language allows a level of societal analysis that is richer and deeper than when using English alone. This type of analysis contributes to the adult students' development of critical thinking and reading skills. The native language combined with the use of a participatory pedagogy also enables programs to develop leadership from the bottom up, including the training of bilingual teachers who are rooted in community knowledge and expertise.

The Role of Literacy

The role of literacy in the first language is also of utmost importance to adult learning. Literacy in the first language allows adults to apply what they know about reading in the first language—such as how to draw meaning from text, use context cues, skim for meaning, and monitor comprehension—to the development of reading in the second language. This is known as transfer (Krashen, 1996; Ovando, Collier, & Combs, 2003) (see also Rivera & Huerta-Macías, chapter 1, this volume). Drawing in all the components of language to learn how to read is a challenge for all beginning readers. Bringing these components to bear in the development of literacy in not only one, but two languages makes the process of learning complex for bilinguals. Using the phonology of two languages, organizing ideas, recognizing words and applying all the available linguistic systems to understand them, making meaning predictions based on syntax, and applying background knowledge to a particular text are some of the skills that bilinguals activate when they encounter text in any language. When utilized, these skills contribute to bilinguals' engagement with texts in cognitive and linguistically sophisticated ways. Capitalizing on these skills, therefore, makes the process of learning and thinking richer for bilinguals.

In chapter 6, Skilton-Sylvester highlights the importance of using the first language at the university level, where the development of literacy has traditionally centered on the development of academic literacy proficiency in standard English. By applying the continua of biliteracy (Hornberger, 1989; Hornberger & Skilton-Sylvester, 2000), she discusses how oral, written, academic, and communal languages can come together to support the biliterate development of college students. She describes how bilingual Korean students converse in Korean about papers that they write in English and how bilingual high school students in a university summer program engage with multilingual texts. The importance of talking in any language about what one is writing and reading makes for stronger academic papers in English; inviting students to engage with texts written by bilingual and multilingual authors broadens their knowledge about the world and their experience with language. Supporting academic biliterate development can also have social, intellectual, and emancipatory results, argues Skilton-Sylvester. The inclusion of both English and the students' native and strongest language in their education honors their linguistic rights and pairs with a social justice orientation.

Many community-based programs, Rivera states, see their role as much more than teaching reading, writing, and English language skills to immigrants; they also describe themselves as agents of change and use the students' native language as a tool to help them achieve their educational goals, improve their lives, challenge oppressive conditions, and contribute to community development (see chapter 3). Social justice is also one of the five orientations that can shape EL/Civics curricula. Powrie in chapter 7 describes how some civic education programs help immigrants challenge the status quo and work together for social justice in an effort to create a better life for themselves, their families, and communities.

The Role of Transfer

The transfer of language and literacy skills and background knowledge from the first to the second language makes it possible for adults to apply what they know and are able to do in their first language to what they need to learn and use in English. This includes transferring reading and writing skills and ways of being in the world to a new language and its cultural paradigm. This phenomenon is of utmost importance when developing educational approaches for immigrants and bilingual adults in the United States, because transfer also applies to the learning of subject matter. This is well documented by Huerta-Macías in chapter 4 on workforce education for Latinos. She explains how rather than waiting for someone to learn English to then be able to participate in work training, bilingual programs can integrate English language development with occupational instruction. The outcome of these programs is that workers begin to learn the skills they need to find a job without having to use their time and financial resources to learn stand-alone English as a second language. Learning English concurrently with upgrading work skills or learning new ones can have positive effects on programs' retention and completion rates since students enjoy the educational benefits right away, such as securing a job with better pay.

Castro and Wiley in chapter 2 note that lack of access to education is more salient than language background as a predictor of success in the labor market. In order not to miss adults who need workforce training and education the most, it must be provided to those with low levels of schooling in their strongest language, especially speakers whose first language is not English or who do not speak English like the local English monolinguals. The Met program described by Huerta-Macías in chapter 4 is a good example of the potential that the use of two languages in instruction has for workforce development. By using two languages rather than restricting education to only English, this program prepares students for jobs with sustainable wages, teaches them English, and opens the doors to higher education and a better standard of living in a way that is educationally sound and efficient. The notion of transfer makes evident that conceptual knowledge, such as learning the safety rules to operate machinery in the workplace, rights and responsibilities as parents, the content of a citizenship test, or the application of a complex theory in an advanced college class, can be more efficiently and effectively discussed and learned in the native language and then applied to the second language. That is, a worker can learn the safety instructions about a particular dangerous machine in Spanish (Huerta-Macías, chapter 4); a student can discuss the premises of an academic paper in Korean and then write the paper in English (Skilton-Sylvester, chapter 6); an immigrant applying for citizenship can understand difficult concepts of U.S. history in Spanish while learning English (Powrie, chapter 7); a community member can learn about how to negotiate wages and safety in the job in Spanish and English (Rivera, chapter 3); and parents can read to their children in their native language to support literacy in English (Quintero, chapter 5). Using the adult students' native language along with English in the educational program expedites immigrants' participation in the fabric of their new society by allowing them to apply their background knowledge to hold jobs, engage in citizenship activities, participate in their children's education, develop their leadership abilities, improve their lives, and continue their education.

The Complexities of Biliteracy and Multilingualism

Literacy and bilingualism involve notions of what is appropriate to do or not to do in a particular environment or context. Along with language, humans learn ways of being in the world. When adults learn a second or third language, they add new ways of being in and perceiving the world (Rivera & Huerta-Macías, chapter 1, this volume). These views and their corresponding ways of interacting allow bilinguals and biliterates the ability to make choices about which language to use in a particular situation and the cultural practices associated with their linguistic choice. The fluidity in the choice of how and when they will use one or the other language makes the assessment of what bilinguals and biliterates know and are able to do in their first, second, and both languages very complex.

In chapter 8 on assessment, Wrigley critically examines notions that simplify the assessment of language proficiency to the use of a single measure, such as one type of standardized test, with bilinguals. The complexities of finding appropriate assessments for bilinguals are multilayered, since effective assessments should be able to capture what adults are able to do in two languages as well as the extent in which they are literate in each language. As stated by Wrigley, some standardized tests "often fail to distinguish between language problems, in which the learner is unfamiliar with the language or concepts of the test item, and literacy problems, in which the learner lacks the requisite reading and writing skills but could easily respond to similar items presented as part of a conversation." Alternative assessments, she recommends, can fill many of the gaps left by large-scale standardized tests and provide a much richer picture of what students know how to do, as well as how well they are able to negotiate various types of literacy tasks.

Bilinguals must also consider which linguistic mode (oral, written, aesthetic, technological, etc.) best meets the communication and cultural demands in each of the languages they know. This interplay between languages and modes of communication takes place everywhere and all the time, and has positive cognitive effects since the engagement with the different modes of communication in each of their languages augments the learning capacity of bilinguals (Rivera & Huerta-Macías, chapter 1). In programs that implement a biliteracy approach, students can use the Internet, for example, and have access to information in not only one but two languages, augmenting the amount of knowledge they have access to and broadening the number of sources from which that knowledge comes. Powrie describes how students in the Socorro program explored Web addresses in English and Spanish that they found via Web Quests that list sites in both languages. Rivera, in the chapter on CBOs, and Powrie, in the one about EL/Civics, describe how students can engage in community-based research projects in two languages. This allows them to not only access broader and diverse amounts of information and subjects, but also to reach a wider audience by documenting and disseminating their findings in both languages and by using technology. By applying their multiliteracies (New London Group, 1996) in both of their languages, bilinguals augment their meaning-making potential and their capacity to deal with complex information, and also to reach higher levels of critical thinking, analysis, and synthesis in a manner that is efficient and culturally appropriate.

Rivera and Huerta-Macías discuss the connections between language and identity. In so doing, they explore the connections that bilinguals and biliterates have to two cultural contexts and their corresponding forms of communication, and also to the literate identities associated with each language and the hybridity they create (see chapter 1). Skilton-Sylvester in chapter 6 describes how bilingual high school students talked about how their bilingual identities were accepted or not accepted in school, and about choosing an American name because their name was difficult to pronounce by mainstream English speakers. These activities show the students' awareness of the real and imagined spaces their biculturalism affords them and the identity choices it creates. For in addition to having the ability to use one or two languages in different modes and contexts, bilinguals also have the facility to successfully navigate across diverse language and cultural communities and their corresponding identities and affiliations.

Final Thoughts and Future Directions

This volume focuses on Latinos because they are the largest group of non-English speakers in the United States. According to the 2000 Census there are over 28.1 million Spanish-speaking persons in the United States who make up 60% of those who speak a language other than English at home. The number continues to grow. At the present time, Latino immigrants have the lowest levels of education, fill the largest percentage of low-wage workers, are more likely to live in poverty, and have the highest unemployment rates and the lowest English literacy levels in the United States (Huerta-Macías, chapter 4, this volume). The low levels of literacy for Latinos are not only due to poor educational systems in their countries of origin, they are also the result of inadequate education for Latinos in the United States, including disproportionately high dropout rates among first- and second-generation Latinos. While adult education programs such as the ones described in this volume provide alternative educational contexts for workers, immigrants, and other language minorities, federal policy falls behind, not yet recognizing the importance of adults' first and second languages in instruction.

The remaining part of this chapter will list possible venues for programs and policies based on the most salient theoretical concepts and the successful experiences of the biliteracy programs described in this book.

1. There is an urgent need for language and educational policy that is informed by reliable national data.

   The United States is in urgent need of a sensible language and educational policy for adult education. Such a policy would take into consideration the many contexts in which adults learn, move between linguistic communities, use literacy in two languages, and engage with texts of different types, in different languages, and in different modes. Such a policy would thus respond better and in a timely fashion to adults' economic and educational needs. In chapter 2, Castro and Wiley stress the need for better national data to inform policy. They also highlight the need for a better understanding about and stronger focus on language diversity and literacy in other languages to inform policy.

2. There is a need for comprehensive assessment of language, literacy, and biliteracy.

National data should provide information beyond levels of oral English proficiency to include how and when adults use literacy in English and other languages. In chapter 8 on language and literacy assessment for bilingual adults, Wrigley emphasizes the need for comprehensive approaches to assessing immigrant, language minority, and bilingual adults. These approaches should include the four elements of biliteracy: the level of literacy in the native language, the level of literacy in the second language (English), and the levels of oral proficiency in the first and second languages. Wrigley further argues for the need for alternative assessments to fill many of the gaps often left by large-scale standardized tests and to provide a much richer picture of what students want to know and how well they are able to negotiate various types of literacy tasks. These types of assessments should allow low literacy Spanish-speaking respondents to demonstrate what they can do with literacy, and include a wide variety of measurements, such as reading profiles and logs, student-teacher interviews and conferences, writing portfolios, simulations, and role-plays. Wrigley also supports current efforts to develop standardized assessments that capture a broader scope of proficiency-related skills through performance-based assessments that mirror literacy tasks reflective of real-life demands.

3. There is a need for a broad delivery system that includes funding for biliteracy services in a variety of settings, such as community-based organizations, the workplace, community colleges and universities, civic education and family literacy programs, and public schools and libraries.

4. There is a need for comprehensive bilingual programs where biliteracy is implemented.

In the section on adult biliteracy in diverse contexts, all authors (Huerta-Macías, Powrie, Quintero Rivera, and Skilton-Sylvester) assert that there is a need to provide Spanish language literacy along with English instruction for adults in a variety of settings. In their respective chapters these authors discuss how and why Spanish language education must be part of workforce development, civics education, family literacy and community-based projects, GED preparation, and college courses. They also offer examples of successful educational programs. Additionally, programs should:

- Honor individuals' human right to speak their home and strongest language. They should be contexts where students' bilingualism and biliteracy are valued and exercised. The native language of the students has a place everywhere, including the university.

- Not wait for students to learn English in order to teach them subject matter knowledge. This is especially important for adults who must earn a living to support their families and should have access to a job right away.
- Teach language and literacy through interesting and relevant content.
- Include the arts—music, storytelling, theater, and museum education—as part of their curriculum. Children's and adults' literature in both of their languages should also be part of the curriculum.
- Offer comprehensive social services and referrals that address the multilayered needs of adults.
- Assess and take into consideration the levels of language proficiency and literacy in both languages in their educational planning and curriculum development.
- Address the dual-language needs of learners in a way that is systematic, coherent, and educationally sound, and allow students to use their first language to think and talk about ideas, to develop critical thinking, to learn to read and write, and to engage with multilingual texts.

5. There is a need for training about language diversity, literacy in other languages, and biliteracy:
- Training should be provided to adult educators about the nature of language development and the role of the first language in thinking and learning (Castro & Wiley, chapter 2, this volume). There is also need for training about language diversity in the United States, which should include education about the languages that are native to the United States and its territories and that have managed to survive and about the coexistence with English of a number of other European languages, including Spanish, since colonization. Training sessions should bring together educators from a variety of contexts and a wide range of experiences to learn from one another.
- Collaborations between adult education programs and universities for the training of bilingual teachers who are knowledgeable about biliteracy should be funded and established.

Regardless of what side of the immigration issue one stands on, one thing is clear: immigrants and citizens who are speakers of a language other than English in the United States need to learn English in order to be part of the democratic process. The question is whether we are going to capitalize on what they already know regarding parenting, citizenship participation, work readiness, education, and community living, or whether we are going to disregard this knowledge. Vygotsky (1978) reminds us that language mediates human activity; the native language of immigrant students can facilitate their incorporation into the fabric of the United States as successful members of the workforce and as happy and productive family members and citizens in the country that is now their home.

References

Hornberger, N. H. (1989). The continua of biliteracy. *Review of Educational Research, 59*, 271–296.

Hornberger, N. H., & Skilton-Sylvester, E. (2000). Revisiting the continua of biliteracy: International and critical perspectives. *Language and Education: An International Journal, 14*, 96–122.

Krashen, S. D. (1996, May 1). Does literacy transfer? *NABE News*, 5–36.

New London Group. (1996). A pedagogy of multiliteracies: Designing social futures. *Harvard Educational Review, 66*, 60–92.

Ovando, C. J., Collier, V. P., & Combs, M. C. (2003). *Bilingual and ESL classrooms: Teaching in multicultural contexts.* New York: McGraw-Hill.

Vygotsky, L. S. (1978). *Mind in society: The development of higher psychological process* (M. Cole, V. John-Steiner, S. Scribner, & E. Souberman, Eds.). Cambridge, MA: Harvard University Press.

Wong Fillmore, L. (2000). Loss of family languages: Should educators be concerned? *Theory into Practice, 39*, 203–210.

Author Index

Author Index

A

AA (African American) educators, 85
academic biliteracy for adults
    assumptions about linguistic diversity,
        133–135, 138
    overview, 131–133
    supporting the development of, 135–49
        Project PATH, 136–143
        writing center example, 143–149
adult basic education (ABE), 108, 124
Adult Competitiveness Challenge, x
adult education. *see also* education; English as
    a Second Language (ESL)
    academic biliteracy for (*see* academic
        biliteracy for adults)
    characteristics of, 22–23
    community-based organizations and, 75–79
    emphasis of, 40
    future direction of, 210–213
    learner resources in, 204–208
Adult Education and Family Literacy Act, 119,
    134–135, 157
adult education policy. *see* policy, education
Adult Literacy Media Alliance (ALMA), 164
Adult Literacy Supplemental Assessment
    (ALSA), 184–185
African American (AA) educators, 85
age-appropriate children's education, 122–123
Aguirre International, 79
ALMA (Adult Literacy Media Alliance), 164
ALSA (Adult Literacy Supplemental
    Assessment), 184–185
alternative assessment of literacy, 196–198
American Institute for Research, 187
American linguistic culture. *see* U.S. linguistic
    culture
American Statistical Association, 39
assessment of language and literacy
    alternative, 196–198
    common approaches to, 30–31
    complexity of, 182–183
    framework for, 195–196
    future direction for, 211
    overview, 181–183

program-based, 190
self-reported, 30–31, 32–37, 39
standardized, 187–190
types of tests, 185–186
what should be assessed, 191–195
autonomous model, 12
average literacy proficiency, 33

B

background knowledge, role of, 204, 206
Basic English Skills Test (BEST), 164
Bilingual Education Program, 39
bilingual instructional model, 101–108
bilingual pedagogy, 80–82
Bilingual Vocational Training (BVT) model,
    100
biliteracy. *see also* literacy
    academic (*see* academic biliteracy for
        adults)
    civics education and (*see* civics education)
    community-based organizations and, 78–79
    complexities of, 208–210
    concurrent approach to, 79
    context and content of, 139–142
    continua of, 139–146
    critical literacy and, 125–128
    defined, xii, 5
    development of, 5–9, 13–14, 79, 135–149
    different contexts of, 16–17
    expressions in environmental print, 58–72
    future direction of, 210–213
    identity and, 20–22
    media of, 143–147
    micro contexts of, 139–146
    multicompetent view of, 138–139
    native language use (*see* native language
        use)
    power weighting in, 139–149
    schooling and, 17–20
    sequential approach to, 79
    sociocultural and historical activity, 13–16
    sociocultural perspectives on, 10–12
    strategies for, 172–176
    transitional program, 79

educational attainment of the Mexican-origin
  population, 45, 48–49
Educational Testing Service (ETS), 31
EFF (Equipped for the Future), 185
El Barrio Popular Education Program
  (EBPEP), 76–7, 83, 85, 86, 87–88,
  89–91
EL/Civics programs. *see* civics education
Elementary and Secondary Act of 1965, 119
ELL (English language learner), 106
employment of immigrants, 4, 5, 97–100
English ability, 49–52
English as a Second Language (ESL). *see
    also* English for Speakers of Other
    Languages (ESOL)
  and the U.S. Census, 39
  assessment in, 183, 187, 188–198
  community-based organizations and,
    75–79, 81, 87, 89–91
  for the elderly, 162–165
  growth of, 5
  in workforce education, 101
  monolingual instruction in, 18–20, 203
  native language use in, 131–132, 163–164,
    172–176, 205–206
  need for, x–xi, 157
English for Academic Purposes (EAP), 144
English for Speakers of Other Languages
    (ESOL), 156–159, 162–163, 167,
    172, see also English as a Second
    Language (ESL)
English language learner (ELL), 106
English Literacy and Civics Education
    Demonstration Grants, 157–158, 162
English Literacy/Civics programs. *see* civics
    education
Equipped for the Future (EFF), 185
ESL. *see* English as a Second Language (ESL)
ESOL. *see* English for Speakers of Other
    Languages (ESOL)
ETS (Educational Testing Service), 31
Even Start Family Literacy Program, 119–120,
    160, 174

F

Family and Community Development Matrix,
    194
family education
  critical literacy, 116–119, 125–128
  native language use in, 116–119, 126–128,
    205

overview, 115–116
personal histories project, 123–125
successful components of, 119–125
  adult education and literacy, 121
  age-appropriate children's education,
    122–123
  intergenerational literacy, 120–121
  parent education, 121–122
Family Initiative for English Literacy (FIEL),
    118–119
FIEL (Family Initiative for English Literacy),
    118–119

G

GED. *see* General Educational Development
    (GED)
General Educational Development (GED), 4,
    82, 90, 101, 108–109, 172
grammar, 6

H

Head Start, 108
HIRE Center, 102
*Historias de la Vida Real: De la Fábrica a la
    Escuela,* 90
hybrid identity, 20–22

I

identity and biliteracy, 20–22
ideological assumptions of literacy, 29, 40–41,
    52–53, 203
ideological model of literacy, 12
IDEPSCA. *see* Instituto de Educación Popular
    del Sur de California (IDEPSCA)
IES (Institute for Education Studies), 187
immigrants
  citizenship of (*see* citizenship)
  classification of, x, 3–5
  dropout rates of, ix, 4, 98–99
  education of, 97–100, 155, 162–165
  employment of, 4, 5, 97–100
  income of, 4, 98–99
Immigration and Naturalization Service (INS),
    163, 168–169, 171
Immigration Facts, 3
immigration, increase in, 3
income of immigrants, 4

inequality, 5
Information and Resources Center for
    Educación Liberadora (IRCEL),
    78–79, 83
initial assessment, 193
INS. *see* Immigration and Naturalization
    Service (INS)
Institute for Education Studies (IES), 187
Instituto de Educación Popular del Sur de
    California (IDEPSCA), 76–77,
    81–84, 88, 90–91
instruction, monolingual, 18–20
intake assessment, 192–193
interdependence theory, 7–8
intergenerational literacy, 120–121, 205
Internal Revenue Service (IRS), 75
International Literacy Day, 91
IRCEL. *see* Information and Resources Center
    for Educación Liberadora (IRCEL)
IRS (Internal Revenue Service), 75

J

Job Placement program, 90

K

King County Bar Association, 89–90

L

language
    assessment (*see* assessment of language
        and literacy)
    distribution, 102, 109–110
    diversity
        assumptions and myths of, 29, 40–41,
            52, 133–135
        with NALS, 31
        in the U.S., 41–42
    policy (*see* policy)
    rights (*see* linguistic rights)
    spoken
        at home, 49–50
        by citizenship, 48, 49–52
        by state, 46–47
    systems of, 6
    use, 38–41
    vitality, 136
language of power, 141–142

Language Use and English-Speaking Ability:
    2000 Census Brief, 39–41
language-as-problem orientation, 134, 143–145
language-as-resource orientation, 143
leadership development, 88
LEP (limited English proficient) adults, 133
LEP Investment Strategy, 100
limited English proficient (LEP) adults, 133
linguistic culture. *see* U.S. linguistic culture
linguistic diversity. *see* language, diversity
linguistic rights, 134–135, 138, 203
linguistically isolated household, 40–43
literacy. *see also* biliteracy
    assessment (*see* assessment of language
        and literacy)
    assumptions and myths of, 29, 40–41,
        52–53, 203
    community-based organizations, 78–79
    development of, 6–7, 13–14, 79
    direct measures of, 30–37
    environment, 136
    expressions in environmental print, 58–72
    family (*see* family education)
    future direction of, 210–213
    languages spoken, 34
    profile, 35
    role of, 206–207
    scores, ix, 4–5, 33, 35–37
    sociocultural construct, 12–13
    strategies, 6–9
    surrogate measures of, 30–31
    three domains of, 31
    transactional process, 9–10
    transfer, 7–9, 206–208
Literacy Involves Families Together Act, 120
Los Jornaleros de Hollywood, 91
Los Jornaleros del Norte, 91

M

Magic Cleaners, 88
media of biliteracy, 143–147
MET. *see* Motivation Education Training
    (MET)
Mexican-origin population in U.S., 42–53
    educational attainment, 45, 48–52
    monolingualism in, 42–43
    state-by-state comparison, 43–47
    U.S.-born, 45, 48–52
micro contexts of biliteracy, 139–146
monolingualism, 29–30
    ideology of English, 40–41, 203